EL NIÑO Y SU MUNDO

Fácil y divertido

ACTIVIDADES PARA APRENDER

El niño de 2 años

Ina Massler Levin
Michael H. Levin

ONIRO

Título original: *Quick & Fun Learning Activities for 2 Year Olds*
Publicado en inglés por Teacher Created Materials, Inc.

Traducción de Elena Barrutia

Diseño de cubierta: Valerio Viano

Fotografía de cubierta: Gertie Burbeck

Distribución exclusiva:
Ediciones Paidós Ibérica, S.A.
Mariano Cubí 92 – 08021 Barcelona – España
Editorial Paidós, S.A.I.C.F.
Defensa 599 – 1065 Buenos Aires – Argentina
Editorial Paidós Mexicana, S.A.
Rubén Darío 118, col. Moderna – 03510 México D.F. – México

© 1996 Teacher Created Materials, Inc.

© 2001 exclusivo de todas las ediciones en lengua española:
   Ediciones Oniro, S.A.
   Muntaner 261, 3.º 2.ª – 08021 Barcelona – España
   (oniro@edicionesoniro.com - www.edicionesoniro.com)

ISBN: 84-95456-67-2
Depósito legal: B-27.894-2001

Impreso en Hurope, S.L.
Lima, 3 bis – 08030 Barcelona

Impreso en España – *Printed in Spain*

Índice

Introducción

Incansables, caprichosos y encantadores. Con dos años los niños llenan nuestra vida con su simpatía, su vitalidad y su entusiasmo sin límites. Dominan el arte de decir no y ponen a prueba nuestra paciencia y nuestra resistencia como padres. Pero también nos cautivan con su capacidad para expresarse, su deseo de agradar y su curiosidad por todo lo que les rodea. Los niños de dos años son adorables, exigentes y agotadores. Y también son muy divertidos.

Cuando nuestras hijas tenían dos años las llevábamos al parque y a la playa, jugábamos con arena y pompas de jabón, cantábamos las mismas canciones una y otra vez y observábamos asombrados cómo iban creciendo. También había veces en las que acabábamos agotados mientras ellas pedían a gritos «más» u «otra vez». Al escribir este libro hemos vuelto a recordar esas experiencias.

Puesto que a lo largo del día hay muchas cosas que hacer, las actividades que se incluyen en este libro están pensadas para familias que llevan una vida ajetreada. Los juegos y los ejercicios que proponemos requieren muy poca preparación y limpieza, y con ellos tanto tú como tu hijo os beneficiaréis de la interacción que se pretende conseguir y de la cercanía que normalmente se establece.

En este periodo se distinguen dos etapas: la primera va de los veinticuatro a los treinta meses, y la segunda de los treinta a los treinta y seis meses. Sin embargo, tú sabes mejor que nadie como padre en qué fase de desarrollo se encuentra tu hijo en cada momento. Por ejemplo, si una actividad consiste en repetir una frase y el niño es incapaz de hacerlo, no te preocupes. Quizá no esté aún preparado para pronunciar esas palabras. Vuelve a intentarlo dentro de una semana o de un mes. Por mucho que te empeñes, si fuerzas las cosas no conseguirás nada. Cuando tu hijo esté preparado para correr, saltar o cantar, lo hará. Si te adaptas a su ritmo apreciarás mucho mujer sus progresos. Si te olvidas temporalmente de tus expectativas podrás ver el mundo a través de sus ojos. Y es posible que jugando con él se despierte de nuevo tu capacidad para jugar. ¡Divertíos juntos!

De dos a tres años

Para un niño, el periodo comprendido entre los veinticuatro y los treinta y seis meses es una época de cambios extraordinarios. A continuación se detallan las principales capacidades que se aprenden durante ese año y el momento aproximado en que comienzan a desarrollarse. Es esencial recordar que cada niño crece y evoluciona a su propio ritmo.

Desarrollo físico
Entre los 24 y los 30 meses los niños:
◆ Mejoran su capacidad motriz
◆ Trepan a todas partes, incluso a sitios prohibidos
◆ Juegan en columpios cada vez más grandes
◆ Chutan una pelota hacia delante
◆ Lanzan pelotas por alto, pero sin apuntar
◆ Pasan con cuidado las páginas de un cuento
◆ Abren tapas de tarros y vuelven a enroscarlas
◆ Giran pomos de puertas con dificultad

Entre los 30 y los 36 meses los niños:
◆ Se mueven continuamente
◆ Les gusta correr
◆ Suben escaleras alternando los pies y las bajan usando un pie cada vez
◆ Saltan de cualquier altura sin calcular bien las distancias
◆ Extienden los brazos y las manos para coger una pelota grande
◆ Hacen dibujos y garabatos
◆ Construyen torres de seis o más bloques
◆ Separan y juntan objetos
◆ Giran pomos de puertas con más facilidad

Desarrollo intelectual
Entre los 24 y los 30 meses los niños:
◆ Comprenden la relación entre causa y efecto en términos de comportamiento personal
◆ Utilizan objetos cotidianos en juegos de simulación

- Imitan en sus juegos situaciones familiares
- Escuchan cuentos grabados y canciones
- Recuerdan secuencias y pueden volver a contar un cuento
- Reconocen signos familiares en su entorno
- Muestran más interés por los programas de televisión infantiles
- Siguen instrucciones de dos pasos
- Usan frases de dos palabras
- Utilizan su nombre para referirse a sí mismos
- Les gusta aprender nombres de objetos nuevos
- Emplean palabras para pedir cosas
- Tienen un vocabulario de más de 200 palabras

Entre los 30 y los 36 meses los niños:
- Comienzan a clasificar objetos en categorías generales
- Tienen más habilidad para hacer rompecabezas
- Prestan más atención cuando escuchan cuentos y ven la televisión
- Recuerdan y siguen instrucciones de tres pasos
- Construyen frases de dos o tres palabras, con verbos incluidos
- Comienzan a utilizar tiempos pasados y plurales
- Preguntan nombres de objetos y los repiten
- Relacionan el nombre y el uso de los objetos
- Distinguen objetos de diferentes tamaños (grandes y pequeños)
- Tienen un vocabulario de más de 500 palabras

Consejos de seguridad

Puesto que la seguridad de tu hijo es de vital importancia, las actividades de este libro se han diseñado con el fin de evitar cualquier tipo de riesgo. Ten en cuenta los siguientes consejos.

Con dos años tu hijo puede trepar. Puede arrastrar una silla y subirse a ella para coger lo que quiera. Guarda los productos tóxicos, las cerillas y los objetos afilados fuera de su alcance en armarios cerrados. No dejes sus juguetes en lugares a los que tenga que escalar para cogerlos. Si es necesario lo hará. Y no olvides que a esta edad puede llegar a las ventanas y pasar por puertas abiertas. Mantenlas bien cerradas.

Los niños de dos años sienten curiosidad por todo. Tu hijo tocará, olerá y probará cualquier cosa, así que debes tener cuidado con lo que dejas por ahí. Cuando estés cocinando pon las asas de las cazuelas hacia dentro para que no pueda tirarlas. Si dejas monedas a su alcance puede encontrarlas y metérselas a la boca. Cuando estéis en el parque o en el jardín no le pierdas de vista y mira qué tiene en las manos. Podría acabar con un bicho en la boca con mucha facilidad.

Cubre los enchufes para que no pueda meter en ellos los dedos ni ningún objeto.

Supervisa sus juguetes. ¿Tienen alguna pieza suelta? Si en la caja se indica que es para mayores de tres años quizá se deba al tamaño de las piezas más que al hecho de que le parezca divertido. Explícale que no puede llevarse nada a la boca. Y si lo hace quítaselo.

Los juegos acuáticos plantean nuevos retos en materia de seguridad. No dejes nunca a tu hijo solo cuando esté bañándose o jugando con agua.

De vez en cuando ponte a gatas y da una vuelta por el territorio de tu hijo para verlo desde su perspectiva. ¿Hay esquinas de mesas que convendría almohadillar? ¿Ves cables de lámparas que podrían caerse al dar un tirón? Si encuentras situaciones de este tipo corrígelas para evitar posibles accidentes.

Ten en cuenta dónde juegas con tu hijo. Cuando estéis en la calle ten mucho cuidado, porque puede salir a la carretera para recoger la pelota. Y dentro de casa puede romper un cristal si la lanza con fuerza.

Siempre que lleves a tu pequeño en el coche, aunque sea para un trayecto corto, ponle en su silla con las correas atadas.

Materiales que conviene tener en casa

Aunque para jugar con un niño de dos años por lo general no hace falta nada —contigo y con él es más que suficiente—, en algunas de las actividades de este libro se utilizan una serie de materiales básicos. Procura reunir todo lo que necesites antes de comenzar cualquier actividad para que no os sintáis frustrados si no tenéis los elementos necesarios para completarla.

Comienza a reunir los materiales y busca un recipiente adecuado para guardarlos. Nosotros utilizábamos un cesto de ropa para almacenar todas estas cosas, y nos resultó muy útil. Era ligero, tenía una gran capacidad y llevaba unas asas que permitían moverlo con facilidad.

No es necesario que dispongas de todos los materiales de la lista antes de comenzar a jugar con tu hijo. Añade y elimina lo que consideres oportuno en cada momento. No hemos incluido utensilios como tijeras y cinta adhesiva porque es muy probable que ya tengas ese tipo de cosas, pero si tus recursos son limitados no olvides que debes reponerlos.

A lo largo del libro encontrarás actividades en las que se emplean estos materiales, pero no tienes por qué limitarte a usarlos tal y como se describen. La práctica y la energía que exija cada actividad te ayudarán a hacerte una idea de cómo puedes utilizarlos. Deja este libro encima del cesto. Después, cuando te apetezca, juega, improvisa y, sobre todo, diviértete con tu hijo.

Lista de materiales

- Cazos y sartenes
- Cucharas de madera y de metal
- Pelotas (de playa, de tenis, grandes y pequeñas)
- Cajas (de varios tamaños, incluida una grande en la que quepa el niño)
- Cesto de ropa
- Cuentos
- Casete
- Radio

- Plastilina
- Manteles de plástico
- Pañuelos
- Varios cuadrados de tela
- Animales y muñecos de peluche
- Coches y camiones
- Juguetes de arrastre (carretilla, carrito de compra)
- Colorante alimentario
- Mezcla para pudín

- Reproductor de CD
- Cintas y CD
- Tubos de papel de cocina
- Instrumentos musicales (campanillas, cajas de arena, palos rítmicos)
- Sombreros (de todas clases)
- Disfraces fáciles de poner
- Bolsos, peines y cinturones viejos
- Recipiente y varita para hacer pompas de jabón

- Lápices de cera grandes
- Papel
- Fichas
- Catálogos
- Tizas

En casa

Introducción

Durante el segundo año de tu hijo pasaréis muchas horas en casa. Además de los ratos que pasará comiendo y durmiendo habrá mucho tiempo para jugar. A veces no podréis salir debido al mal tiempo. Aprovecha esas ocasiones para jugar con tu pequeño.

Tu casa es uno de los mejores lugares del mundo para jugar, en el que tu hijo debería sentirse cómodo y seguro. Puesto que se trata de un entorno familiar, en él se enfrentará a nuevas experiencias sin ningún temor.

Para cuando tu hijo cumpla dos años deberías haber adoptado las medidas de seguridad necesarias. Sin embargo, puesto que puede arrastrar muebles y subirse a ellos, no olvides guardar las cosas que no quieras que coja fuera de su vista. Si es posible despeja una zona grande para que corra y salte y coloca una estera en el suelo para marcar los límites. Si en tu casa hay escaleras tendrás que vigilarle o ayudarle cuando suba por ellas. Dale toda la libertad que puedas dentro de casa. Nosotros cedimos a nuestras hijas uno de los armarios bajos de la cocina, en el que guardábamos los cacharros que nos parecían divertidos para jugar y lo que les gustaba a ellas.

Si hay algún lugar en el que no quieres que entre, comienza cuanto antes a cerrar la puerta y a decirle: «En el cuarto de la plancha no se entra». (Aunque deberías tomar las medidas oportunas por si acaso alguien deja la puerta abierta.)

Por otro lado puedes aprovechar la oportunidad para enseñar a tu hijo algunas tareas domésticas. Conseguir que resulten divertidas es muy fácil, puesto que si las haces con él y añades una canción puedes convertir casi cualquier cosa en un juego. En esta sección encontrarás muchas actividades cuyo fin es completar una tarea. Este tipo de actitudes ayudan a fomentar el sentido de la responsabilidad. No obstante, recuerda que tu hijo sólo tiene dos años, y que el objetivo principal es que se divierta mientras aprende.

Batiendo huevos

Materiales

Cuenco
Huevos
Batidor

Actividad

Casca unos cuantos huevos en un cuenco grande. Si quieres utilizarlos más tarde hazlo tú misma. En caso contrario deja que lo intente el niño. Hay un cincuenta por ciento de probabilidades de que los huevos caigan en el cuenco, aunque también es probable que haya trozos de cáscara.

Enseña a tu hijo el batidor y dile cómo se utiliza. Ayúdale a batir los huevos, mostrándole cómo se forma una sustancia amarillenta al mezclar la clara y la yema. Cuando los huevos estén batidos eres tú quien debe decidir si vas a utilizarlos (y cómo).

Limpieza

Materiales

*Trapo de polvo o
    plumero*

Actividad

Si no te importa que los muebles no queden impecables tu hijo se lo pasará en grande ayudándote a quitar el polvo. Dale un trapo suave o un plumero y deja que limpie. Puede ser de gran ayuda a la hora de limpiar las barras de las sillas o las patas de las mesas, porque llegará a esas zonas mucho mejor que tú. Nuestra hija pequeña quería tener su propio plumero, y le compramos uno pequeño con plumas naranjas. Jamás hemos vuelto a tener la casa tan limpia.

todo en orden

Materiales

Juguetes que no estén en su sitio

Letra de la canción (véase abajo)

Actividad

Este juego es excelente para poner las cosas en su sitio. Si hay juguetes esparcidos por todas partes puede resultar agobiante, así que procura ponerlo en práctica sobre la marcha, por ejemplo cuando veas que tu hijo ha terminado con un juguete y va a coger otro.

Cuando se hayan acumulado varias cosas o tengas un juguete con muchas piezas, como una serie de bloques, juega con tu hijo a poner todo en su sitio. Piensa en una canción infantil cuya música se ajuste a la letra siguiente (por ejemplo, «En la casa de Pepito»), luego coge uno de los juguetes con los que haya estado jugando y dile: «Vamos a jugar a un juego especial que tiene su propia canción. Cada vez que acabemos de usar un juguete buscamos su caja y lo volvemos a meter dentro mientras cantamos. Lo más divertido es que al terminar podemos sacar otros juguetes».

Canción

Así es como recogemos las cosas, recogemos las cosas,
recogemos las cosas.
Así es como recogemos las cosas,
y guardamos los juguetes.
Así es como recogemos las cosas, recogemos las cosas,
recogemos las cosas.
Así es como recogemos las cosas,
y sacamos otro juguete.

Casas y torres

Materiales

Bloques de construcción

Actividad

A los niños les encanta hacer casas y torres con bloques de construcción tanto como derribarlas. Enseña a tu hijo a apilar los bloques para que se mantengan en equilibrio y no se caigan inmediatamente. Cuando se caiga alguno dile que lo coloque de nuevo. Después podréis hacer otra casa o cualquier otro edificio.

Construir una ciudad con bloques puede dar pie a una interesante conversación. Pregunta a tu hijo qué estáis construyendo y dónde se encuentra. Anímale a que ponga en la ciudad muñecos, coches y otros juguetes. Por lo general hasta los treinta meses los niños sólo levantan torres con varios bloques, pero los más mayores pueden hacer estructuras más complejas.

Los bloques de madera suelen ser caros, aunque la inversión merece la pena. Si no quieres comprar un juego de bloques puedes hacer unos bloques sencillos, ligeros y económicos siguiendo las instrucciones que se detallan a continuación.

Intrucciones para hacer bloques

Busca cajas de cartón de diferentes tamaños, por ejemplo cajas de zapatos con tapa, cajitas de regalo para joyas, cartones de leche y cajas de comida.

Elige un papel adhesivo con un dibujo que te guste y forra con él las cajas. Puedes utilizar más de un tipo de papel.

Asegúrate de que el papel se adhiere a la parte exterior de las cajas.

juegos con pelotas de tenis

Materiales

Pelotas de tenis
Tubo en el que vienen
  las pelotas
Lata de café grande

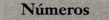

Actividad

Dentro de casa se puede jugar con pelotas de tenis de muchas maneras. En algunos casos resulta tan divertido como al aire libre. Compra un tubo de pelotas para jugar en casa y evitar que se manchen cuando llueva.

Números

Para realizar esta actividad sienta al niño en tu regazo. Coge el tubo y saca las pelotas una a una mientras las vas contando. Di: «Una pelota, dos pelotas y tres pelotas. ¿Puedes volver a meterlas dentro?». Ayúdale a meterlas de nuevo en el tubo y cuéntalas una vez más: «Una, dos, tres».

Rodar

Pon la lata de café con el fondo contra la pared y enseña a tu hijo a rodar una pelota por el suelo para meterla en la lata. Como antes, ve contando las pelotas cuando las hagas rodar. Si entra alguna en la lata cuéntala al sacarla. Recuerda que para que al niño le resulte divertido la distancia no deber ser muy grande.

Lanzar

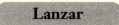

Pon la lata de café boca arriba. Dale a tu hijo las pelotas de tenis, una a una, y enséñale a lanzarlas en la lata de café y a sacarlas para jugar de nuevo. A medida que crezca puedes darle más pelotas para que las lance.

15

Vacía la basura

Materiales

*Cestas pequeñas de
basura*
Bolsa o caja grande

Actividad

Para un niño de dos años incluso vaciar la papelera de su habitación puede ser divertido. Además de hacer algo podrá ayudarte en las tareas domésticas. Da una vuelta por la casa con tu hijo y enséñale las cestas de cada habitación o las que quieres que vacíe. Lleva una bolsa grande de papel o una caja en la que quepa el contenido de la cesta. Enséñale a cogerla sin tocar nada de lo que haya dentro. Explícale por qué usamos cestas de basura y por qué es importante echar en ellas las cosas sucias. Después puedes pedirle que te acompañe al cubo del patio. Y no olvides ver cómo recoge el camión la basura de la calle.

Imanes para el frigorífico

Materiales

Frigorífico
Imanes grandes

Actividad

La parte inferior o lateral del frigorífico puede ser una zona de juego estupenda para tu hijo. Así estará entretenido mientras cocinas. Dale varios imanes para que juegue con ellos. Ten en cuenta que deben ser grandes para que no pueda tragárselos. También deberían ser fáciles de agarrar y manipular. A él le encantará elegir sus propios imanes, sobre todo si vais a un lugar especial y queréis llevaros un recuerdo. De esa forma cada vez que juegue con los imanes puedes hablarle de esa excursión.

Hay una gran variedad de imanes para elegir. Cuando tu hijo se canse de jugar con ellos utilízalos para colgar en el frigorífico las obras de arte que haga en la escuela.

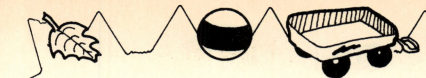

Al aire libre

Introducción

A los niños les encanta jugar al aire libre. Sin embargo, después del entusiasmo inicial es posible que tu hijo necesite algún estímulo para decidir qué puede hacer. Si le ayudas a descubrir la naturaleza que le rodea le gustará cada vez más jugar fuera de casa.

Al realizar algunas de las actividades de esta sección ten en cuenta su seguridad. Los niños no deberían asustarse al aire libre, pero no debemos olvidar que pueden hacerse daño con facilidad. Si le indicas dónde puede hacerse daño le ayudarás a comprender que debe tener cuidado. Agárrale de la mano en las zonas donde pueda caerse. No le lleves a ningún lugar donde haya piedras sueltas o afiladas. Cuanto más pequeño sea mayor será la necesidad de que juegue en zonas amplias y llanas.

Aunque las actividades de esta sección han sido pensadas para el jardín, muchas de ellas se pueden realizar en un parque. En los parques suele haber instalaciones que potencian las actividades físicas. Recuerda que tu hijo es aún pequeño, y algunos aparatos serán demasiado grandes para que disfrute con ellos. Si quiere subirse al tobogán, enseguida te darás cuenta de que tendrás que bajar con él. Las relaciones sociales que se suelen establecer en el parque os permitirán a los dos jugar con otros niños de dos años y con sus padres.

No es necesario que planifiques todo lo que vais a hacer al aire libre. Tu hijo te dirá muy pronto qué es lo que más le gusta. Y con un poco de imaginación podréis crear vuestras propias actividades en el jardín de casa.

Insectos

Materiales

Insectos inofensivos
Tarro para cazar
  insectos

Actividad

Vete de cacería con tu hijo por el jardín. ¿Qué tipos de criaturas hay? ¿Veis algún saltamontes o un desfile de hormigas? Busca un insecto inofensivo y utiliza el tarro para cazarlo. (Los mejores son los que tienen un cristal de aumento en la tapa.) Observa al insecto. Habla de su color, mira si tiene alas y escucha el sonido que haga. Después libéralo.

Dibujos de tiza

Materiales

Tiza
Cemento

Actividad

Cuando haga buen tiempo dale a tu hijo unas tizas y deja que se lo pase en grande decorando la acera, el patio o el camino de entrada. Anímale a hacer dibujos grandes con tizas de varios colores. (Las especiales para aceras son más grandes y más manejables para manos pequeñas.) Haz un dibujo junto a él y no olvidéis firmar vuestras obras de arte.

Puedes dejar en el suelo los dibujos de tiza hasta que llueva, o limpiarlos con una manguera. Para borrar algunas tizas de colores hay que frotar con energía, así que piensa bien dónde vais a dibujar.

Caja de arena

Materiales

Caja de arena
Juguetes de arena
(cubo y pala)
Regadera de plástico
Agua

Actividad

Si no tienes una caja de arena puedes realizar esta actividad en el parque o en una playa. Asegúrate de que tu hijo tiene a mano un cubo y una pala. Hay una gran variedad de juguetes de arena, entre ellos los que giran cuando se echa arena en ellos y los moldes de diferentes formas. Sin embargo, lo más probable es que pase la mayor parte del tiempo llenando el cubo con arena y vaciándolo de nuevo. Cuando juguéis con la arena habla con él y pregúntale qué está construyendo.

También puedes enterrar en la arena juguetes pequeños y pedirle al niño que los busque.

No le pierdas de vista en ningún momento para que no se coma la arena. Si la caja de arena está sobre una superficie de cemento conviene que tengas a mano una escoba y un recogedor, porque si echa arena fuera podríais resbalaros.

Paseo por la naturaleza

Materiales
Aire libre

Actividad

Lleva a tu hijo a dar un paseo por el jardín o alrededor de la manzana. Agárrale de la mano y muéstrale algunas de las maravillas de la naturaleza. Si es otoño dile que se fije en las hojas que se ponen amarillas. Si es verano enséñale las flores en todo su esplendor.

También puedes buscar un árbol y observarlo con tu hijo en diferentes épocas del año. Cuando lo hagas dile si las hojas se están cayendo o cambiando de color. Si ves un pájaro en el árbol señálaselo y dile que no haga ruido para que pueda oír cómo canta. Y si quieres puedes sacar fotos a lo largo del año para que el niño vea cómo crece el árbol.

Colección de piedras

Materiales
Piedras grandes
Caja o cesta

Actividad

A los niños les gusta recoger cosas. Aprovecha la curiosidad de tu hijo y anímale a que coleccione piedras. Aunque sea pequeño puede cogerlas él mismo. Después decidirás si debe guardarlas o no. Cuando crezca un poco llévale al jardín y dile que busque diferentes tipos de piedras. Las mejores para coleccionar son las que tienen alguna característica especial. Dale una caja o una cesta para que ponga en ella las piedras.

Cuando haya elegido varias piedras ayúdale a decidir qué va a hacer con ellas. Por ejemplo puede formar una figura en el jardín o colocarlas en su habitación para mirarlas cuando le apetezca.

21

En el cielo

Materiales
Manta

Actividad

Procura hacer esta actividad cuando tu hijo necesite un pequeño descanso. Sal fuera y túmbate con él sobre una manta. Después mira al cielo y asegúrate de que se vea el sol sin que os dé directamente en los ojos. Pregunta a tu hijo de qué color es el cielo y qué ve en él. ¿Ve aviones o helicópteros? ¿Hay alguna nube? Anímale a que mire hacia arriba y te diga lo que vea.

Como alternativa, haz lo mismo una noche despejada de verano. ¿Cuántas estrellas puedes contar? Señala la luna y deja que el niño aprecie la diferencia entre el cielo diurno y nocturno.

Vamos a volar una cometa

Materiales
Cometa
Cuerda
Día de viento

Actividad

Monta una cometa o compra una que tenga una cola larga y vistosa. Lleva a tu hijo al jardín o a un parque en el que no haya postes eléctricos. Dile que vais a volar una cometa con la ayuda del viento y enséñale a soltar la cuerda poco a poco.

Para esta actividad conviene que haya más de un adulto, puesto que alguien tiene que vigilar al niño mientras el otro corre con la cometa. Si tu hijo se queda quieto en su silla puedes ir tú solo; en caso contrario es una buena idea que os acompañen otros miembros de la familia o algún amigo.

Ramo de flores

Materiales

Flores para coger

Actividad

Lleva a tu hijo de paseo para coger flores. Antes de hacerlo asegúrate de que las flores no tengan espinas ni pesticidas. Ayúdale a componer un ramo pequeño para poner en agua. Recuerda que lo que para ti son malas hierbas a tu hijo le puede encantar. Con las flores silvestres que crecen en el campo se pueden hacer unos ramos preciosos.

Corre, corre

Materiales

Ninguno

Actividad

Juega a correr con tu hijo. Corre a su lado, delante de él, detrás de él y agarrándole de la mano. Como es probable que le guste correr de cualquier manera, esta actividad le resultará muy divertida.

Corre hacia un árbol en el jardín. O dile que corra él primero y te espere para enseñarle a hacerlo por turnos. Estos juegos no tienen por qué ser competitivos. Disfrutad corriendo juntos y animándoos el uno al otro.

Como alternativa prueba con otro tipo de movimientos. Dile que:

◆ salte con los dos pies
◆ ande hacia atrás
◆ ande a cuatro patas
◆ dé vueltas en círculo

Molinillo

Materiales

Molinillo

Actividad

Compra un molinillo que le guste a tu hijo o haz uno tú mismo siguiendo las instrucciones que se detallan a continuación. Saca el molinillo al jardín y muéstrale cómo lo haces girar soplando o moviéndote. Después sujétalo y corre con él. Dale al niño un molinillo y dile que lo haga girar, primero soplando y luego corriendo con él.

A nosotros nos gustaban los molinillos de plástico de colores vivos. Son muy vistosos y duran mucho. Aunque a veces los hacíamos en casa. Como verás es muy sencillo.

Molinillo casero

Instrucciones

1. Haz un corte diagonal en las cuatro esquinas de un cuadrado de papel. Asegúrate de que los cortes tengan la misma longitud y deja un trozo pequeño en el centro.
2. Dobla las cuatro esquinas hacia el centro para formar el molinillo.
3. Sujeta las esquinas con una chincheta y clávala en una goma de borrar pequeña.

Corre con el viento

Materiales

Día de viento

Actividad

Cuando hace viento es casi imposible tener a un niño de dos años dentro de casa. Disfruta de lo que nos ofrece la naturaleza; abriga a tu hijo y sácale a la calle para que corra con el viento.

Una vez fuera comprueba en qué dirección sopla el viento. Luego dale la mano al niño y deja que te guíe mientras corréis con el viento por detrás.

Música y movimiento

Introducción

Puesto que a los niños de dos años les encanta moverse, ¿por qué no combinas la pasión natural de tu hijo por la música y el movimiento con algunas actividades dirigidas en las que podáis participar los dos? Verás cómo te diviertes.

Ante todo debes recordar unas cuantas cosas. Tu hijo sólo tiene dos años. No esperes que lo haga todo perfecto. Si tú quieres bailar ballet y él prefiere bailar rock & roll, déjale. Si está cantando una canción y se equivoca en alguna palabra no dejes de cantar para corregirle. Cuando acabe vuelve a cantar la canción con él con la letra correcta. No reprimas su espontaneidad porque no haga las cosas bien.

Cuando puedas incluye en estas actividades a otros miembros de la familia. Un hermano mayor que ya sepa contar puede enseñarle una canción de números, y es posible que los abuelos se animen a participar en un desfile.

La música suele ser relajante incluso a esta edad. Las nanas que le cantabas a tu hijo cuando era pequeño pueden ser adecuadas al terminar el día. Además, a los niños les gusta que haya canciones en el ritual que realizan antes de dormirse.

Por otro lado puedes usar música de fondo. Por ejemplo, puedes poner música clásica suave mientras esté jugando, o sus cintas favoritas cuando le lleves en el coche. Recuerda que tú también tendrás que escuchar esas canciones, así que elígelas con cuidado. En tiendas de discos y librerías infantiles encontrarás una gran variedad de cintas, algunas de ellas grabadas por cantantes famosos.

La silla de la reina

Materiales

Letra de la canción
(véase abajo)

Actividad

Dale la mano a tu hijo y canta esta canción tradicional andando despacio en círculo. Cuando digas «y de culo se desmayó», deberíais caeros al suelo con cuidado.

Como variación prueba con las alternativas que encontrarás a continuación. Haz lo que indique la letra y muy pronto descubrirás cuál le gusta más a tu hijo.

En esta actividad puede participar toda la familia: mamá, papá, los abuelos y los hermanos mayores. Diles a estos últimos que no den tirones a su hermano pequeño.

La silla de la reina

A la silla de la reina, que nunca se sienta,
un día se sentó, y de culo se desmayó.

Variación 1
A la silla de la reina, que nunca corre,
un día corrió, y de culo se desmayó.

Variación 2
A la silla de la reina, que nunca salta,
un día saltó, y de culo se desmayó.

Orquesta

Materiales

Tazas de metal
Sartenes, cazos y
tapas
Cucharas de madera
o de acero
inoxidable

Actividad

Anima a tu hijo a componer su propia música. Llévale a la cocina y elige con él algunos «instrumentos». Con un cazo con asa y una cuchara de madera puede tocar el tambor. (Si utiliza una cuchara de acero inoxidable el sonido será diferente.) Y si golpea suavemente dos tapas del mismo tamaño con una cuchara tendrá un xilófono casero.

Dale a tu hijo la oportunidad de crear distintos sonidos y de cantar cualquier canción con la música que componga. Y no olvides que también tú puedes practicar.

Canciones

Materiales

Canciones
Cancioneros
Cintas

Actividad

A los niños les entusiasma cantar. Podrías pasarte todo el día cantando con tu hijo, bien tarareando las sintonías de sus programas favoritos o intentando seguir las canciones de la radio. Aunque sólo cantes en la ducha y no lo hagas muy bien, tu hijo pensará que eres un virtuoso. Intenta aprender la música y la letra de unas cuantas canciones que te parezcan adecuadas. Si quieres comienza con nanas, cuyas melodías suelen ser familiares. Busca en tiendas de discos cintas y CD que contengan canciones fáciles de aprender. Si te gustan los musicales, la ópera o el rock no pases por alto estos géneros. Cuando hayas aprendido una canción cántasela a tu hijo. Canta en el coche, en la bañera o en el parque. Practica siempre que puedas.

Graba una canción

Materiales
Grabadora
Cinta virgen
Canciones familiares

Actividad
Cuando hayas aprendido unas cuantas canciones, grábalas y pónselas a tu hijo. Anímale a que cante contigo y no te sorprendas cuando comience a cantar su propia versión. Luego grábale a él sin que se dé cuenta. Ponle la grabación y observa cómo reacciona al escuchar la melodía familiar.

Completa la frase

Materiales
Letras de canciones

Actividad
Elige varias canciones que te gusten; las que riman son más fáciles para esta actividad. Después canta una de ellas y anima a tu hijo a que cante contigo. Cuando creas que conoce bien la canción omite una palabra para ver si es capaz de decirla. Una de las favoritas de nuestras hijas era «En la vieja factoría». Cuando nosotros cantábamos «Con el gato», ellas decían «miau» con gran entusiasmo. Luego seguíamos cantando y aplaudiendo su acierto. Esta actividad es excelente para desarrollar el lenguaje y la capacidad musical.

Osito de peluche

Materiales

Poema (véase abajo)
Oso de peluche

Actividad

Dile a tu hijo que finja que es un osito de peluche mientras le recitas esta poesía. Enséñale los distintos movimientos que hace el oso y luego practica con él. Anímale a recitar la letra contigo.

 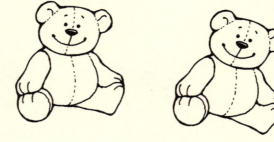

Osito de peluche

Osito de peluche,
date la vuelta *(gira despacio)*.
Osito de peluche,
saca la lengua *(enséñale la lengua)*.
Osito de peluche,
toca el suelo *(agáchate y toca el suelo)*.
Osito de peluche,
péinate el pelo *(pásate la mano por la cabeza)*.
Osito de peluche,
sube la escalera *(simula que subes una escalera)*.
Osito de peluche,
corta con las tijeras *(separa y une los dedos corazón e*
índice).
Osito de peluche,
baja del coche *(simula que te bajas de un coche)*.
Osito de peluche,
di buenas noches
(junta las manos, apoya la cabeza en ellas
y di «Buenas noches»).

Desfile

Materiales

Música de marcha
Sombrero para
desfilar

Actividad

Pon música de marcha o cualquier canción con un ritmo animado y haz un desfile con tu hijo. Tenéis varias opciones. Podéis desfilar los dos solos en la cocina, o por la calle con otros niños. Para que el acontecimiento resulte más vistoso dales unos «sombreros para desfilar». Les encantará. Sigue las instrucciones que se detallan a continuación para hacer estos sombreros.

Sombreros para desfilar

Materiales
- Una hoja de periódico
- Tijeras
- Grapas, cinta adhesiva o cola
- Lápices de cera o rotuladores

Instrucciones
1. Dobla una hoja de periódico por la mitad por el pliegue ya marcado.
2. Con el pliegue hacia arriba, dobla hacia abajo las dos esquinas y únelas en el medio. Formarán dos triángulos con un borde inferior de unos cinco centímetros.
3. Dobla hacia arriba el borde de ambos lados.
4. Para que el sombrero quede más fuerte y se adapte mejor al niño, corta los extremos de la tira inferior y dóblala hacia arriba una vez más.
5. Si quieres puedes meter hacia dentro los extremos de la tira y sujetarlos con grapas, cinta adhesiva o cola.
6. Deja que tu hijo decore el sombrero con lápices de cera o rotuladores.

Sesión de baile

Materiales
Radio

Actividad

Los niños de dos años son unos bailarines natos. Aunque a esta edad no están preparados aún para nada serio, pueden ser el alma de la fiesta si les gusta la música.

Elige una música que os agrade a los dos. Para ello puedes buscar en la radio una emisora de música o poner una cinta. Luego comienza a bailar con tu hijo. Podéis agitar las manos, subir y bajar los brazos o mover todo el cuerpo.

Si tienes problemas para moverte utiliza la imaginación. Imagina que sois los protagonistas de un espectáculo musical, que cantáis en un coro moviendo los hombros y las piernas o que bailáis juntos en una película de Fred Astaire y Ginger Rogers. Déjate llevar por el ritmo de la música y la imaginación.

Uno, dos, tres, ya

Materiales
Una zona abierta y segura para correr

Actividad

A los niños de dos años les encanta correr. Convierte este ejercicio en un juego para enseñarle a tener un poco de paciencia y los tres primeros números. Dile que vais a correr, pero que tendrá que esperar a que cuentes para empezar. Después cuenta «Uno, dos, tres» señalando los números con los dedos. Al llegar al tres grita «Ya» y deja que el niño comience a correr a tu lado. Cuando estéis los dos cansados podéis dejar de correr.

La chata Merenguela

Materiales

*Letra de la canción
    (véase abajo)*
Tazas de té, tetera
Zumo y galletas

Actividad

Con esta versión de la canción popular «La chata Merenguela» podrás enseñar a tu hijo buenos modales. Verás cuántas veces te pide que la repitas. Comienza cantándola con él. Cuando digas «La chata Merenguela» señálate con las dos manos. En el segundo verso ponte las manos en la cintura y mueve el cuerpo hacia los lados siguiendo el ritmo de la melodía. Al decir «Toma el té en tacitas» simula que coges una taza y te la llevas a la boca. Y en el último verso estírate los ojos para que queden rasgados. Cuando acabes la canción puedes tomar el «té» con tu hijo. A él le bastará con un poco de zumo y unas galletas. Pero utiliza una tetera y tazas de verdad o de juguete y explícale cómo se sirve el té.

La chata Merenguela

La chata Merenguela, cui, cui, cui,
como es tan fina, tico, tico, ti,
toma el té en tacitas,
de porcelana china.

33

Rimas y canciones de números

Materiales

Canciones de números
Animales de peluche

Actividad

Tu hijo se lo pasará en grande contando. Aunque no se lo tome muy en serio enseguida dirá «uno, dos, tres, cuatro». Las canciones de números son muy divertidas para aprender a contar. Si tienes alguno de los animales que se mencionan en las rimas utilízalos en esta actividad. Dáselos al niño y dile que los mueva cada vez que oiga su nombre.

Además de las canciones que se incluyen a continuación, puedes buscar otras en libros de rimas y poemas.

Los elefantes

Un elefante se balanceaba
sobre la tela de una araña.
Y como veía que resistía,
fue a buscar a otro elefante.
(Repite la estrofa con el dos, el tres, el cuatro...)

El uno es un soldado

El uno es un soldado haciendo la instrucción.
El dos es un patito que está tomando el sol.
El tres una serpiente, el cuatro una sillita.
El cinco es una oreja, el seis una guindilla.
El siete es un bastón, el ocho son las gafas
de mi tío Ramón.
El nueve es un globito atado a un cordel.
El cero, una pelota para jugar con él.

ABC

Materiales
Cualquier canción

Actividad

Cuando te parezca oportuno puedes enseñarle a tu hijo el abecedario cantando. Aquí hemos utilizado la música de la canción «Vamos a contar mentiras», pero puedes recurrir a cualquier otra que te guste. Cántasela cuando esté en la bañera, mientras le des la comida o en el coche. No esperes que aprenda enseguida las letras ni sus sonidos. A esta edad lo que les divierte es cantar por cantar. Aún tardará algún tiempo en cantar bien la canción.

También es una buena idea que le enseñes las letras en un tablero magnético o en libros que contengan el alfabeto. Naturalmente, todo el mundo comentará que es un niño precoz, y te sentirás muy orgullosa.

ABC

A be ce de e efe ge,
a be ce de e efe ge,
hache jota i ka ele, tralará,
hache jota i ka ele, tralará,
ka ele eme ene o...

Cu erre ese te u uve,
cu erre ese te u uve,
uve doble equis y griega y zeta,
uve doble equis y griega y zeta,
y volvemos a empezar.

juegos acuáticos

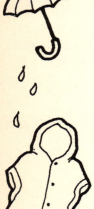
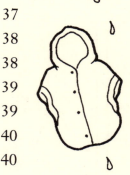

Introducción

¿Qué tendrá el agua que atrae tanto a los niños de dos años? ¿Serán las sensaciones que notan al moverse en una bañera llena de agua templada? ¿Las ondas que se forman al tirar en ella una piedra? ¿O los arco iris que se ven a través de los aspersores los días calurosos de verano? Sea cual sea la razón, a los niños les fascinan el agua y los juegos acuáticos.

Estos juegos cambian cada vez que se utiliza un nuevo recipiente o una forma distinta de agua. Pero las reglas son siempre las mismas. Para divertirte jugando con tu hijo ten en cuenta estas sencillas reglas:

◆ No le dejes nunca solo cuando juegue en el agua o cerca de ella.
◆ No le dejes jugar con agua demasiado caliente o demasiado fría.
◆ Puesto que las superficies pueden estar resbaladizas, vigila al niño en todo momento para que no se caiga.
◆ Decide si es seguro que beba el agua antes de que empiece a jugar. De este modo evitarás riesgos y no tendrás que repetirle que no beba el agua un montón de veces.
◆ Ten una toalla y ropa de repuesto a mano cuando dejes al niño jugar con agua.

Recuerda que con estos juegos también tú te mojarás, pero os lo pasaréis en grande.

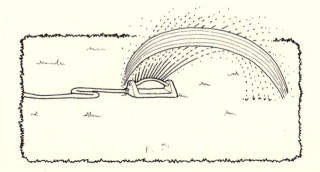

trasvase de agua

Materiales

Agua
*Recipientes
irrompibles*
*Bolsa de plástico de
cierre hermético*

Actividad

Con esta actividad podréis pasar unos ratos estupendos. Lo único que tenéis que hacer es echar el agua de un recipiente a otro. El truco consiste en buscar muchos recipientes de distinto tipo. Los más evidentes son las jarras y los vasos, pero también puedes usar moldes de pasteles y cestas de plástico. Los botes vacíos de ketchup y las bolsas de plástico de cierre hermético ofrecen también muchas posibilidades.

Este juego se suele hacer en la bañera, pero también puede ser muy divertido en el lavabo, en el fregadero de la cocina o en el jardín.

Vamos a lavar el coche

Materiales

Un coche
Agua
Cubo
Trapos o esponjas
Manguera
Jabón (opcional)

Actividad

Aunque para los adultos lavar el coche suele ser un trabajo tedioso, a los niños de dos años les encanta ayudar a sus padres en esta tarea. Si eres de los que se preocupan mucho por su coche, dile a tu hijo que lave su «coche» o su triciclo mientras tú limpias el tuyo. Pero no te sorprendas si el que se lava es él.

Dale un trapo o una esponja y un cubo de agua y enséñale a mojar el trapo y a escurrirlo para limpiar el coche con él. La tarea especial de nuestras hijas consistía en lavar y secar los neumáticos. Los dejaban impecables.

A los niños pequeños les gusta lavar el coche con una manguera, aunque para ello es necesario tener paciencia y estar dispuesto a mojarse. Si les dejas hacerlo no olvides bajar la presión del agua.

Pintando la acera

Materiales

Cubo de agua
Brochas o rodillos
Superficie de cemento

Actividad

Enseña a tu hijo a utilizar brochas grandes y rodillos. Dale varios rodillos y brochas de distinto tamaño y un cubo de agua y deja que pinte con ellos la acera o el patio. Como el sol lo secará todo lo único que tendrás que hacer es tirar el agua y recoger las brochas y el cubo. No olvides admirar la obra de arte de tu hijo.

Seguridad: Puesto que el suelo quedará resbaladizo, vigila al niño por si acaso quiere pisar sus dibujos. Ponle unos zapatos con suela de goma. Y no le dejes nunca solo cuando esté jugando con un cubo de agua.

Domador de mangueras

Materiales

Una manguera

Actividad

Dale a tu hijo la oportunidad de que dome una manguera. Antes de conectarla enséñale de dónde sale el agua. Deja que intente abrir la llave y luego explícale que el agua comenzará a salir enseguida. (También es una buena idea recordarle que sólo puede hacerlo cuando esté con mamá, papá u otra persona mayor.) Si la manguera está enrollada como una serpiente cógele la mano y pásasela por el tubo.

Después abre despacio la manguera. Si el agua sale muy deprisa el niño podría asustarse. Déjale que agarre la manguera. Si quiere beber el agua dile que lo haga sin tocar la boquilla. Cuando consiga sujetar bien la manguera déjale que se divierta regando o moviéndola por el jardín. Y cuando aprenda a dominarla sube un poco la presión.

Flota o se hunde

Materiales

Bañera
Agua
Objetos que floten
*Objetos que se
  hundan*

Actividad

A los niños les encantan los objetos que pueden empujar y salen de nuevo a la superficie. Pero también les fascinan los que se quedan en el fondo. Para que esta actividad sea segura además de divertida elige los objetos con cuidado. Pruébalos y comprueba si son lo bastante grandes para que el niño los agarre con facilidad y no se los pueda meter en la boca. Cuando tu hijo intente hundir uno de ellos pregúntale: «¿Flotará o se hundirá?». Y después dile: «Mira cómo flota el patito».

Algunos de los objetos que mejor flotan son los patos de goma, los juguetes hinchables y las cucharas de madera. Y para hundir puedes usar cucharas de metal, toallitas y pastillas de jabón.

Aspersores

Materiales

Aspersores
Toalla seca

Actividad

Si tienes aspersores en el jardín deja que tu hijo se refresque con ellos cuando haga calor. Déjale que corra a su alrededor contigo. Para que disfrute con esta actividad el agua no debe estar muy alta; bastará con que os mojéis los pies. Dile que te persiga entre los aspersores y deja que te pille; luego intercambiad 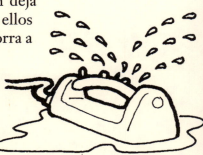 los papeles y cógele tú a él. Ten una toalla a mano para que podáis secaros.

De charco en charco

Materiales

Charcos pequeños
Botas

Actividad

Cuando deje de llover saca a tu hijo a la calle o al jardín para que pise charcos. Asegúrate de que lleva la ropa apropiada para esta apasionante aventura. Ayúdale a buscar charcos y anímale a que chapotee y salte en ellos. A algunos niños les encanta correr por los charcos. Averigua qué es lo que más le gusta a tu hijo y únete a él.

Paseo bajo la lluvia

Materiales

Una lluvia fina
Ropa adecuada para la lluvia

Actividad

Cuando no llueva mucho sal con tu hijo a dar un paseo. No olvides ponerle un impermeable, unas botas y un gorro. Coge un paraguas por si acaso comienza a llover con fuerza, pero sobre todo para que pueda llevarlo él.

Mientras paseáis habla de la lluvia y de cómo crecen las cosas con ella. Busca hojas que tengan gotas grandes de agua o muéstrale cómo cae el agua de los tejados. Habla también del color del cielo. Con un poco de suerte quizá veáis un arco iris.

Baños divertidos

Materiales
Bañera
Juguetes para la bañera

Actividad

Probablemente ahora tu hijo pasará en la bañera más tiempo que nunca, así que procura que se lo pase bien. Dale muchos juguetes de distinto tipo. Aunque los barquitos y los patos de goma son divertidos también puede jugar con un bote vacío de ketchup o con una pistola de agua. Enséñale a tirar los barcos con la pistola de agua y a usar el bote de ketchup para intentar hundir el pato.

De vez en cuando saca los juguetes y sécalos, porque si están siempre húmedos pueden oler o escurrirse entre los dedos.

Y lo que es más importante, no dejes nunca a tu hijo solo en la bañera. Aunque sólo sea un segundo y haya poca agua, las bañeras son muy peligrosas.

Qué frío hace

Materiales
Agua
Recipientes
Congelador

Actividad

Deja que tu hijo vea qué le pasa al agua cuando se enfría mucho. Esta actividad es muy interesante sobre todo para los que viven en zonas donde no nieva. Dale unos cuantos recipientes de distinto tamaño y deja que los llene de agua y los congele.

Explícale que el agua tarda un rato en congelarse, pero no esperes que lo entienda. Cuando los recipientes estén congelados saca los bloques de hielo y deja que los toque y juegue con ellos. Si quieres introducir una variación pon en el agua objetos pequeños. En ocasiones especiales haz helados con zumos para comerlos más tarde.

Regando las plantas

Materiales

Plantas
Regadera o jarra

Actividad

Si le das a tu hijo una regadera se lo pasará en grande ayudándote a regar las plantas. Las de plástico con asa grande y boca ancha son las más fáciles de manejar.

Explícale que a las plantas les gusta el agua y que necesitan beber un poco de vez en cuando. Después dale una regadera no muy llena y dile que te acompañe a regar las plantas. Ayúdale a echar el agua colocando bien la boca. Si te parece que echa demasiada, la próxima vez pon menos agua en la regadera. Con el tiempo podrá regar las plantas él solo, si no te importa que derrame agua en el suelo de vez en cuando.

juego de escurrir

Materiales

Esponjas
Cuencos o moldes
Agua

Actividad

Aunque es probable que a tu hijo le guste limpiar la mesa con una esponja húmeda, también se divertirá escurriendo una mojada. Dale unas cuantas esponjas de diferentes tamaños y dos cuencos: uno vacío y otro con agua. Enséñale a empapar la esponja en el cuenco de agua y a escurrirla en el vacío. (También puedes usar moldes de pasteles.) Deja que disfrute empapando todo el agua y escurriéndola. Cuando termine da la vuelta a los cuencos y dile que comience de nuevo. Con un poco de suerte conseguirá echar algo de agua en el cuenco. Esta actividad se puede hacer en el jardín o en una bañera vacía.

Chapucerías

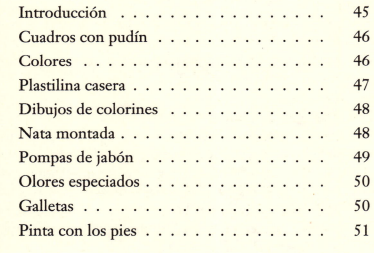

Introducción

A los niños de dos años les encanta chapucear y ensuciarse. Además de revolverlo todo suelen dejar sustancias pringosas por todas partes. Intenta pensar que las chapucerías son experiencias de aprendizaje para tu hijo. Puede que tengas una mancha de pintura en el techo, pero también tendrás un bonito dibujo colgado en el frigorífico. Con los siguientes consejos para limpiar y guardar las cosas la experiencia te resultará menos frustrante.

Procura buscar una zona para este tipo de actividades. Si tienes un cuarto de juegos puedes colocar en él una mesa pequeña, y cuando haga buen tiempo basta con sacar una mesa vieja al jardín. Otra buena alternativa es el suelo, sobre todo cuando hay varios niños trabajando al mismo tiempo.

Cubre con papel la zona de trabajo y pon una sábana grande debajo. También puedes usar papeles de periódico, aunque suelen crear problemas cuando se mojan. Lo mejor es un mantel viejo de plástico.

Antes de comenzar estas actividades ponle a tu hijo un delantal o una bata. Nosotros teníamos una ropa especial para «hacer chapuzas». (Las camisas viejas de papá son unas batas perfectas.) De ese modo no pasará nada si se ensucia.

Si tu hijo no quiere ayudarte con la limpieza plantéale esta tarea como un juego. Intenta motivarle haciendo una carrera para recoger los papeles o cantando una canción mientras guardáis las pinturas.

Ten a mano trapos o esponjas. A los niños de dos años les gusta mucho limpiar, y aunque no quiten bien todas las gotas, algo es algo. El papel de cocina resulta más práctico, porque después se puede tirar.

Aunque tengas que ocuparte de la limpieza tú sola, disfruta con tu hijo de estas actividades. Intenta ver las cosas desde su punto de vista. Lo que para ti es un engorro, para él es sinónimo de «diversión».

Cuadros con pudín

Materiales

Pudín preparado
Cuchara
Papel de cera
Cinta adhesiva

Actividad

Antes de comenzar esta actividad, prepara un pudín siguiendo las instrucciones del envase o compra uno ya hecho. (Ten en cuenta que si lo haces tardará varias horas en enfriarse.) Corta varios trozos grandes de papel de cera y cubre con ellos la zona de trabajo.

Pon unas cuantas cucharadas de pudín sobre el papel y enseña a tu hijo a pintar con los dedos. Anímale a hacer figuras y espirales y ayúdale a trazar un círculo, un cuadrado y un rectángulo.

Como variación, utiliza pudín de diferentes sabores para darle la oportunidad de que mezcle distintos colores.

Colores

Materiales

Vasos de plástico
*   transparente*
Agua
Colorante alimentario
*   (no tóxico)*

Actividades

Llena dos o tres vasos de plástico con agua y ayuda a tu hijo a echar en ella un poco de colorante. (Mira las instrucciones del paquete.) Remueve el agua y dile que observe cómo cambia. Deja que intensifique el color añadiendo unas cuantas gotas más de colorante.

Intenta mezclar diferentes colores para ver qué combinaciones podéis crear. En muchos paquetes se indica la cantidad que se necesita para conseguir algunos colores.

También puedes echar unas cuantas gotas de colorante en otros líquidos, por ejemplo leche o soda, para ver qué ocurre.

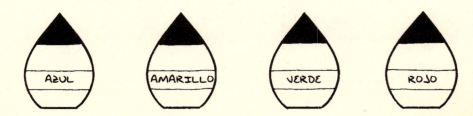

plastilina casera

Materiales

Cuenco grande
1 taza de sal (250 ml)
1 taza de harina
  (250 ml)
¹/₂ taza de agua
  (125 ml)
Recipientes o bolsas de
  plástico de cierre
  hermético
Colorante
  alimentario
Mantel de plástico
Varios «utensilios»

Actividades

Mezcla la sal, la harina y el agua en un cuenco y añade unas cuantas gotas de colorante. Guarda la plastilina en recipientes o bolsas de plástico de cierre hermético. Cuando tu hijo se sienta creativo pon la plastilina sobre un mantel de plástico y deja que se divierta tocándola con los dedos. Pregúntale si es dura, blanda o áspera.

La plastilina es muy útil para enseñar diferentes formas. Haz varias y dile a tu hijo cómo se llaman. Cógele los dedos y ayúdale a moldear un cuadrado, un círculo, un triángulo y un rectángulo. Si quiere crear sus propias figuras, déjale. Utiliza las figuras para hacer cosas, por ejemplo una casa con cuadrados o un animal con triángulos.

Para modelar figuras con plastilina basta con los dedos, pero puede resultar más divertido con algunos utensilios. Aunque se pueden comprar, es muy probable que en la cocina tengas muchos adecuados. El favorito de nuestras hijas era el prensador de ajos que usábamos para hacer espaguetis. Los moldes de galletas, los ralladores de huevo y los tapones de botellas pueden ser muy creativos. Como siempre, asegúrate de que tu hijo no se pueda hacer daño con ellos. Luego remángate y juega con tu pequeño.

Dibujos de colorines

Materiales

Lápices de cera
Papel blanco
Bote o cesta
Cinta adhesiva
    (opcional)

Actividad

Dale a tu hijo varias hojas de papel blanco o cubre una zona grande con papel de envolver y deja que pinte donde quiera. Los lápices de cera grandes son los más fáciles de manejar. Sujeta el papel a la mesa con cinta adhesiva para que le resulte más fácil pintar. Y deja los lápices juntos en un recipiente, por ejemplo en un bote de plástico o en una cesta con asas.

Recuerda que al principio sólo hará unas cuantas marcas. Quizá quiera utilizar sólo un color, y puede que se salga del papel. Pero no importa siempre que se divierta pintando.

Limpiar las marcas de pintura es muy sencillo. Si el niño se sale del papel limpia la mesa con un detergente suave.

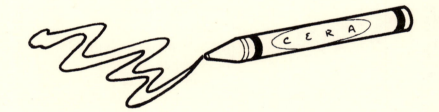

Nata montada

Materiales

Bote de nata montada
Mantel de plástico

Actividad

Cubre la mesa con un mantel de plástico y echa encima un poco de nata montada para que tu hijo dibuje con ella. Ayúdale a echar la nata del bote. (Esto sólo debería hacerlo con tu ayuda. Los niños no deben jugar con aerosoles.) Traza sus iniciales o su nombre completo.

Si no es alérgico a la leche deja que pruebe su obra de arte antes de limpiarla.

pompas de jabón

Materiales

Agua jabonosa
Varita para hacer
pompas

Actividad

Las pompas de jabón son muy divertidas. Túrnate con tu hijo para hacer pompas y cogerlas. Verás qué bien os lo pasáis. Las varitas de plástico que vienen en los recipientes pequeños pueden ser suficientes para él. Enséñale a soplar con cuidado para formar pompas y dile que no se las meta en la boca. Advertencia: el agua jabonosa puede hacer que el suelo resbale, así que piensa cuál es el lugar más conveniente para este juego.

Agua jabonosa

◆ Un recipiente grande con tapa
◆ 4 litros de agua
◆ Una taza (250 ml) de detergente líquido
◆ 40-60 gotas de glicerina

Mezcla todos los ingredientes y remueve bien.

Varita para hacer pompas

◆ Una percha
◆ 9 metros de hilo de algodón
◆ Unos alicates
◆ Unas tijeras
◆ Cinta adhesiva

Dobla el gancho de la percha para darle la forma que desees y enrolla los extremos para hacer un asa. Para evitar que haya bordes cortantes cubre el asa con cinta adhesiva.

Olores especiados

Materiales

Cuencos
Cucharas
Varias especias

Actividad

Con las especias que tienes en la despensa puedes pasar unos ratos estupendos con tu hijo. Elige dos o tres especias con un olor agradable, por ejemplo canela, clavo y jengibre. Nosotros dejábamos que nuestras hijas las olieran de los botes, pero si quieres puedes echarlas en varios cuencos. Identifica los olores y dile a tu hijo en qué comidas se suelen utilizar esas especias.

También puedes dejar que el niño eche una pizca de cada especia en un trozo de papel para que las pruebe. Esta actividad se puede repetir con distintas especias.

Galletas

Materiales

Masa de galletas
Moldes de galletas
Rodillo
Bandeja de horno
Harina
Espátula
Decoraciones para galletas (opcional)

Actividad

A los niños de dos años les gusta hacer galletas con moldes. Los de plástico con formas sencillas son los más adecuados para ellos, porque no tienen figuras intrincadas. Si no tienes moldes de galletas puedes usar vasos de plástico.

Compra o prepara masa para hacer galletas. Cubre la superficie de trabajo con harina y después aplana la masa con un rodillo hasta que tenga un grosor de poco más de un centímetro. Después enseña a tu hijo a utilizar el molde para cortar la masa y ayúdale a poner las galletas en la bandeja con la espátula.

Según el interés que tenga, podéis decorar las galletas antes de hornearlas.

pinta con los pies

Materiales

Papel de envolver
Pinturas para pintar
  con los dedos
Molde de pasteles
Toallas o toallitas
  húmedas

Actividad

Coge un trozo grande de papel de envolver y colócalo en una zona en la que tu hijo pueda moverse y se limpie con facilidad, por ejemplo el césped del jardín o la bañera. Si quieres ponle al niño unos pantalones cortos o un traje de baño.

Echa un poco de pintura en el fondo del molde. (Debe haber suficiente para cubrir las plantas de los pies del niño.) Pon el molde cerca del papel y ayuda a tu hijo a meter en él los pies, uno cada vez. Dile que levante un pie y deje que la pintura gotee en el molde. Después dile que apoye ese pie en el papel y repite la operación con el otro. Luego déjale que pinte con los pies andando de un lado a otro o en círculos. Anímale a que trace figuras o a que dé pasos grandes para que varíe la distancia entre ellas. A continuación ayúdale a limpiarse los pies para que los meta en otro molde de pintura. Si te apetece puedes usar dos colores diferentes al mismo tiempo.

Deja que se seque la obra de arte y utiliza el papel para envolver regalos especiales.

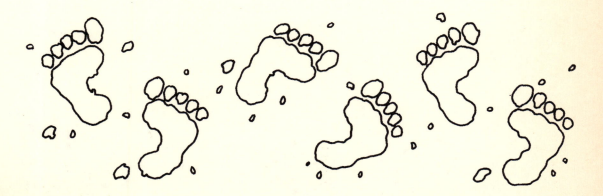

Ratos de espera

Introducción

Muchas veces tendrás que esperar con tu hijo en la cola del supermercado o en la consulta del médico. O puede que tu hijo mayor participe en una función escolar y tengáis que esperar a que se levante el telón. En cualquier caso habrá momentos en los que tendrás que entretenerle mientras esperáis.

Con las actividades de esta sección te resultará más fácil pasar esos ratos. En muchas de ellas utilizarás objetos que normalmente llevas en el bolso, el bolsillo o la bolsa de los pañales. Para otras conviene que prepares algunas cosas. Y hay otras que se realizan con los objetos que suele haber en los sitios donde esperamos.

Esperar nunca es divertido, pero si vas preparado puede ser más llevadero de lo que te imaginas. Además de tener un repertorio de actividades que no exigían mucha preparación, nosotros siempre salíamos de casa con unos tentempiés especiales.

Para empezar mira dónde estás. ¿Puedes dar un pequeño paseo con tu hijo antes de que os llamen? ¿Hay alguna zona en la que podáis correr? Compruébalo y corre con él de distintas formas. (Véase página 23.)

Sólo tú sabes cuánto tiempo es capaz de esperar tu hijo. Puede que se te acaben las ideas antes de que llegue tu turno, pero con un poco de preparación y unos tentempiés especiales la espera se te hará más corta. Para evitar una situación incómoda, no esperes hasta que tu hijo se ponga pesado para empezar a jugar.

No obstante, si comienza a dar la lata intenta mantener la calma. Si es necesario vete al comienzo de la cola y pregunta si pueden atenderte ya. Te sorprenderá lo amable que puede ser la gente para no tener que oír los berridos de un niño de dos años. Como último recurso quizá tengas que darte por vencido y volver a casa. Pero antes pon en práctica las actividades de esta sección.

tarjetas de crédito

Materiales

Tarjetas de crédito

Actividad

Si llevas tarjetas de crédito en la cartera podrás jugar con tu hijo a este sencillo juego. Pon unas cuantas tarjetas delante de él. Al principio se limitará a apilarlas, pero cuando crezca un poco podrá ordenarlas como le indiques. Si tienes dos tarjetas doradas dile que las ponga juntas. También puedes enseñarle tu nombre en una de ellas y decirle que lo busque en las demás. Y puedes inventarte juegos con cualquiera de las características que tienen en común las tarjetas de crédito, como los logotipos, los colores y los números.

Con este juego tu hijo estará un rato entretenido si no le das todas las tarjetas a la vez. A nuestras hijas les gustaba sacarlas de la cartera y volverlas a meter. Este juego casi siempre daba resultado cuando tardaban en servirnos en el restaurante.

Mira qué tengo en el bolso

Materiales

Objetos o juguetes

Actividad

Antes de ir a algún lugar donde tengas que esperar, echa un vistazo por casa y mete en el bolso algunas cosas que le gusten a tu hijo, por ejemplo un cuento, un catálogo, unas cartas, cochecitos o una caja nueva de pinturas y un bloc. No ocupan mucho y el niño se alegrará de verlas en un sitio diferente. Para jugar con algunas cosas conviene que haya una mesa y una silla, así que piensa dónde vas a ir antes de salir de casa.

Conejito

Materiales

Rotulador
Pañuelo

Actividad

Para este juego conviene usar pañuelos grandes. Lleva siempre unos cuantos cuando salgas. Aunque no hagas conejitos con ellos puedes ponértelos sobre la cabeza para entretener a tu hijo. Para hacer un conejito forma una bola en la mano con el pañuelo y después levanta dos orejas. Si no utilizas un pañuelo almidonado las orejas quedarán caídas, pero a tu hijo no le importará. Coge el rotulador y dibuja los ojos con dos puntos y la boca con una línea. Luego deja que el conejito hable a tu hijo. Puede decirle a qué estáis esperando o qué haréis al salir de allí. Cuando acabes puedes meter al conejito en su madriguera colocando la otra mano en la cadera y pasándolo por el hueco. Con un poco de suerte no tendréis que esperar mucho.

Marionetas

Materiales

*Rotulador de punta
fina*

Actividad

Estas marionetas son muy fáciles de hacer y muy divertidas. Lo único que necesitas es un rotulador para dibujar caras en tus dedos. Los mejores son el índice y el pulgar. Haz los ojos y la nariz con unos puntos y la boca con una línea. Estas marionetas pueden hablar a tu hijo o contarle cuentos. También puedes dibujar marionetas en sus dedos y decirle que las haga hablar.

juegos con monedas

Materiales
Monedas

Actividad

Si tienes monedas en el bolso o en el bolsillo podrás hacer más llevaderos los ratos de espera. Deja que tu hijo las saque de tu monedero y las vuelva a meter. Dile que las ponga en montones antes de tirarlas. Enséñale a clasificarlas por tamaños.

También puede hacer caras con las monedas. Dile que te ayude a formar con ellas un círculo y a poner los rasgos de la cara. Cuando ponga una moneda en la zona de los ojos dile que se toque los ojos. Haz lo mismo con las distintas partes de la cara.

Intenta hacer girar las monedas. Tu hijo se divertirá viendo cómo dan vueltas, e incluso puede que consiga hacerlas girar con un poco de práctica.

Recuérdale que no debe llevarse el dinero a la boca y, como es lógico, no le pierdas de vista.

Péiname el pelo

Materiales
Cepillo o peine
Espejo (opcional)

Actividad

Puesto que le habrás peinado el pelo a tu hijo más de una vez antes de salir de casa, no hará falta que se lo vuelvas a peinar. Pero puede que él se lo pase bien cepillando el tuyo. De ese modo estará entretenido un buen rato, sobre todo si os turnáis para peinaros el uno al otro. Este juego será aún más divertido si usáis dos cepillos y un espejo para ver los resultados. (Ten en cuenta que no conviene realizar esta actividad antes de una cita de trabajo o en la mesa de un restaurante.)

Cuentos de bolsillo

Materiales

Cuentos pequeños de cartón

Actividad

Con la cantidad de cuentos pequeños que hay ahora en el mercado no te resultará difícil reservar unos cuantos para los ratos de espera. Lleva siempre alguno de los favoritos de tu hijo, aunque muchas veces será uno nuevo el que capte su atención, sobre todo si le dejas sujetarlo mientras leéis. A nuestras hijas les gustaban los cuentos de cartón. Tenían poca letra y colores llamativos, y se entretenían mucho pasando las páginas.

Veo, veo

Materiales

Ninguno

Actividad

Procura realizar esta actividad en un lugar en el que tu hijo se pueda mover un poco. En el juego tradicional se dan pistas para adivinar lo que estás viendo, pero en este caso conviene que lo simplifiques un poco. Por ejemplo, puedes decirle: «Veo un cuadro en la pared. ¿Lo ves tú? ¿Puedes enseñármelo?». Si tu hijo ve el cuadro puede acercarse a él y señalarlo. Si no lo encuentra ve con él hacia donde esté y dile: «Éste es el cuadro que he visto».

Lectura

Introducción

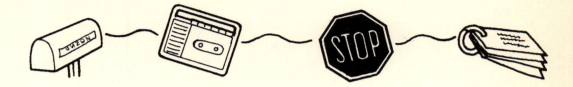

Los estudios indican que el hecho de leer a los niños es muy importante para formar buenos lectores. En cualquier caso, de ese modo desarrollan la capacidad de escuchar desde pequeños, lo cual no es poco si lo consideramos desde nuestra perspectiva como adultos. Para sentarse y escuchar hace falta tiempo y paciencia.

Además de aprender a leer, con la lectura se descubre el mundo. Si leemos a los niños en voz alta les damos la oportunidad de desarrollar el lenguaje y el sentido del ritmo. Enseguida comienzan a ver la relación entre los sonidos y las palabras escritas, y gracias a los dibujos ven cosas que no existen en su mundo.

Los ratos de lectura te permitirán comunicarte con tu hijo y acercarte a él. Coge un cuento y una manta, acurrúcate con él en una butaca y comienza a leer. Con cada cuento compartiréis una aventura diferente y podrás mostrarle nuevos lugares y personajes. Las palabras que leas le ayudarán a ampliar su vocabulario. Y las imágenes que le enseñes aumentarán su repertorio visual.

En muchas familias la hora del cuento es todo un ritual, que se puede realizar a primera hora de la mañana o antes de ir a la cama. Cuando vuelvas a casa del trabajo dedica un rato a leer con tu hijo para restablecer el contacto con él.

Hay miles de libros para elegir: cuentos sin palabras, cuentos para la bañera, cuentos desplegables y cuentos con formas. No olvides incluir algunas de tus poesías favoritas, cuentos de hadas y algunos clásicos. Y recuerda que tu hijo puede tener sus preferencias.

Los cuentos son un regalo estupendo. Anima a tus familiares y amigos a ampliar vuestra biblioteca. Si lees a tu hijo un cuento cada día, en un año habrá escuchado 365 historias; y tú tendrás 365 oportunidades de abrazarle. ¡Feliz lectura!

Vamos a leer

Materiales
Varios cuentos

Actividad

Si respetas la capacidad de atención de tu hijo disfrutarás mucho leyéndole. Puede que sea capaz de escuchar un cuento entero y pedir otro, o puede que tenga suficiente con dos páginas. Sea cual sea su reacción, respeta su ritmo y no le fuerces. Cuando esté preparado para escuchar lo hará.

Los ratos de lectura suelen ser momentos de cercanía. Para ello sienta al niño en tu regazo o cerca de ti y elige con él un cuento. Procura que sea una historia que te guste; si no te interesa mucho se notará en la forma de leerla. En cualquier caso intenta mostrar cierto entusiasmo, aunque sea la enésima vez que lees esa historia.

Lee con expresividad, cambiando el tono de voz para cada personaje. Anima a tu hijo a mirar las letras y los dibujos contigo. De vez en cuando puedes señalar una palabra o una letra. Cuando acabes hazle unas cuantas preguntas sobre la historia. «¿Te ha gustado el tren?» «¿Qué han cenado los niños?» Cuando crezca un poco intenta plantearle algunas preguntas que no se respondan con un sí o un no. Dale tiempo para pensar las respuestas.

Hojeando catálogos

Materiales

Catálogos

Actividad

Si tienes suerte recibirás un montón de catálogos por correo. Mira el buzón con regularidad y guarda todos los catálogos que lleguen. Si quieres puedes dejarlos en un lugar al que tenga acceso tu hijo. Después, cuando tengas unos minutos, siéntate con él para mirar un catálogo. Lee alguna de las descripciones de los productos. No hace falta que leas todas las palabras. Anímale a que te diga en qué zona de la página está el impermeable amarillo o el tren de juguete.

Los niños de dos años no suelen cansarse de los catálogos cuando crecen. Ten siempre unos cuantos a mano y reemplaza los que se vayan estropeando por otros nuevos. Si no recibes catálogos por correo, busca en una revista un producto que pueda interesarte y llama al número que se indique para que te envíen el catálogo.

Revistas

Materiales

Una revista con muchas ilustraciones

Actividad

Nunca falla. Cuando crees que tienes un rato libre para leer una revista, tu hijo se une a ti. Aprovecha esas ocasiones para jugar con él y enseñarle cosas. Dile que vas a leer una revista y explícale qué es con palabras sencillas: «Una revista es un conjunto de historias sobre temas diferentes, que tiene fotografías y anuncios». Luego muéstrasela y señala los anuncios y las fotos. En algunos casos quizá debas hojear la revista antes para decidir qué ilustraciones quieres mostrar a tu hijo.

Cuentos táctiles

Materiales

Cuentos táctiles

Actividad

A veces leer con un niño de dos años que no para de moverse es todo un reto. Si tu hijo quiere participar en la experiencia prueba con un cuento táctil. Estos cuentos incluyen en las páginas diferentes texturas que los niños pueden tocar mientras se lee la historia.

Para potenciar el aprendizaje comienza a establecer relaciones con tu hijo. Si el material que está tocando es suave pregúntale: «¿Qué otras cosas suaves solemos tocar?». Al terminar la sesión de lectura no olvides algunas de las texturas que hayáis tocado en el cuento. A lo largo del día, cuando encuentres algo suave, dile que lo toque y pregúntale: «¿Cómo es? ¿Es suave como el conejito del cuento?».

Lee y toca

Materiales

Papel grueso
Anillas
Punzón
Tijeras
Cola o cinta adhesiva
Rotulador
Materiales con distintas texturas

Actividad

Haz un cuento táctil con texturas diferentes, por ejemplo con bolas de algodón, papel de lija, trozos de moqueta y papel de aluminio arrugado. No te limites a usar telas y papeles; seguro que encuentras otras cosas que también resultan adecuadas. Pega los materiales en cartulinas o fichas grandes y escribe debajo con un rotulador si la textura es rugosa, suave o resbaladiza. Perfora unos agujeros en los bordes de las fichas y sujétalas con unas anillas. Luego siéntate para leer y tocar este cuento con tu hijo.

Cuentos grabados

Materiales

Grabadora
Cintas vírgenes
Cuentos

Actividad

Graba algunos de los cuentos favoritos de tu hijo para que pueda escucharlos en cualquier momento. Comienza diciendo: «Soy la madre de Helena y voy a leer para ella *Los tres cerditos*». Luego graba la historia mientras se la lees.

Los cuentos grabados son especialmente útiles para escuchar en el coche o cuando tengas que salir y dejes al niño con otra persona.

Viaje a la biblioteca

Materiales

Biblioteca pública
Bolsa para cuentos

Actividad

Puesto que es imposible tener muchos cuentos en casa, la biblioteca pública puede resultar de gran ayuda. Si todavía no eres socio, éste es el momento de que te saques el carné.

Ve a la biblioteca a menudo. A los niños de dos años les suele parecer fascinante. Muchas bibliotecas tienen una zona especial de libros infantiles. Si tienes alguna duda pregunta al bibliotecario y saca varios cuentos. Nuestro único problema era acordarnos de devolver todos los cuentos, así que siempre llevábamos la misma bolsa y contábamos los libros que sacábamos.

Cuando vayas a la biblioteca pregunta si tienen actividades especiales para niños. En algunas hay juegos y puzzles con los que tu hijo se puede entretener un rato mientras tú echas un vistazo en la sección de adultos. En otras suele haber cuentacuentos. Cuando nuestras hijas eran pequeñas la biblioteca era para ellas como su segunda casa, y ahora siguen yendo con regularidad.

Cuento personalizado

Materiales

Papel grueso
Anillas
Punzón
Tijeras
Cola o cinta adhesiva
Fotos de tu hijo

Actividad

Tu hijo disfrutará de lo lindo leyendo una historia en la que aparezca él. Coge algunas fotos suyas, pégalas en fichas o trozos de cartulina y luego escribe una historia en la que él sea el protagonista. El texto debe ser muy sencillo, con comentarios breves de las fotos. Para ello puedes utilizar las fotografías de un viaje o una excursión especial. A tu hijo le encantará oír su nombre. Por ejemplo:

Página 1: Éste es Juan en su sillita.
Página 2: Aquí está Juan en el jardín.
Página 3: Ahora Juan está echando la siesta.
Página 4: Estamos en casa de los abuelos.

Si no quieres recortar y pegar las fotografías, puedes ponerlas en un álbum de fotos y escribir debajo el texto.

En el coche

Materiales

Señales de tráfico

Actividad

Mientras vayas conduciendo por la autopista o la autovía muestra a tu hijo las señales de tráfico grandes. Cuando salgas lee en voz alta lo que ponga en letrero y dile: «Ésta es nuestra salida. Se llama Rosaleda. Rosaleda empieza por R». Así sabrá que ésa es la salida que cogéis para volver a casa y comenzará a reconocer la letra R.

Rótulos y etiquetas

Materiales

Cualquier cosa con un rótulo

Actividad

Los adultos sabemos que leer resulta útil para muchas cosas, pero los niños no. Ayuda a tu hijo a comprenderlo leyéndolo todo. Cuando te sientes a desayunar muéstrale la caja de cereales y lee los rótulos. Señala las palabras y dile qué significan. Cuando eches el detergente en la lavadora lee lo que ponga en el paquete. Si pones una cinta en el casete lee los títulos de las canciones en voz alta. Sirve cualquier cosa que se pueda leer.

Rimas y poemas

Materiales

Rimas y poemas (Véase la sección «Música y movimiento»)

Actividad

Si quieres pasar un rato estupendo con tu hijo léele poesías y rimas. Elige unas cuantas que te gusten, sobre todo las que recuerdes de tu infancia en libros con ilustraciones de colores. Después siéntate con tu hijo para leerlas juntos. Cuando crezca un poco comenzará a reconocer las palabras que riman y las repetirá contigo.

Busca algunas rimas menos conocidas. Suelen ser muy divertidas, y los niños se entretienen mucho cuando las aprenden y son capaces de recordarlas.

Esta actividad te permitirá además ampliar el vocabulario de tu hijo, porque en muchas rimas y poesías antiguas se utilizan algunas palabras con diferente significado.

Desarrollo del lenguaje

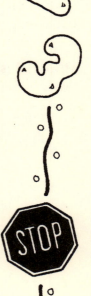

Introducción

Hace un año tu hijo sólo sonreía y gorjeaba cuando le decías algo. Ahora es capaz de responder con palabras. Dice que no con un tono contundente, y es probable que acompañe los síes con una sonrisa irresistible. La comunicación puede ser maravillosa.

Ya puedes comenzar a mantener con él conversaciones interesantes. ¿Te acuerdas de cuando era pequeño y sólo hablabas tú? Ahora además de hablar tendrás que hacer algo mucho más difícil: escuchar. ¿Cómo es posible que eso sea un problema?, te preguntarás. Con dos años los niños comienzan a unir las ideas y las palabras, y para escucharlos hace falta mucha paciencia.

Aunque ahora puede decirte si quiere leche o zumo, tendrá que pensarlo antes de decirlo. A veces te resultará más fácil darle lo que tú quieras en vez de esperar a que lo pida, y puede que te cueste dejar de hacer comentarios del tipo «Juan quiere un zumo». Pero si hablas por él no le harás ningún favor. Recuerda que necesita tiempo para contestar. Los adultos procesamos la información con mucha más rapidez que los niños, y tenemos un vocabulario extenso. Cuando nuestras hijas eran pequeñas solíamos contar en silencio hasta diez antes de esperar a que respondieran.

Como adultos también tenemos la responsabilidad de hablar bien para darles un buen ejemplo. Si quieres que tu hijo utilice frases completas debes hacerlo tú antes. Si le hablas con balbuceos él te imitará. Tenlo en cuenta, puesto que eres la persona a quien escuchará con más frecuencia.

Con las actividades de esta sección te resultará más fácil comenzar a hablar a tu hijo. Además de enseñarle a expresarse, te ayudarán a abrir vías de comunicación con él desde la infancia y a establecer las bases de su capacidad verbal.

Estribillos comerciales

Materiales

*Rimas o estribillos de
anuncios*

Actividad

Aunque a ti no te gusten mucho la radio o la televisión,
tu hijo entrará en contacto con estos medios. Utiliza los
estribillos musicales de varios productos para ampliar su
vocabulario. Cuando veas la televisión o escuches la radio, presta atención a los estribillos pegadizos y cántalos
con el niño. Explícale qué significan algunas palabras y
luego anímale a que cante contigo. Tanto el ritmo de la
música como las palabras le ayudarán a aumentar su vocabulario.

Fichas ilustradas

Materiales

*Fichas
Tijeras
Cola o cinta adhesiva
Fotografías de cajas o
revistas*

Actividad

Dedica un rato a hacer fichas ilustradas para hablar de
ellas con tu hijo. Busca dibujos y fotografías que le puedan gustar en revistas, cajas de cereales y cajas de juguete-
tes, recórtalas y pégalas en unas fichas.

Luego siéntate con el niño, enséñale las fichas una a
una y háblale de lo que haya en ellas: «Veo un gatito que
se parece al nuestro». Anímale a hablar de lo que vea en
las fichas. Al principio sólo responderá con una palabra,
pero cuando crezca un poco te sorprenderá con detalles
en los que quizá tú no te hayas fijado.

Deja las fichas a mano para cuando tengas unos minutos para sentarte con tu hijo. Si llevas unas cuantas en
el bolso te resultarán muy útiles para jugar en los ratos de
espera.

Stop

Materiales
Señales de tráfico

Actividad
Cuando vayas con tu hijo en el coche o andando por la calle comienza a mostrarle las señales de tráfico. Los stops son perfectos para esta actividad, porque son rojos y grandes. Cada vez que te acerques a una señal de stop di: «El rojo significa que debemos pararnos. ¿Ves la señal de stop roja?». El hecho de que os paréis le ayudará a comprenderlo mejor. Cuando te detengas en un semáforo en rojo explícale que la luz roja significa lo mismo que la señal roja. **Seguridad:** Aunque sea capaz de relacionar los colores y las palabras, no esperes que comprenda bien cuándo debe esperar o avanzar.

tengo dos años

Materiales
Ninguno

Actividad
A partir de ahora perderás la cuenta de las veces que la gente le pregunta a tu hijo «¿Cuántos años tienes?». Enséñale a responder «Dos» poco antes de que cumpla dos años. De esa manera, cuando alguien se lo pregunte en su fiesta de cumpleaños, aunque no responda verbalmente reconocerá la pregunta.

Dile también cómo se forma el número dos. A los niños de dos años les suele resultar difícil levantar los dedos índice y corazón, pero puedes enseñarle a levantar el índice de las dos manos y a ponerlos juntos. Nuestras hijas hacían chocar sus deditos y gritaban como locas que tenían dos años cada vez que podían.

Vamos a contar

Materiales
Ninguno

Actividad

Aprender a hablar y a contar suelen ser procesos paralelos. Plantea los números como un juego para enseñar a contar a tu hijo. Cuando subáis las escaleras pregúntale: «¿Cuántas escaleras crees que hay?». Luego agárrale de la mano y cuéntalas mientras las subís. En el supermercado elige un producto envasado y cuenta los paquetes. Hazlo despacio para que el niño pueda seguirte. Cuando sepa contar mejor sáltate un número para ver si es capaz de decirlo. Comienza del uno al diez, y no te preocupes si durante un tiempo mezcla los números. Cuanto más repitas este juego más fácil le resultará decir las palabras.

Coge el correo

Materiales
Correo

Actividad

A los niños de dos años les encanta coger el correo. Cuando vayáis al buzón deja que saque todo el correo y mire las cartas antes de dártelas. A medida que te las dé dile para quién es cada una. Si le envían algo a él no olvides señalar su nombre. Si hay revistas explícale qué contienen y hojéalas con él al volver a casa.

Algunos días sólo recibirás propaganda, pero tu hijo estará encantado. Con los folletos de juguetes y los sobres de cupones podréis hablar de muchas cosas. Y lo mejor de todo es que podrá guardarlos. Con el tiempo te darás cuenta de que merece la pena que te envíen esos catálogos que no has solicitado.

Conversación matutina

Materiales
Ninguno

Actividad

Enseñar a los niños a organizarse es muy importante. Si hablas con tu hijo por la mañana puede convertirse en un ritual que le ayudará a desarrollar su capacidad de expresión y a poner cierto orden en su vida. Después de darle los besos y los abrazos de rigor prepara una lista de preguntas sencillas para tu hijo. Cuando se establezca esta rutina estará deseando escuchar las mismas preguntas todas las mañanas. Aunque al principio sólo hables tú, enseguida comenzará a preguntar y responder.

Comienza el día preguntando:
1. ¿Qué día es hoy?
   Hoy es martes.
2. ¿Cuál es la fecha de hoy?
   Dos de junio.
3. Vamos a mirar por la ventana. ¿Qué ves?
   Veo nuestro árbol. Está lleno de hojas verdes.
4. ¿Llueve o hace sol?
   Esta mañana hace sol.
5. ¿Hace frío o calor?
   Hace calor. Hoy puedes ponerte pantalones cortos.
6. ¿Hay nubes en el cielo?
   Esta mañana no hay nubes.

Charla televisiva

Materiales

Televisión

Actividad

Aunque no veas mucho la televisión, es muy probable que a tu hijo le llamen la atención las imágenes y los sonidos que salen de ese aparato. Si es así, puedes convertir la televisión en un aliado para desarrollar su capacidad de expresión.

Selecciona los programas con cuidado. Hay algunos excelentes para niños. A veces los vídeos resultan más adecuados, porque se pueden controlar mejor.

Después de ver el programa elegido con tu hijo hazle algunas preguntas sobre lo que habéis visto.

Cuando su hermano mayor vuelva de la escuela dile que le pregunte al pequeño qué ha hecho durante el día. De ese modo le incluirás en su vida. Además, un niño de cinco o de diez años hablará de cosas diferentes. Antes de que te des cuenta el pequeño comenzará a preguntarle al mayor qué ha hecho en la escuela.

Si tienes un vecino al que le guste hablar con los niños dile que se pase por vuestra casa a menudo. Los niños que oyen hablar a mucha gente suelen desarrollar mejor el lenguaje. El hecho de oír a otras personas que tienen un vocabulario y unas expresiones diferentes les ayuda a tener una visión del lenguaje más completa. Al principio puede que le cueste responder, pero si el vecino tiene paciencia tu hijo comenzará muy pronto a conversar con él.

juegos de simulación

Introducción

Los niños de dos años hacen simulaciones con frecuencia, por ejemplo cuando juegan a los disfraces, imaginan que montan a caballo o mantienen una conversación mientras acuestan a sus muñecos.

Simular es el arte de dejarse llevar por la imaginación, y los niños de dos años son unos expertos en esta materia. Además, los padres podemos aprender muchas cosas si observamos cómo actúan nuestros hijos y participamos en sus juegos. A los que vivimos en el mundo real nos puede parecer ridículo ponernos un sombrero o fingir que estamos merendando, pero a través de este tipo de juegos podemos saber cómo nos ven nuestros hijos. Cuando cantamos canciones o les leemos cuentos a la hora de ir a la cama muchas veces nos imitan y hacen lo mismo con sus muñecos. ¿Cuándo fue la última vez que te pusiste a gatas y rugiste como un león? Tu hijo se lo pasará en grande si te imaginas que estás en la selva o en una granja. Anímale a que te enseñe todo lo que sabe sobre los movimientos y las voces de los animales.

Los accesorios son muy útiles para los juegos de simulación. Normalmente se utilizan sombreros o platos, pero las pelotas y los bloques son también estupendos, porque pueden representar muchas cosas. Y si añades unos cuantos muñecos, animales o coches de juguete puedes montar una granja, una carretera, un supermercado, un parque o un zoo. Al principio quizá tengas que crear tú el escenario para que tu hijo comience a jugar, pero cuando crezca un poco también lo hará él.

Aunque las cocinas de juguete y los bancos de trabajo son muy prácticos para este tipo de juegos, también se pueden hacer cocinas, casas y establos con cajas de diferentes tamaños. Utiliza cestas, cazuelas, cuencos o cualquier objeto que pueda ser otra cosa para tu hijo. Cuando nuestras hijas eran pequeñas hacíamos meriendas imaginarias, íbamos al zoo con animales de peluche y cazábamos osos sin salir de casa. Observando cómo simulaban, participando en sus juegos y viendo cuánta imaginación tenían nos lo pasábamos tan bien como ellas.

Disfraces

Materiales

Ropa grande
Espejo de cuerpo
   entero (opcional)

Actividad

Tu hijo se lo pasará en grande disfrazándose. Para ello busca ropa y accesorios que se puedan poner y quitar con facilidad, como sombreros, bolsos y zapatos. Las prendas demasiado largas y las que tienen cordones o hebillas no son nada prácticas. Con un sombrero vaquero y un simple chaleco tu hijo podrá simular que es otra persona. En vez de limitarte a mirarle disfrázate con él. Ponte un sombrero y crea una situación que tenga que ver con vuestros disfraces. Deja que el niño se mire en un espejo de cuerpo entero mientras simula que es lo que quiera ser.

Dale de comer al bebé

Materiales

Muñecos o animales
   de peluche
Cuchara
Cuenco
Vaso

Actividad

Puesto que para los niños de dos años comer es muy importante, este juego es para ellos algo natural. Deja que tu hijo finja que da de comer a un muñeco o a los animales de peluche. Puede hacerlo con platos de juguete o con cuencos y cubiertos de verdad. Si todavía utiliza la silla alta puede poner en ella al muñeco. Cuanto más mayor sea más se divertirá con este juego. Sin embargo, lo que más le gustará será darte de comer a ti. Y quizá quiera también un vaso para darte algo de beber.

Bloques multiusos

Materiales

*Bloques de
construcción*
Muñecos
Otros juguetes

Actividad

Los bloques son extraordinarios para los juegos de simulación. Un simple bloque cuadrado puede convertirse en un coche, una almohada para un muñeco o un plato de comida. Anima a tu hijo a jugar con bloques cuando le recuerdes el día que pasasteis en la playa o la visita a casa de la abuela.

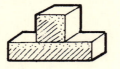

Arre, caballito

Materiales

*Tubos de cartón
largos*

Actividad

Tu hijo se lo pasará en grande simulando que monta a caballo. Dale un tubo largo de cartón y enséñale a subirse a su caballito. Dile que diga «Arre» mientras da una vuelta por el jardín. Si quieres puedes cabalgar con él.

¿Puedes hacer lo mismo que yo?

Materiales

Ninguno

Actividad

Para empezar con este juego simula que eres un pájaro. Después dile a tu hijo: «Mírame. Soy un pájaro que está moviendo las alas. ¿Puedes hacerlo tú?». Cuando comiences a mover las «alas» intentará imitarte. Haz lo mismo con otros animales, por ejemplo con un león que ruge o con un pez que nada. Así podrá simular que es otra cosa.

Gala musical

Materiales

Música

Micrófono (opcional)

Actividad

Dale a tu hijo la oportunidad de ser la estrella de un espectáculo. Tú puedes ser el público o participar con él en la gala. Deja que simule que canta una canción. (Quizá te sorprenda cantando de verdad.) Con un micrófono real o imaginario será aún más divertido. Anima a tu hijo a cantar con el micrófono y a moverse. Podéis cantar juntos una canción para el resto de la familia o animar a los demás a unirse al espectáculo.

Conversaciones telefónicas

Materiales

Teléfono de verdad o
de juguete

Actividad

Tu hijo lleva varios meses viendo cómo hablas por teléfono, y probablemente interrumpiéndote. Dale un teléfono para que pueda hablar también él. Si le compras uno de juguete asegúrate de que el cable sea corto para que no pueda enrollárselo alrededor del cuello. Si le das uno de verdad es mejor que quites el cable.

Dile que hable por su teléfono. También puedes simular que comienza a sonar, cogerlo y dárselo diciendo que es el abuelo o la abuela. Luego anímale a que mantenga una conversación con la persona que ha llamado.

Para que el juego resulte más divertido, consigue otro teléfono de juguete para conversar con tu hijo.

Zona de juegos

Materiales
Zona especial

Actividad

Tu hijo ampliará muy pronto su mundo imaginario buscando lugares especiales para jugar. Puede que se meta debajo de la mesa y se imagine que es una cueva. O que la parte posterior del sofá sea para él un parque o una playa. Deja que tenga su propio espacio, sobre todo si sus hermanos mayores quieren estar a todas horas en ese lugar. Algunos niños de dos años crean su espacio en el parque en el que jugaban de bebés. Respeta su territorio y entra en él sólo cuando te invite.

Marionetas de papel

Materiales
Bolsas de papel
Pinturas o
*   rotuladores*

Actividad

Dibuja caras y cuerpos en dos bolsas pequeñas de papel con un rotulador. Recuerda que debes hacer la boca en el pliegue para poder abrirla y cerrarla cuando las marionetas «hablen». Ayuda a tu hijo a decorar las marionetas. Ponte una bolsa en la mano, dale la otra a tu hijo y enséñale a manejarla. Las marionetas pueden hablar entre sí o contar cuentos. Si das una marioneta a cada miembro de la familia podéis pasar un rato estupendo.

Bibliografía

Información para padres
Estos libros pueden servirte de ayuda cuando tengas alguna duda sobre el desarrollo de tu hijo.

Allison, Christine, *I'll Tell You a Story, I'll Sing You a Song*, Dell, 1987.

Ames, Louise, *Your Two-Year-Old: Terrible or Tender*.

Blaustine, Jan, *The Joy of Parenthood*, Simon and Schuster, 1993.

Brazelton, T. Berry, *Touchpoints*, Addison Wesley, 1992.

Caplan, Theresa y Frank, *The Early Childhood Years: The 2 to 6 Year Old*, Putnam, 1983.

Decker, Celia Anita, *Children: The Early Years*, The Goodheart-Willcox Co., Inc., 1991.

Fisher, John J. (ed.), *Johnson and Johnson—From Baby to Toddler*, Putnam, 1988.

Jessel, Camilla, *From Birth to Three*, Bantam Doubleday Dell, 1990.

Kelly, Marguerite, y Parsons, Elia, *The Mother's Almanac*, Doubleday, 1975.

Leach, Penelope, *El bebé y el niño*, Grijalbo Mondadori, 1993.

Riverside Mother's Group, *Don't Forget the Rubber Ducky*.

Ryder, Verdene, *Parents and their Children*, Adams-Hall, 1993.

Silver, Susan, *Baby's Best*, Simon and Schuster, 1995.

Spock, Benjamin, y Rothenberg, Michael, *Dr. Spock's Baby and Child Care*, Simon and Schuster, 1992.

Trelease, Jim, *The New Read-Aloud Handbook*, Penguin, 1989.

White, Burton, *First Three Years of Life*, Simon and Schuster, 1995.

EL NIÑO Y SU MUNDO

Títulos publicados:

FOR BRADY

THIS IS A STORY OF WHAT I WAS,
NOT WHAT I AM.

—Robert Graves, *Goodbye to All That*

I, CLAUDIA

MARY McCoy

Carolrhoda LAB
MINNEAPOLIS

Carolrhoda Lab™
An imprint of Carolrhoda Books
A division of Lerner Publishing Group, Inc.
241 First Avenue North
Minneapolis, MN 55401 USA

For reading levels and more information, look up this title at www.lernerbooks.com.

Cover and interior images: Manekina Serafima/Shutterstock.com; Marcel Jancovic/Shutterstock.com; Ezepov Dmitry/Shutterstock.com; kraifreedom Studio/Shutterstock.com; gashgeron/Shutterstock.com; M88/Shutterstock.com; Miloje/Shutterstock.com; Dream_master/Shutterstock.com; A_Lesik/Shutterstock.com; Ka_Lou/Shutterstock.com; Todd Strand/Independent Picture Service.

Main body text set in Janson Text LT Std 10.5/15.
Typeface provided by Linotype AG.

Library of Congress Cataloging-in-Publication Data

Names: McCoy, Mary, 1976– author.
Title: I, Claudia / Mary McCoy.
Description: Minneapolis : Carolrhoda Lab, [2018] | Summary: "Over the course of her high school years, awkward Claudia McCarthy finds herself unwittingly drawn into the dark side of her school's student government, with dire consequences" —Provided by publisher.
Identifiers: LCCN 2017038714 (print) | LCCN 2018007836 (ebook) | ISBN 9781541523753 (eb pdf) | ISBN 9781512448467 (th : alk. paper)
Subjects: | CYAC: Conduct of life—Fiction. | High schools—Fiction. | Schools—Fiction. | Student government—Fiction. | People with disabilities—Fiction. | Family life—California—Los Angeles—Fiction. | Los Angeles (Calif.)—Fiction.
Classification: LCC PZ7.1.M43 (ebook) | LCC PZ7.1.M43 Iah 2018 (print) | DDC [Fic]—dc23

LC record available at https://lccn.loc.gov/2017038714

Manufactured in the United States of America
3-47220-26213-2/4/2019

During our first session, you told me, "Claudia, you are what we call an excellent historian."

You meant it in the therapist's sense of the word, my ability to reflect upon my own troubles, their causes, and contributing factors, and craft a narrative around them: the story of my rise, my disgrace, the long string of humiliations and failures that had brought me to your couch, a box of tissues at my side.

I had just mentioned Charles I of England, who was hounded by Oliver Cromwell and the Roundheads, arrested, made the subject of a farcical trial, and sentenced to death. The day of his trial was cold, and Charles wore two shirts so that no one would see him shivering when he placed his head on the block and think that it was because he was afraid.

The idea of putting a king on trial was novel to the English people—so novel, in fact, that no one noticed until it was too late that Oliver Cromwell and his New Model Army were batshit insane and that they'd just replaced an innocuous king with a full-blown tyrant.

I was not trying to say that Charles I was the best king England ever had. However, out of them all, he certainly wasn't the one most deserving of public execution.

"Are you saying you feel like Charles I?" you asked.

"Of course not," I said.

He was a 17th-century English king. He had a son to avenge him, who would return from exile, overthrow Cromwell, and regain the throne. He was guaranteed a place in history. We have nothing in common.

I was just saying that, in some small way, I might have understood how he felt standing before the executioner's block.

PART I

THE REIGN OF AUGUSTUS

THE HONOR COUNCIL

SENIOR CLASS REPRESENTATIVES:
AUGUSTUS DEAN, PRESIDENT
MARCUS RIPPA

JUNIOR CLASS REPRESENTATIVES:
MAISIE MCCARTHY, VICE PRESIDENT
TY BERMAN

SOPHOMORE CLASS REPRESENTATIVES:
LIVIA DRUSUS
REBECCA IBAÑEZ

FRESHMAN CLASS REPRESENTATIVES:
ZELDA PARSONS
JESSE NICHOLS

I

THE FUTURE IS COMING FOR YOU

I asked where we should start, and you said the beginning, which did not clarify things at all. The historian imposes beginnings upon her narrative; they are not naturally occurring things.

I could begin with the founding of the Imperial Day Academy in 1898 and its subsequent rise to prominence among the elite families of Los Angeles County. Or I could begin in the late 1990s when my parents bucked the glittery tech company trend of settling in the Bay Area or the Pacific Northwest, and instead based their start-up, DeliverMe, in Los Angeles. I could start with my birth, or with the day that Augustus and Livia became a couple, or with the day that Livia became a menace.

When you said none of that would be necessary, annoyance tugging at the corners of your mouth, I told you that I'd start with the ninth grade. It seemed as good a place as any to start.

I entered ninth grade with a piece of prophecy and a piece of advice from a fortune-teller, and they served me well up until the recent chain of events that led to me being here and talking to you.

The night I came into this information, I had gone to Venice Beach with my older sister, Maisie, and her friends:

Augustus, Livia, Marcus, Julia, Ty, and Cal. They were all older than I was, already students at Imperial Day, already distinguishing themselves despite the fact that most of them were still underclassmen, and were it not for Maisie, I would never have been invited to join them at all.

Maisie is two years older than I am and was about to start her junior year at Imperial Day. She has long, dark hair that she wears parted down the middle with bangs. She is always drawing, and when my family goes out to dinner at our favorite Italian restaurant, Maisie orders for all of us with an accent, which impresses the waiters.

Everybody loves Maisie, but more importantly, Maisie loves me.

Maisie loves me in a way most people do not. She never acts like I am an embarrassment or an obligation. She didn't have to invite me to the beach with her friends that evening, but she did anyway. My parents would have been content to leave me moldering in my room with a history of Weimar Germany or a playlist of Ken Burns documentaries. I would have been content with that, too, but when Maisie stuck her head into my bedroom and said, "A bunch of us are going to Venice tonight, Claudia. You should come," I found myself getting up off the floor and putting on a clean t-shirt.

Marcus was driving when they came to pick us up, though the Lexus belonged to Augustus, who only had his learner's permit. Augustus rode shotgun, and Marcus's long-time girlfriend, Julia, sat in the backseat looking like a 1940s film star in her cat-eye sunglasses. I was pleased to see that Augustus's girlfriend, Livia, was not in the car. Livia had a summer internship at Google, Augustus explained, and since their offices were in Venice anyway, she was going to meet us there.

"How did she manage *that*?" Julia asked, and I was pleased to hear in her tone evidence that Livia's charms were not universally admired, even if my sister was best friends with her.

"Her dad knows someone," Augustus said. He said it without judgment because at Imperial Day, everybody's dad or mom knows someone. Not necessarily someone who could get a Google internship for a high school freshman who couldn't even code—Livia's dad was especially well connected—but at least someone who could get you good seats at the Hollywood Bowl or write you a rec letter for Stanford.

In any case, I was grateful for whatever nepotism had made it possible for me to enjoy the drive to the beach without her. Something about Livia always made my stutter come out.

With the others, it was easier. Marcus, who was a rising senior, was so much older that I barely registered as a person to him, and Augustus was so popular that he could afford to be magnanimous. Besides, he liked my sister, and I found a little bit of shelter under the umbrella of his admiration for her.

We parked, then walked over to the Venice Skate Park, where we found Ty and Cal leaning on the railing and watching the skateboarders whizzing around the banks of the flow bowl. Cal carried a board with him and swaggered toward us as if he had already skated, even though I could tell he hadn't. There wasn't a drop of sweat on him and the board looked like it had never been used.

Julia noticed it, too.

"Are we going to get to watch you skate, Cal?" she asked with a smirk.

He turned his piggy eyes on her and cackled in the straitjacket-ready way I would come to know far too well over the next three years.

"No, Julia!" he said, holding his skateboard out to her like a burnt offering. "I'm going to watch *you* skate!"

Julia took a stutter-step back from his outstretched arms, but had no retort. Cal had a flair for verbal repartee that came in from the side, slightly cockeyed with an absurdist bent. You never knew how to respond to it, and if anything, Julia looked like she wished she'd kept her mouth shut in the first place. I understood. Cal made me almost as nervous as Livia did, and I dreaded the idea of doing anything that might draw his attention.

We said our hellos, and then we turned to watch the skateboarders, whose feats were so dazzling and hypnotic that we barely spoke to each other.

Maybe this won't be so bad, I thought. Maybe next, somebody would suggest going to the movies so we could all sit in the dark for two hours not talking and then go home. I was just thinking how perfect that would be, when I turned around and saw Livia coming our way.

She peeled off her pink cardigan as she walked, and her white sundress suddenly transformed from office- to beachwear in a way it only ever does on the pages of *Marie Claire*. She propped her sunglasses on top of her head as she sauntered up to Augustus and stood on tiptoes to kiss him on the cheek.

"How was work?" he asked, and she said, "Fine," and they both sounded at least forty.

The thing that might surprise you after hearing the way I've just talked about Livia is that she isn't pretty. Not that I have any right to talk. I'm just saying that if you didn't know her and saw a picture of her, you might be surprised that someone with the conventional, symmetrical, Captain America prettiness of Augustus was dating her.

Maisie hugged Livia, which started a cascade of unwanted hugs. Julia had to hug Livia because otherwise it would have looked like a snub. As Augustus's best friend and Julia's boyfriend, Marcus had to hug her next. Ty was the sort of stiff, taciturn person for whom hugs were acutely painful but who would never do anything that seemed rude, so he hugged her, and then Cal hugged her probably a little longer and closer and more creepily than Livia would have liked. Once this had all been dispensed with, Livia's eyes fell at last on me.

"I wasn't expecting to see you here, Claudia," she said, and if she'd said, *What the hell are you doing here, Claudia?* it would have sounded equally gracious and warm. Needless to say, we did not hug.

"M-M-Maisie invited me," I said, folding my arms across my chest.

There it was: my stutter, reliable as a German train schedule.

"Oh, that was nice of her," Livia said, giving a pitying look to Augustus. Then she suggested we all get some food because she was dying of hunger, which of course, was a ludicrous overstatement.

We drifted away from the skate park and walked down the boardwalk, past beach cafes and taco stands. Nobody could agree on where to go, not even my ordinarily easygoing sister, who insisted on sushi even though everybody else refused to eat it because the Health Department had given the stand a B.

Undeterred, Maisie split off from the group to get her Dragon Roll, though not before inviting me to join her. Maisie was always thoughtful like that. I considered going with her. It would have been nice to have had a few minutes alone with her, away from her friends who made me so nervous. It would have been worth the food poisoning I almost certainly would have gotten. If I had it to do over again, I *would* have gone with her, but at that moment, all I could think was that Maisie might have wanted a break from her loser kid sister, and so I stayed behind with the others, looking longingly over my shoulder. She shouted that she'd catch up with us and disappeared into the crowd.

On one side of the boardwalk were semi-legitimate businesses—the places where you could buy bikini tops and pizza by the slice. On the other side of the boardwalk people had set up card tables and canopies from which they sold homemade jewelry, painted rocks, and pamphlets filled with conspiracy theories about aliens and the Illuminati and the lizard people. You walked faster past these people, avoided eye contact. If you got into a conversation with the henna tattoo lady, you might be lost, and found again years later selling toe rings at a rickety card table of your own.

I struggled to keep up with the others, my bad leg starting to ache as it did whenever I tried to walk too far or too fast, and I was mentally willing myself not to keel over in the sand when we passed the fortune-teller's booth.

The hand-lettered sign in front of it read, BE PREPARED! THE FUTURE IS COMING FOR YOU!

I noticed it in the way you notice when you walk past a dog tied up in someone's yard, barking like it wants to eat your face.

Bead curtains hung from three sides of the canopy so that it was almost dim inside. Behind a card table sat a man with sand-colored dreadlocks. He wore several layers of clothing despite the heat. Nobody stopped and nobody paid any attention to him, and he didn't seem to mind until I walked past. Then he became agitated, rocking back and forth on his stool and calling out to us.

"Hey, Blondie!" That was to Livia. "C'mere. All of you come here. I've got something to tell you. No one may ever have this knowledge again. Power. Betrayal. Corruption. Destruction. If I was you, I'd want to know about it."

There was something about his voice when he said "Destruction"—something low and rumbly that made me shudder. I recovered quickly, but Livia picked up on it right away, perpetually on the lookout as she was for any display of human frailty. I knew immediately that she would veer back toward the fortune-teller, leading the rest of our group behind her.

"How much for this knowledge that no one may ever have again?" Livia asked.

"Twenty bucks," the fortune-teller said. The whites of his eyes were the color of Dijon mustard, and as we drew closer, smells of patchouli and grain alcohol wafted toward us.

"Yeah, I'm not doing that," Marcus said, before turning to Julia. "Come on, let's get something to eat."

Marcus was on scholarship, and even if he wasn't, he was much too sensible to throw away twenty dollars on a boardwalk fortune-teller. Besides, why did he need a fortune-teller? His future was as good as written. Sweet, beloved, genius poor kid bounces around foster homes until he lands at Imperial Day, and soon thereafter moves in with Augustus's family, practically like a second son. His college application essay would probably be optioned for film.

"Who's first? I don't have all day," the fortune-teller said as Marcus and Julia turned away and set off down the boardwalk toward the chicken flautas stand. He sounded impatient, even though it wasn't like we were falling over each other to sit down at his seedy-looking table.

Livia turned to me and smiled sweetly.

"Why don't you go first?" she said.

"I don't have twenty dollars," I said, even though I did.

"Too bad," the fortune-teller said. "I have some *especially* extraordinary things to tell you."

Livia turned toward the others. "We'll throw in five dollars each for her." It was a command, not a question.

"That's really not necessary," I said, inching back from the fortune-teller's stand.

"It's no trouble," Livia said, reaching in her baby-blue Bottega Veneta clutch.

"I d-d-don't want to have my fortune told," I said, a little more forcefully than I'd intended, which of course made me stutter all over the place.

Livia looked like a sadistic dentist who'd just prodded a sore tooth. She held out her hand and, just like that, Ty and Cal each pitched in a five-dollar bill. Only Augustus held back, eyeing my obvious discomfort. He'd shell out five bucks for a laugh, but not for a cruel one.

"She doesn't want to do it, Livia," he said.

Livia shrugged as though that fact was entirely beside the point.

"Come on, Maisie's sister," Cal said. "It's not like he's going to give you herpes. Probably."

I could feel my throat start to tighten as I inhaled the mixture of incense and cheap liquor wafting from the fortune-teller's booth. My head spun, and I held a hand to my nose even though I knew it was rude.

It wasn't this particular fortune-teller. It wasn't his odor or grotesque looks. The truth is that I don't like fortune-tellers.

No. That's not the truth. The truth is that I'm afraid of fortune-tellers.

I'm a historian. Fortune-tellers are my natural enemies. I deal in a past that happened. They deal in a future that won't.

The idea of having a stranger look into my eyes and down at my palm, then tell me all about myself, made me want to go into hiding. I didn't want to be seen or known, and I certainly didn't want any of it to happen with Livia, Cal, and the rest of them watching.

But more than any of that, I didn't want to hear my fortune because even if it was a scam, even if I had nothing to be afraid of, it was *me* we were talking about.

I knew it would be terrible, and I knew it would be the truth.

After kicking in the last five dollars herself, Livia put four bills down on the fortune-teller's table and pulled her hand away like she was afraid of accidentally touching something. Then she pushed me forward and sat me down on the three-legged stool.

There I was, face-to-face with the fortune-teller. I was frozen in my seat, arrested by his gaze and deranged grin. I shook Livia's hands from my shoulders and scooted up close to the fortune-teller's card table. If I was going to be forced to have my fortune read, at least I could have some privacy. The man seemed to understand, leaning in and lowering his voice.

"How old are you?" he muttered.

"Fourteen," I muttered back.

He nodded knowingly. "Ninth grade, right?"

"Yes."

"Ninth grade is where it all started to go wrong for me," he said, sucking on a tooth.

That was one of the many things about fortune-tellers that drove me nuts, the way they tricked you into doing their work for them, acting like they were making small talk when really, they were trying to pin you down. I didn't respond. I wasn't going to make it that easy for him.

"Do you like school?" he asked.

"Yes," I said.

Then he surprised me.

He cocked his head to the side and said, "So it's people you don't like."

"I like people fine." I tried to sound casual about it, but it probably came off sounding defensive anyway.

"Then people don't like *you*," he said, sucking his tooth again as he sized me up. "You start a lot of fights?"

I sniffed, enjoying a moment of vindication—and a little bit of relief. There was nothing magical about this person. He was doing a cold reading, and not doing a very good job of it either.

"I'm a pacifist," I said, looking back over my shoulder. Augustus and Ty were keeping a respectful distance, and Cal's attention had drifted toward a busty woman in a slingshot bikini and roller skates, twirling down the bike path. But Livia hung on every word I said, no doubt filing it away for some moment in the future when she could use it against me.

"You know who else was a pacifist?" The fortune-teller reached across the table and gripped my forearm. I could feel my skin begin to itch at his touch, could almost see the fleas hopping from his arm to mine. I tried to pull away, but he only tightened his grip.

"You ever heard of Good King Wenceslas?" he asked.

"Like in the song?" I asked, finally wrenching my arm out of his grip, not caring how rude it might seem. But the fortune-teller seemed too worked up to care.

"Murdered by his own brother, Boleslav the Cruel," he

said. "To get a dukedom. With a name like that, you'd think Wenceslas would have seen it coming."

"What does that have to do with me?" I asked.

He lowered his voice further and craned his neck down so that the ocean breeze carried his words away and Livia, who wasn't even trying to conceal her eavesdropping, was frustrated in her efforts and finally rejoined Augustus, Ty, and Cal.

"Because, Claudia, I want you to know that I am also a student of history."

His words shot down my spine like ice water.

He overheard one of them, I thought. Livia must have said my name within earshot of his table.

However, I knew this was not the case. And how could he have known I was a historian?

The fortune-teller's lips curled back to reveal two silver canine teeth, probably the ones he'd been sucking.

"What's the matter?" he asked, pleased with himself. "Cat got your tongue? Now, tell me. What is it that you'd like to know?"

I could have asked anything. Often I think about that and wish I'd asked about something meaningless, like what the weather would be like on October 16 or whether I'd be pretty in ten years. Other times, I wish I'd asked about love and whether I was always going to be alone. That would have been useful information.

But I didn't, and what I asked was so broad, so stupid, I don't know what kind of answer I even expected to get.

"What's high school going to be like?" I asked.

The fortune-teller didn't hesitate.

"The answer is all right there," he said, nodding toward Augustus and Ty and Livia and Cal. "Your little friends over there."

I looked over my shoulder in disbelief.

"Those people aren't my friends."

The fortune-teller clasped my hands. This time, I didn't recoil from his touch.

"Of course they're not. And you're going to destroy them all. You're going to leave them reeling, their ambitions unrealized, their dearest hopes and wishes thwarted. And when all of them have fallen away, you alone will be left standing with the kind of power that people would lie and cheat and steal for, the kind of power that everyone wants. Everyone except you."

The skeptic in me pulled my hands away, started to get up from the table, but the historian in me won out. I stayed put and let the fortune-teller's words sink in.

His eyes darted toward Augustus, then down the line: Ty, then Cal, before meeting mine again.

"Gold. Silver. Then clay. Then bronze."

"Augustus is gold?" I asked, frantic to remember every word even if I didn't understand what they meant. He'd looked at me when he said *bronze*. Did that mean I was bronze? Was that supposed to be a good thing?

Without answering my question, the fortune-teller cut his eyes toward Livia and he whispered to me, "And her? She's the fire that forges you all. You want to keep from getting burned, Claudia? Play up that stutter of yours. Play up the limp. But whatever you do, Claudia, play dumb and keep your head down. You do that, and you just might make it out of Imperial Day Academy in one piece."

I'd never told him where I went to school. That I knew for sure.

II

A STUDENT OF HISTORY

Nothing I do matters.

You might think that I'm upset about this, that after years of absorbing contempt from my peers and disappointment from my parents, it was inevitable that I would end up here in your office.

But you'd be wrong if you think I'm that fragile.

You see, I almost died when I was born. I was hospitalized for months, an incubator baby with translucent skin and a dozen tubes sticking out of me, and for most of that time, I was alone. My mother and father were busy cleaning up the mess that was our family business and attending to my siblings, so mostly I lay mewling in the Neonatal Intensive Care Unit by myself. Very few pictures of me exist from that time. Two-pound babies are not very lovely to look at, and I suppose no one wanted to get all that attached to me in case I failed to pull through.

Lest you think my parents neglectful monsters, I don't hold this against them. The time surrounding my birth was a difficult one for them. You see, my parents were, in the parlance of the early 2000s, internet pioneers. They had started a string of successful online businesses that catered to busy people who were too important to have time to do their own errands, but not important enough to have personal assistants to do those things for them. So my parents created DeliverMe, an online service to deliver their diapers and groceries, run background checks on their nannies, and order their takeout.

Along the way, they transformed themselves from Caltech-educated nerds into the class of moneyed Angelenos. They lost their schlubiness, moved from Pasadena to Los Feliz, and then to Pacific Palisades when they had kids. They acquired the trappings of Angeleno success: a pool they never used, a personal trainer, Botox, teeth whitening sessions, an electric car, a storage unit for their wine, and a stylist for special occasions.

My mother was not quite seven months pregnant with me when she discovered that my father's assistant, Melinda, had stolen credit card numbers from 75 percent of DeliverMe's customer base.

My mother's suspicions had been aroused when she found Melinda, whom she'd never liked, flirting with the head of DeliverMe's security operations, a doughy, acne-scarred, unreconstructed geek named David. My mother valued David for his home-brewed encryption software and the firewalls he guarded like a sworn member of some ancient warrior guild, but she was not sure what Melinda saw in him and doubted the purity of her motives.

As a result, the next time Melinda went to lunch, my mother went to her desk and saw that the little idiot had left her Hotmail account logged in. A cursory search revealed hundreds of emails, each containing long strings of credit card numbers and expiration dates. Calmly, my mother summoned her own assistant to guard the door while she printed off one email after another, placing them carefully into a folder.

That was when the contractions began, but instead of telling someone or lying down or going to the doctor, my mother called her lawyer. She called the police. She called my father and spelled out the extent of Melinda's betrayal. She met with a PR consultant about damage control, and—most of all—she waited for Melinda's arrest. But as quickly and quietly as my mother had acted, Melinda must have sensed the axe was about to fall because when the police descended upon her one-bedroom carriage house in WeHo, she was already on a plane to Argentina with enough stolen credit card numbers to comfortably fund a long exile.

I think it was being thwarted like that, being denied her vengeance, that sent my mother into full-on, movie cliché, water-breaks-in-the-elevator labor, causing me to come into the world far more prematurely than anyone would have liked.

My parents' business ultimately recovered from the Melinda Incident. And mostly, I recovered from the trauma of my early birth. I still have the usual preemie problems: allergies and asthma. I've had three heart surgeries and steroids shot into my lungs. I've worn glasses since I was three (though now I sometimes switch them out for contact lenses). And then I have a few other ailments, impediments, maladies, and shortcomings.

There's the stutter that, despite my speech therapist's assurances, never quite resolved itself and a sibilant "S" that still gives me trouble if I try to pronounce the letter while thinking about it too much or not enough. And my right leg is three inches shorter than the left one, causing me to walk with a limp (though it's really only noticeable when I get tired or if you're looking for it).

On top of everything else, no one would ever call me my parents' loveliest child.

They have two other children, both intelligent, attractive, talented in all the ways parents hope for. Charlie is at Harvard Business School now and has little to do with any of us, least of all me. He does not come into this story. Serves him right, the snob.

And I've already told you a little about Maisie, though not about what happened to her—what Livia did to her, I should say.

So my parents have all the legacy they need. My siblings will achieve great things, marry into good families, produce lovely children themselves, and do and be all the things my parents ever hoped for.

It used to be that first sons inherited property, second sons went into the military, and third sons were given over to the church as thanks to God for the other two. But since my parents are not religious, I became a student of history.

People always say that history is important because those who don't learn from its mistakes are doomed to repeat them.

I'm not sure that's true. *I* believe that history is important because if you're still standing on the other side of it, it means you won. You survived. It's in the past, and what's behind you can't hurt you.

Not as long as you can outrun it.

As far as most people were concerned, what I did was putter around with dates and dusty old books and microfilm, and who was going to bother to ask me about that? I was glad to be thought bookish and eccentric, but ultimately harmless. I was grateful for my unremarkableness, for my parents' indifference to me, that my classmates found me boring or strange.

Nothing I did mattered.

And because of that, I was free.

"You said you wanted to begin this story in the ninth grade, Claudia."

"And I do. It's just that to fully understand the Claudia McCarthy ninth-grade experience, you need context."

"What sort of context?"

"I've told you what kind of person I am, or at least what kind of person I was when I entered the Imperial Day Academy. Now you need to know exactly what kind of a rat factory it was, so you can understand that a person like me had no business being sent there in the first place."

"Then I suppose you'd better tell me about it."

III

A Rich Person Who Felt Guilty about Something

The Imperial Day Academy is sometimes called "the Empire" because its graduates are spread throughout every Ivy League school and Fortune 500 company in the world. Once I realized I would be going there, and that there was no getting out of it, I decided that I owed it to myself to learn a little something about the place. As a historian, I knew that the version of events presented on the school website would be sanitized and scrubbed clean of all truth and human interest, so I dug deeper into the historical record until I found the real dirt.

The Imperial Day Academy was founded in 1898, and like many things in Los Angeles, it was founded by a rich person who felt guilty about something. Paul Chudnuff was an oil tycoon whose only daughter, Faith, had an intense friendship with a distressingly middle-class girl named Violet Hayes. Chudnuff was unnerved by it and suspected that something unseemly—by 1898 standards, anyway—was going on, so he put a stop to it. He forbade the girls from seeing one another anymore, which went over even more poorly than you might have expected.

Faith and Violet ran off in the night with nothing but the clothes on their backs and attempted to hop a train to San Francisco. They weren't stupid girls, but they were sheltered, with heads full of romantic ideas. Miraculously, they weren't crushed beneath the wheels or stabbed by hoboes. They got on the northbound train without incident, but then the weather turned as night fell. The next morning, railroad bulls found the girls in a boxcar huddled together and frozen nearly to death.

It was with a mixture of guilt, shame, worry, and anger that Paul Chudnuff made his way to San Francisco to collect them. The girls' injuries were very severe—both had lost appendages to frostbite—and it was already in the papers. Some foolish person had even told reporters how Chudnuff had interfered in the girls' friendship.

The whole train ride up, Chudnuff reasoned that if Faith had been in a more rigorous environment, surrounded by a better sort of person than the neighbor girl, her head would have been filled with more serious things. She would have cultivated her mind, filled it with philosophy, rhetoric, oration, and history instead of dime novels about train-hopping tramps.

According to his biographers, by the time Chudnuff reached San Francisco, he'd hatched the idea for the Imperial Day Academy. It would be a school governed by honor, by decency, by obedience to one's parents and teachers. It would be coeducational so that male and female students might "mix freely and learn early to enjoy one another's society," by which he really meant "not turn queer," but you know, potato, po-TAH-to.

The more he thought about the school, the more he liked the idea. It appealed to his sense of himself as a classicist and a scholar. What's more, he knew that it would change the newspaper headlines from "OILMAN'S DAUGHTER LOSES FOOT" to something far more noble.

The school would be elite. It would be rigorous, but in his feverish scheming, Paul Chudnuff would not be satisfied with starting a good private school, or even an excellent one. It had to be really revolutionary. For starters, it would be a meritocracy. Chudnuff's school would admit only the brightest and most talented, regardless of their ability to pay (but with the unspoken understanding that *most* of the students *would* be able to pay because that was just how these things worked). But more important than that, the students would learn to govern themselves, and take on the responsibility and duty to rout out whatever was not fine or fitting. To uphold these ideals, each student would sign an honor code when he or she entered Imperial Day, vowing not to cheat, steal, lie, or otherwise demonstrate character unbecoming, and to report any instances of misconduct witnessed. And that was the kernel of thought that would become the Imperial Day Academy Honor Council, created to uphold the school's honor code. We have a student council like most schools do, only ours is called the Senate—another of Paul Chudnuff's classicist touches. The Senate has the appearance of running things, but the real power lies with the Imperial Day Academy Honor Council, and everyone knows it.

The Honor Council consists of eight members, two from each class, elected by their peers, and all infractions are reported to them. They conduct the investigations, provide counsel to the accused, call the witnesses, render the verdicts, and dish out the sentences, which can range from probation or community service for a minor infraction to expulsion for a serious one. The principal may overrule a decision, though in my perusal of the Honor Council archives (disappointingly scanty—nothing but member rosters and a page or two of statistics about how many cases were heard each year), I learned that this executive privilege has not been exercised in over a decade—certainly not during the tenure of Dr. Graves, who is seldom known to leave his office, much less meddle in the affairs of the Honor Council.

Lots of schools have honor codes, but what Paul Chudnuff created at Imperial Day was a whole culture. Overseeing all of it is the Honor Council, which has the power to do whatever it wants to uphold that code; whose members hold in their hands all of our fates and decide whether we will be cast out in disgrace or permitted to remain.

The Honor Council knows everything that happens at Imperial Day, every dark secret, every misdeed.

Paul Chudnuff took the ideas of honor and righteousness and linked them to power.

And to a certain kind of person, power like that is irresistible.

IV

SOMEONE I KNEW FIRSTHAND TO BE A TERRIBLE PERSON

"This isn't the Griffith School," Maisie said as she walked me to homeroom on the first day of my freshman year at Imperial Day Academy. I felt a little bit babyish about this, but also grateful to have my sister by my side.

And when she said that this wasn't the Griffith School, I knew what she really meant. Three years of middle school had taught me to brace myself for certain kinds of meanness, to anticipate, deflect, and when all else failed, to flee. The existence I'd made for myself in middle school had allowed me to survive, but it was no way to live. After three years of keeping my head down, of being invisible, of sheltering at a lunch table with people whose common status as rejects failed to bond us together in any meaningful way, what I needed was a friend. A real friend. A friend who wasn't also my sister. Some of my former classmates at Griffith had found their way to Imperial Day, but most had not. As I looked around the hallways, the faces I saw were almost all new. This was encouraging.

"You're going to find your people here, Claudia. I know it."

We stopped in front of my homeroom door.

"Are you ready?" Maisie asked.

"Do I have to?"

"Unless you can think of a reasonable, legal alternative."

"I'll be homeschooled," I said.

"Our parents have better things to do than homeschool your ass."

"I'll have a private tutor then," I said. "Like a 17th-century dauphin. Or a child actor."

Maisie gave me a sad smile because she knew that I was kidding, but she also knew that the reason I was kidding was because I was scared.

"Do you want a hug?" she asked, holding out her arms to me. "Or would that be embarrassing?"

I wanted a hug more than anything.

"Go," I said, shooing her out of the doorway. "You'll be late. I promise not to run away and become a child actor."

"Or a 17th-century dauphin," she said, giving my arm a squeeze. "Find me at lunch, okay? I'll save you a seat."

Having lunch with Maisie was both good and not good. On the one hand, it was the only time during the day when I was guaranteed to see her. The second she saw me, Maisie always stopped what she was doing to drop some little bit of sunshine into my day: she'd show me a batch of Gerald Ford campaign buttons that had gone up for sale on eBay, or a close-up picture of the dude who is, absent any context, depicted on the Bayeux Tapestry with his 11th-century cock and balls dangling freely. What I'm saying is, Maisie knew how to make me smile.

On the other hand was the rest of our lunch table. The upperclassmen Honor Council representatives all ate together: Augustus and Marcus; Julia, who wasn't on the Honor Council, but had a certain status nonetheless because she was Marcus's girlfriend; Maisie and Ty; and, much to my dismay, Livia, who was only a sophomore, but as Augustus's girlfriend, held court over the entire table. Everyone was in her thrall, including my sister. Especially my sister.

The nice thing about having been in middle school during my sister's first two years at Imperial Day was that I could tell myself that certain things weren't happening, that my sister wasn't becoming closer and closer to someone I knew firsthand to be a terrible person.

But that first day of school in the Imperial Day cafeteria, Livia walked through the door, spotted my sister, and shouted from across the room, "There she is!" And Maisie pointed at her and shouted back, "There's my girl!"

And then, when they came running up to each other, Livia stopped in front of my sister, threw up her hands and said, "Who run it?" And at the same time they both said, "*You* run it," pointed at each other, crossed their arms, bumped them together, then hugged, like the whole routine was some long-standing inside joke/secret handshake the two of them had, its origin story entirely mysterious to me.

Being at Imperial Day and sitting with Maisie at lunch meant that I could no longer ignore my sister's friendship with Livia.

I didn't know then, on the first day of my freshman year, that the Honor Council would come to be synonymous with corruption and tyranny. The fact that my sister was the junior class Honor Council representative didn't jar me in the least. She was lovely and honorable and decent and good and universally liked. Of course she was on the Honor Council.

But her friendship with Livia? That worried me from the start.

V

EVERY BIT AS AWFUL AS THE LIE

There are lots of reasons to dislike Livia.

She walks around like she has a stick up her ass.

She thinks she's the only person who knows how to do anything properly, like the rest of us are giant idiots and she has to save us from ourselves.

She knows where everybody's weak spot is, and she always seems to know how to push and prod it until it gives.

There are lots of reasons to dislike her, and depending on who you are, there are also some reasons to hate her, but there was only one reason that my sister's friendship with Livia scared me. Maisie was already a freshman at Imperial Day preparing for her first Honor Council campaign, but Livia and I were still together at the Griffith School. Livia was in eighth grade and I was in seventh when the incident in question happened, and it was very difficult for me to come by reliable information because I was in the wrong grade to have access to firsthand sources. Information was on lockdown because everyone was trying to keep the younger students from finding out anything about it.

My sources eventually included a conversation between staff in the front office, on whom I eavesdropped while pretending to photocopy a John Updike short story for a teacher; Livia's former best friend, Octavia Resnick; her victim, Cassidy Jones; and, of course, the newspaper accounts that surfaced. I went so far as to track down a few of their sources and re-interview them, just to verify their stories.

I'm telling you this so you understand: This isn't gossip. This is history.

And it matters.

What happened was this: An eighth-grade girl named Cassidy Jones accepted an invitation to a school dance from a boy named Victor Merriweather, who is unimportant to this history save for his distinction of having been Livia's seventh-grade boyfriend. According to Octavia, it was not that Cassidy agreed to go that enraged Livia so much as the fact that Cassidy failed to ask Livia's blessing beforehand.

Right on the heels of Cassidy's offense, the eighth-grade language arts teacher, Mr. Arnold, caught Livia with a *To Kill a Mockingbird* cheat sheet concealed under the sole of her shoe during a quiz. Mr. Arnold handled the matter discreetly. He asked Livia to stay after class, where he informed her that she'd receive a zero. Then he lectured her about what waited around the corner at Imperial Day Academy, the Honor Code. Was she willing to jeopardize her future over the outcome of a 10-point quiz?

Livia nodded her head, feigned regret, and meekly accepted her punishment, but inside she seethed. She was especially irate after receiving a B+ for the course, rather than the A her carefully compiled point spreadsheet showed that she had earned, even factoring in the zero on the *To Kill a Mockingbird* quiz.

However, Livia kept her rage to herself and was not suspected when an anonymous letter arrived in the inboxes of several middle-school administrators stating that Mr. Arnold and Cassidy Jones were having a sexual relationship. The letter alleged that Mr. Arnold had written Cassidy poetry and given her a prepaid cell phone. They'd had sex in his car at the end of a little-traveled cul-de-sac overlooking the 101 freeway. They'd also had sex at Mr. Arnold's house on a day when both he and Cassidy had called in sick.

It was all shockingly well documented. Office records showed that Mr. Arnold and Cassidy had indeed been absent from school on the same day. The clerk at a convenience store near the school said that he remembered Mr. Arnold purchasing a pair of cheap, prepaid cell phones on at least one occasion. A sheaf of love poems written in a decidedly adult hand was found in Cassidy's locker, though she denied ever having seen it before.

Not a bit of suspicion fell on Livia, and poor Cassidy was judged and found guilty from the second the story got out. She was a girl who'd always had boyfriends, who'd developed early, who wore skintight shirts and jeans and loomed large in the fantasy lives of most heterosexual males in the eighth grade, and possibly more than one creepy staff member. For this, she was immediately assumed to be complicit in the whole thing.

In addition, she was on partial scholarship. Her parents were no one you had to suck up to. She wasn't like Astrid Murray, who, despite being a known asshole, was treated with inexhaustible goodwill by her classmates because her parents were moderately famous actors.

The school was thrown into chaos. People could talk of little else, although at the same time, you weren't *supposed* to talk about it. Nobody enjoyed talking about it. It wasn't the kind of story that made you feel scandalously in-the-know. It was the kind that made you feel dirty for having brushed up against it.

What was lost in all of this was that, from the beginning, Cassidy had said that the story was a lie, and she had never wavered from this. She'd told the principal, she'd told the police, she'd told her parents, and yet, the investigation carried on because no one believed her. Her grades suffered and she came perilously close to losing her scholarship, but still, she came to school every day, staring straight ahead, speaking to no one. She took notes in class and handed in all her assignments on time, avoiding the pitying, curious, disgusted looks from her teachers.

It was when the police had hit a roadblock in their investigation—not quite enough evidence to move forward, too much to back away—that Octavia came forward and outed Livia as the letter-writer.

At first, no one believed Octavia any more than they had believed Cassidy. But then, Octavia began to recite lines of verse, verbatim, from the sheaf of poetry that had been found in Cassidy's locker. Octavia confessed that she and Livia had written the poems together. It was a joke, a shitty one, but Octavia had only done it as a way to commiserate with her friend. Everybody knew that if a girl with boobs as big as Cassidy Jones's had a cheat sheet under her shoe, Mr. Arnold would have acted like he didn't see a thing. Octavia had never intended to show the poems to anyone, and she'd sworn she had no idea what Livia had planned to do.

Mr. Arnold had never had sex with Cassidy, Octavia said. Nobody had done anything. Livia had made the whole thing up. This news detonated in the hallways of the Griffith School as the case began to disintegrate. Mr. Arnold came back to work, and a handful of people (though fewer than you'd expect) told Cassidy they were sorry for what she'd gone through.

Now it was Livia who was in exile. People avoided her in the halls or stared openly, whispering behind their hands. The more people learned about what Livia had done—and how mild the original provocation was—the more disgusted they became. The school administrators cancelled the hearing to decide Mr. Arnold's fate, and instead set a date to determine whether Livia would be permitted to remain at the Griffith School. The LAPD considered bringing charges against her, though Mr. Arnold gallantly came forward and begged them not to punish a confused, immature girl who couldn't have known how out of control her accusations would become.

Cassidy could have spat in Livia's face, slapped her, punched her, torn out her hair, and hardly a teacher at the Griffith School would have lifted a finger to discipline her. However, she did none of these things. The day the news broke, she walked up to Livia, looked her in the eye, and asked, "Why me?"

Legend has it that Livia sneered and replied, "Why not?" However, a more credible source at the scene confirms that Livia said nothing at all, that she pretended she hadn't heard and walked away. I consider this to be the likelier account because Livia knew how much trouble she was in. She knew how close she was to losing everything she valued, everything she was. If ever her indomitable spirit was cowed in the slightest, I believe it must have been then.

Just when things looked darkest for Livia, the story took an ugly turn.

A girl came forward, a girl no one had ever thought of much before, a girl who tended to walk invisibly through the halls, a girl who was the last girl in the world you'd expect to be involved in any of this. Jill Hathaway.

Jill Hathaway was painfully shy, with a shock of overgrown

black hair. She always carried around a black Moleskine note-book filled with poetry she'd written, some of it very good. She had an intensity about her, a seriousness that said all of this pain and isolation and alienation was for *something*, like she was making a study of it to tease out later, strand by strand, for her art.

So, yeah, I think you see where this is going. The truth was every bit as awful as the lie. The fact was this: Mr. Arnold would never have pursued a girl like Cassidy Jones. A girl with friends. A girl who talked, a girl who spoke up for herself. And had he known that Jill Hathaway was the kind of girl to keep a journal, perhaps he would have set his sights elsewhere.

I've always found it curious that Jill's Moleskine notebook turned up when it did, in the inbox of Ms. Garza, our middle-school guidance counselor. Maybe Jill wanted it to be over, too. Or maybe it wasn't Jill who turned the journal in at all.

All I know for sure is that Ms. Garza called Jill into her office and gradually drew from her a tearful confession that she and Mr. Arnold had been sleeping together since October. There was proof. Jill had emails from an account he'd set up just for contacting her. She had a mix CD he'd made for her and an obscene text. She said that she'd wanted to end it, but didn't know how and was too scared. He wouldn't stop send-ing her messages, wouldn't stop watching her. Even when she tried to avoid him, he was always there, following her around, lurking around in the hallway by her locker, parking his car outside her house.

And here's what happened next. People began to say that it was *Livia* who had given Jill the courage to come forward by accusing Mr. Arnold of having an affair with an eighth grader. No one seemed to remember the fact that Mr. Arnold was entirely innocent of the *particular* crime Livia had accused him of. Everyone just decided it was because of Livia that he had been brought to justice.

I don't enjoy telling you this story. It isn't gossip that I relish knowing, but then again, it's not gossip. It's the truth. It is history, and if you want to understand Livia, this is where you have to start.

So, if she was such a monster, why was my beatific older sister such good friends with her?

I guess that's partly my fault.

Like I said, Maisie wasn't there when it happened, and by the time the story trickled out, Livia had dropped out of it entirely. Mr. Arnold's crimes were so abominable that Livia's all but disappeared in their shadow.

Livia also got to Imperial Day a year before I did. She had a whole year to worm her way into my sister's life. Maisie talked about her, went places with her, had her over to our house, and the whole time, I wondered, *Does she know?* She *had* to know.

But if Maisie knew, then why were she and Livia always up in her room with the door closed? Why were they always laughing their heads off, then stopping abruptly when I knocked on the door?

Part of me wanted to tell my sister my version of the story, but something always stopped me.

I was afraid of sounding jealous.

I was afraid Maisie wouldn't believe me. Worst of all, I was afraid that Maisie already knew what Livia had done, and she didn't care.

If any two people had mixed feelings over the revelations about Mr. Arnold, they were Cassidy Jones and Octavia. Cassidy never quite managed to shake off the stories. There was always something about the way people treated her, like she was still unclean even if the stories weren't true.

As for Octavia, that was the end of her friendship with Livia, which meant the end of her time as a person who mattered. She slunk through the Griffith School, then Imperial Day, silently willing everyone to forget she was once a person they noticed.

Some people seek out obscurity; others have it thrust upon them. Octavia was one of the latter.

She did what she needed to do to survive. And so did Livia. It was a long time before Livia was successfully betrayed again, and it was the last time she was caught at any of her tricks.

By the time the older girls finished eighth grade, this was the historical record: Cassidy would always be a slut. Jill would always be a victim. Octavia would always be an outcast. But by the time Livia was in ninth grade and running for Honor Council, nobody ever remembered to call her a liar.

VI

BALLS THE SIZE OF CHURCH BELLS

For the first month at Imperial Day, I was in survival mode. I went to class. I raised my hand just enough to keep my participation scores out of the toilet. I clung to Maisie at lunch and during the rare moments when we saw each other in the hallway like she was a barrel bobbing in shark-infested waters.

But by the end of September, I'd begun to realize that I wasn't going to fail out and I wasn't going to die. I wasn't going to be brutalized by upperclassmen any more than I could handle. The whispers behind hands, giggles, and pitying looks when I talked or was forced to serve a volleyball in gym class— that kind of thing was going to happen, and I'd made my peace with it a long time ago. The important thing was, I realized it wasn't going to get any worse.

I thought about what Maisie had told me on the first day of school, that I'd find my people at Imperial Day, and I decided that it was high time I started looking for them.

I volunteered my services in the fall theatrical production of *Little Shop of Horrors* and was made assistant stage manager, mostly because no one else wanted the job. Imperial Day Academy is not the sort of place where you get a lot of people wanting to be assistant anything. I covered the news beat for the school paper, reporting on school board meetings, the show choir, and the trials and travails of the academic decathlon team.

Maisie was right. It wasn't like the Griffith School. People did seem to like me once they got to know me a little, like I was an unexpectedly good record from the dollar bin. It was nice to be seen with fresh eyes by people who didn't know yet that they weren't supposed to like me.

So when Soren Bieckmann announced to the cast and crew of *Little Shop of Horrors* that his parents were out of town and we were all invited over to his house for a party, it dawned on me that I was *included* in that invitation and that, if I wanted to, I could go.

I was so excited by the prospect of having plans on a Friday night that I failed to consider that my sister might have a problem with it.

You see, Soren Bieckmann was himself a problem. Had he been less rich or less white, he would have done a dozen stints in juvie by his sophomore year, but since he *was* these things, people considered him reckless, fun, and generally a good person to know if you liked prescription medications. Despite his reputation, he always managed to skate on the right side of the Honor Council, and nothing ever stuck to him but rumors.

Soren's parents were never around, and he must have gotten lonely rattling around in that big Brentwood house all by himself because he filled it up with people every chance he got. There was almost always something going on at his house on the weekends, and they were the kind of parties everybody was still talking about on Monday morning. People got together and broke up and had screaming fights and cried in the bathroom.

There was spectacle and drama, blood and vomit. The ancient Romans went to the Colosseum to watch gladiator battles and see elephants fight rhinos to the death. Imperial Day students went to Soren's parties.

"Absolutely not," Maisie said when I told her where I was heading that Friday night.

She was on her way out, too, for frozen yogurt and a movie with Livia, and when she said it, something inside me rankled. Was this the trade-off for her taking me under her wing at Imperial Day, that I could only hang out with people she approved of?

"I'm not going to *do* anything," I said, referring to the drinking, screwing, and recreational drug use that I'd been told came standard at any Soren Bieckmann affair.

"Then why go at all?"

"Because I was invited. Because the alternative is sitting in my room reading a book about the Tower of London. Because I feel like being around some *people* for a change."

"You're welcome to join Livia and me."

Maisie was trying to be nice, but the look I gave her at the suggestion made her throw up her arms in exasperation.

"Fine, do what you want," she said. "But be careful. And check in. Let me know that you're okay."

"I'll be fine," I said, annoyed by Maisie's fussing. If she could spend Friday nights with Livia, I didn't think she had any moral high ground to tell me how to spend mine.

But then I felt myself soften. It was hard for me to be upset with Maisie, and after all, she was only worried about me. If I had faith in my own ability to avoid being lured into a life of vice, didn't it make sense that Maisie could do the same thing and remain unscathed by her friendship with Livia?

"I'll text you," I added, then gave Maisie a quick hug before brushing past her to wait outside for my Uber, ready to embark on my first night of adventure, of spectacle, of freedom.

And as I discovered upon walking up the long winding driveway to Soren's house, Julia had had the same idea. If I had to run into someone from the Honor Council lunch table at a party like this, I was glad it was her. Like me, Julia wasn't on the Honor Council. Like me, she was sitting at the table because of somebody else. If she hadn't been Marcus's girlfriend, Augustus probably wouldn't even have known her name, much less broken bread with her on a daily basis. But unlike me, Julia was undeniably cool, with her bright red lipstick and black liquid eyeliner. Nobody at Imperial Day dressed like her. She wore knee-high lace-up boots with vintage dresses and strings of pearls with her Misfits t-shirt. She looked like she'd as soon kick you in the kneecap as look at you, and if I'd possessed any swagger or style whatsoever, I would have aspired to be just like her.

As I mentioned before, Marcus lived with Augustus's family. They bought his clothes. They fed him and let him drive their car, but he didn't have wads of spending money like the rest of us did. He and Julia spent a lot of weekend nights eating Chipotle and watching Netflix. He never liked to take money from them, not even when they insisted. He was their perfect, deferential, appropriately grateful ward, and he never did anything that would suggest even a hint of trouble.

Except, I guess, having a girlfriend like Julia, a girl you could tell from a glance didn't fit in with Maisie and Livia. If she had, maybe she would have been out getting frozen yogurt with them instead of sitting on Soren Bieckmann's front steps drinking from a flask.

The first thing she did was point to the flask and say, "Before you think about telling your sister, I'm only having one drink."

She sounded like she'd had three, at least.

"I'm not telling anyone," I said, even though both the drinking and not reporting the drinking were Honor Code violations. I felt a pang of guilt about keeping it from Maisie, and yet, at the same time, I thought about all the lunch periods Julia spent sitting quietly while everybody else blathered on about Honor Council business. What Julia did with her own time outside of Imperial Day didn't seem like anyone else's business.

"Where's Marcus?" I asked.

"I don't have to spend every Friday night with Marcus." She said it in a snappish way.

"No one said you did."

"It was implied," Julia said, taking a long pull on her drink. "It was strongly implied."

"I'm sorry," I said. "I didn't mean to imply anything."

"What are *you* doing here anyway, Claudia?"

I'd been dreading a moment exactly like this one—when someone pointed out that I didn't belong there.

"I was in-in-vited," I said, cursing my nervous stutter as I said it.

"You don't say. How do you know Soren?"

Her diction was perfect, right up until she got to Soren's name and slurred the hell out of it.

"He's playing Mr. Mushnik in *Little Shop of Horrors*," I said. "I should know. He's been late to the last three rehearsals."

"Mr. Mushnik?" Julia asked. It took her three tries saying it before she laughed and gave up. "Oh. Then you probably know him better than I do. Cal's in that play, isn't he?"

"He's Orin," I said. Cal had moved on from his poser skater days and was now playing an ether-huffing sadomasochistic dentist who beats the shit out of his girlfriend, Audrey. It was the role he was born for, and it let him bully his way around the sets and granted him ample opportunity to grab the backup singers' tits backstage.

"So you're in a play, you're at a party. It seems like Imperial Day agrees with you," Julia said, adding, "No offense, but I'm kind of surprised."

"None taken," I said. "I'm as surprised as you are."

Julia opened her purse, putting the flask inside and taking out a compact and a tube of lipstick.

"He's working on scholarship applications," she said as she dabbed the deep red on her lips.

"I beg your pardon?"

"You asked where Marcus was. I'm telling you."

"That sounds very responsible, I guess," I said.

"Marcus is very responsible. Some college will be quite lucky to get him."

"What about you?" I asked.

She laughed again and snapped her compact shut.

"Between you and me, Claudia, it's kind of a shit deal."

"Being Marcus's girlfriend?"

"Especially since everybody seems to think I should spend Friday nights chained to his wrist."

"I'm sorry."

"The thing is, it's not like we're going to get married or anything. But it kind of takes the romance out of things when your boyfriend acts like he's just killing time with you until he can start his real life."

"You could always break up with him now," I felt like a

different person when I said it, the kind of person who dispensed reckless and world-weary romantic advice like she knew what she was talking about. And I liked the way it felt.

The front door swung open and Julia sat up and whipped her head around, frantic that whoever it was might have overheard me, but it was just two seniors who could barely stop making out long enough not to fall down the stairs. They disappeared around the side of the house without even noticing that Julia and I were there.

"I guess I could," Julia said softly. "Seems like a lot of work though. It's not like I'd get to keep sitting at the lunch table with Augustus and your sister if I did that."

"So sit somewhere else. Find new friends."

This was the kind of person I wanted Julia to think I was, someone who could shrug her shoulders and say "Fuck it" about anything. I'd already defied whatever expectations she'd formed about me at the lunch table, and I wanted to keep doing it.

"You make it sound so easy," she said, laughing bitterly.

We looked through the big picture window into Soren's house. I could see the living room, some kind of den past that, and, further back, people wandering in and out of the kitchen, opening the refrigerator door. All kinds of people filled the rooms, a perfect cross-section of Imperial Day. If I was being cynical, I'd say that the demand for pharmaceuticals and an unsupervised environment transcended social boundaries. Of course, it might also have been that everyone just really liked Soren.

In the living room, couples sprawled on the long leather couch, their limbs tangled together as they slobbered on and groped each other. In the corner, a cluster of voyeurs pretended to play Cards Against Humanity while a drinking game of some kind raged on around the credenza. In the den, a group of guys crowded around a video game, staring vacantly and blowing shit up. Most of the people I saw were upperclassmen, but I recognized a girl from my biology class and a couple of crew underlings from *Little Shop of Horrors*.

And then Ty passed by the window.

Julia flung herself back.

"Shit," she said.

She pulled me down behind the rosemary bushes, and careful not to be seen, we watched the temperature of the rooms change as Ty walked through them. People set down their red plastic cups, stopped their conversations, angled their backs slightly away from him. Only the couples making out on the couch seemed not to notice.

"What's he doing here?" Julia asked.

"Having fun?" I suggested, though the thought of Ty enjoying himself at a social gathering seemed far-fetched.

Then Augustus stepped into view, a bottle of Snapple in his hand. Julia gasped, and sat down in the dirt beneath the window, knees tucked to her chest like she was willing herself to be as small and invisible as possible.

"I need to get out of here," she said, stunned into a momentary sobriety.

"What's the matter?" I asked. It was strange seeing Augustus here, I was willing to admit, but Julia's reaction seemed extreme.

"Do you honestly think Soren invited two Honor Council representatives to his party?"

I shook my head, and Julia gave me a nudge toward the front door.

"Find out what they're doing here," she said.

"I c-c-can't," I said, suddenly nervous at the thought of it.

"I need to know if they saw me."

"I'm sure nobody saw you."

"Claudia, please."

I saw real worry on Julia's face. She was afraid of what would happen to her if Augustus and Ty saw her here, and I realized that she was right—being an Honor Council girlfriend really was a shit deal.I hadn't been drinking, I hadn't taken anything. I had every right to be there, and I had every right to walk up to Ty and Augustus, say hello, and ask a few friendly questions, didn't I? We did sit together at lunch every day. I could do this. I could do this for Julia.

"Okay, I'll go."

Taking a deep breath, I walked through the front door. A few heads turned to see who was there, but when they saw it was me, people went back to what they were doing. It wasn't as loud as it should have been, considering half the school seemed to be there. The music was turned down low and people's voices sounded like they were at a museum rather than a party. Everyone kept stealing looks into the kitchen, where Augustus and Ty had corralled Soren. Augustus was doing most of the talking while Ty stood looking vaguely disapproving, though also like he sort of wanted a beer.

I inched up on the conversation from the side so I could listen to what they were saying. I was not eavesdropping, I told myself. I was collecting data for the historical record—and, of course, for Julia.

"We're not here to make anyone uncomfortable," I heard Augustus say to Soren. "But we all agreed that there should be an Honor Council presence at off-campus parties this year."

Soren pushed his floppy bangs out of his eyes and said,

"Not trying to be a dick here, but what if people don't want an Honor Council presence at parties this year? Like, you guys are welcome at my house whenever you want, but I guess I'd prefer it if you were here as civilians."

The thing was, he didn't sound like a dick, which was probably the reason he had lasted as long as he had at Imperial Day. There was something aw-shucksy stoner about everything that came out of his mouth. He acted like he couldn't imagine ever getting in trouble for anything, and so mostly, he didn't.

"This is a good thing for you, too," Augustus said. "People will be safe. You and your parents aren't going to be on the news because somebody wrapped their car around a tree after a party at *your* house."

"I appreciate that," Soren said, "but some people won't. They'll just have parties somewhere else and make sure you don't find out about them."

Ty let out a snort and folded his arms across his chest.

"We'll find out about them," he said.

Augustus frowned at him, not because what Ty said wasn't *true*, but because Augustus never would have said it so gracelessly. I always got the feeling that the more elegant points of politics were lost on Ty entirely, that if you couldn't explain it with a football metaphor or a motivational poster, you might as well save your breath.

"What Ty is saying is that Imperial Day isn't that big a school," Augustus said, and that was when he noticed me in the kitchen doorway. "Claudia, there you are."

He said it like he'd been *expecting* to see me.

And that was when I knew.

What were two Honor Council representatives doing at a party to which they certainly hadn't been invited?

They were here because Maisie knew I would be here and told them about it. Or more likely, they were here because Maisie told Livia, and Livia told Augustus. Maybe the idea of an "Honor Council presence" at parties like Soren's had been Livia's idea in the first place. It would be like her to do something like that. Whatever way I looked at it, though, two things were true:

1. This happened because I'd confided in my sister and she'd gone to the Honor Council with it, and
2. The Honor Council was sticking its nose where it wasn't wanted, and it was my fault.

"G-g-gentlemen," I said, nodding to each of them before turning to Soren. "I was just looking for s-something to drink."

"There's Coke in the fridge, Claudia," Soren said, giving Augustus a pointed look. "Nothing but Coke in my very Honor Code–compliant fridge."

Augustus took me by the shoulder and steered me toward the fridge, probably to make sure I didn't go looking for anything stronger than a soda.

"I'm not trying to tell you what to do, Claudia, but going to parties like this is a good way to get yourself an Honor Code violation."

"Can you do that?" I asked. I hadn't gotten the sense that the Honor Code was binding outside the walls of Imperial Day.

"We should have been doing it all along," Augustus said. "If the Honor Code is supposed to mean anything, it has to be in effect at all times."

His eyes shone like an idealist, like a true believer, but I immediately saw the more frightening implications, especially for someone like Julia. According to the Honor Code, the minimum sentence for drinking was a week's suspension.

"Are you handing out Honor Code violations tonight?"

"You know I can't talk about that."

Augustus nodded to Ty, who looked relieved to be dismissed from making conversation with Soren. He went back into the living room, cruising from one cluster of people to another and putting everyone on edge again. Augustus started in the other direction, toward the pool, but before he went out the door, he turned back to me and said, "You can have fun, Claudia. Just be careful."

I limped toward the front door as fast as my bad leg would carry me. I had to get Julia out of there in a hurry. She wasn't an idiot. If she'd known the Honor Council was planning to crash the party, she would have stayed home with her flask. If the minimum sentence for an alcohol-related violation was a week's suspension, the Honor Council vice president's girlfriend was sure to get at least double that. They'd make an example of her, just to show they weren't playing favorites.

Outside, I found Julia nodding off in the rosemary bushes.

"We need to go," I said, tugging on her arm. "Come on, I'll walk you home."

Julia grumbled as I pulled her to her feet, and the flask slipped from her fingers. These were not the drinking habits of a person who wanted to blow off a little steam, I realized. Julia had been drinking like a person who needed to obliterate something.

She reached down to pick up the flask, but I shook my head and gave her arm another tug.

"I'll buy you another one."

"Full of scotch?"

"Full of whatever you want," I said, and she followed me through the yard and down to the sidewalk. She wasn't very steady on her feet, and I ended up pulling one of her arms over my shoulder to keep her from veering into the street or somebody else's yard. It was just over a mile from Soren's house to Julia's, and I hoped my leg would be able to bear her weight as well as my own for that distance.

We'd slogged two blocks in silence when suddenly, Julia lifted her chin from her chest and said in a clear voice, "Marcus isn't a bad person. He just makes me feel like one."

"You're not a bad person," I said.

"I shouldn't stay with somebody because I'm afraid of finding a new place to sit at lunch. That's bullshit."

The words sounded like she'd run through them in her head, practiced saying them under her breath over and over again, while I was in the kitchen with Augustus. I nodded in agreement. Maybe it was the alcohol giving her courage to say these things aloud, but it seemed like maybe they had been a long time coming.

"You'll still be my friend, though, right, Claudia?"

At this, she tripped over a piece of sidewalk that had been pushed up by a tree root, and I tightened my grip to keep her from cracking her head open. At first, I wasn't sure I'd heard her correctly, and then once I was, I was too shocked to answer. My knees and ankles groaned as she leaned into my shoulder, and it dawned on me that someone wanted to be my friend. Someone cool and intimidating. Someone who looked down her nose at half the people at Imperial Day. Someone who was exactly the kind of person I wanted to be friends with. Someone who was currently wasted, but someone who maybe liked me anyway.

That was when I heard the police siren.

"Fuck," Julia said, as we turned around to see a black and white cruiser coming down the street behind us, red and blue lights on. Her eyes cleared, the liquid courage replaced by stark fear. I held tight to her waist to keep her from running.

"Let me handle this," I whispered. "Don't move."

There had only been one short whoop of the siren to get our attention. This was a nice neighborhood, after all, and the LAPD didn't want to disturb the residents on a Friday night. Not like the neighborhoods where helicopters circled overhead pretty much nonstop. The officer rolled down his window as the cruiser pulled up alongside us. He looked us up and down, his eyes lingering on Julia's chest a moment too long.

"Have you girls been drinking?" he asked.

The confidence I'd felt when I told Julia that I'd handle it drained away. What had I been thinking? I had no experience defying authority figures and no idea whether I could actually pull it off, but I knew that I had to. I had to save Julia. I thought about Joan of Arc, and reasoned that if an illiterate peasant girl could talk her way into an audience with the Crown Prince of France and convince him that God wanted her to lead an army into the Siege of Orleans, I could surely match wits with the LAPD.

I made my eyes wide, as though I was scandalized by the officer's very suggestion, then looked over at Julia. She was holding it together fairly well, all things considered. Her feet were planted. She'd stopped swaying from side to side.

"No, officer," I said. "W-w-we haven't been drinking."

"What are you doing out so late? Do your folks know where you are?"

"Of c-c-course they do. She t-t-tutors me in math and history and English. All the s-s-subjects really," I said, laying on thick my assortment of verbal ticks and oddities. "N-n-now she's walking me home. I know it's late, but we really got going on some quadratic equations, and I completely lost track of the time."

The police officer looked skeptical. "Then why does it look like you're holding each other up? Did all those quadratic equations render you unable to walk straight?"

I heard the tiniest whimper escape Julia's lips. She was starting to crack.

"I-I-I-I-I," I said, but that was as far as I got before my asthmatic wheeze overcame me and I fell to the curb, gasping for breath. If you're not used to my asthma attacks, I am told they are extremely upsetting. I am told that I appear to be dying. Actually, it was my own mother who told me that. She said it like she was accusing me of having them that way on purpose.

Julia sat down next to me and rubbed my back while I rummaged in my pocket for my inhaler and jammed it into my mouth. The police officer stared, trying to figure out whether I was going to expire within the next thirty seconds and whether he was going to have to do something about it.

"Is she okay?" he asked Julia.

"I think so," Julia said, her voice careful and measured.

"I'm sorry," I said looking up at the officer from the curb, wearing my most pitiful look. "It's my leg. It doesn't work so well. This one is shorter than the other. John F. Kennedy suffered from a similar condition. Also Little Richard and St. Ignatius of Loyola, founder of the Jesuit order. Anyway, you can breathalyze me if you want to, but that's why she was holding me up."

I held both legs out straight in front of me to demonstrate the veracity of this claim. The officer stared at me for a moment, a baffled look on his face, then shook his head and turned to Julia.

"Can you get her home all right?"

Julia nodded, and I chimed in, wanting to rescue her from having to do any more talking than was necessary. "It's not far. Only a c-c-couple more blocks."

"Well, you girls be careful. Lot of creeps out there." Then he turned to Julia again. "It's nice of you to help her out on your Friday night."

Julia lowered her eyes and muttered, "Thank you, sir," and then he rolled up his window and drove off.

The moment he'd turned the corner, Julia let out a huge sigh, tipped backwards into someone's flower garden, and began to giggle like a loon.

"That. Was. Amazing," she said, throwing her arms up over her head and kicking her legs up in the air, taking out a clump of calla lilies along the way. The porch light went on, illuminating the slate walkway. I grabbed the flailing Julia by an ankle.

"We need to get out of here *now*," I said.

"Claudia, you've got balls the size of church bells."

"Shut up and *move*, Julia."

She scrambled to her feet, still laughing, and I dragged her down the sidewalk until we'd put a little distance between ourselves and the respectable citizens we'd roused from their evening's slumber. My leg really was starting to hurt by then.

"You should spend the night at my house," Julia said, eyeing my limp. "I'll drive you home in the morning."

I was grateful she'd offered. I wasn't sure I had more than a few blocks left in me at that point and didn't want to call Maisie to come get me so late at night, even if I was stone-cold sober. The thought of facing my sister, now that I'd had my first taste of what the Honor Council actually *did*, now that I knew Maisie was a part of it, made me feel queasy.

Still, I'd promised her that I'd check in, so I did. I told her the truth, where I was, what I was doing, who I was with. The only thing I omitted was that I was aiding and abetting a fugitive from the law.

When we got to Julia's house, she let us in through the side door into a mud room where we took off our shoes, then quietly made our way through the house, up the stairs to Julia's room. At the end of a long hallway, I could hear what sounded like the engine of an airplane.

"It's a fan," Julia said. "My mom can't sleep without a lot of white noise. Then she sleeps through everything."

As soon as we got into her room, Julia fell into the king-size bed without getting undressed or pulling back the covers. Eyes already closed, she pointed to the other side of the bed.

"I hope you don't mind sharing," she said.

"Do you want some water?" I asked. "Some ibuprofen?"

But by then, her mouth had dropped open and she was snoring lightly.

I texted my parents to let them know where I was. Then I turned out the light and got into bed, lying on top of the covers just like Julia was. It had been a strange evening. In my fourteen years, I'd had very few nights away from my own bed. I'm sure it doesn't come as the hugest surprise to learn that I hadn't been invited to many sleepovers.

But Julia chose me. Julia decided that she wanted to be *my* friend, and that had never happened before.

It was nice to be over at somebody's house on a Friday night.

On the other side of the bed, I heard Julia mumble softly, "Thanks, Claudia."

As my eyes adjusted to the darkness, I stared up at the ceiling, looking for patterns in the swirls of plaster, a smile on my face. My eyelids started to grow heavy, and I was struck by how good and normal I felt.

Julia had confided in me about her love life and I'd saved her from the cops and she'd called me her friend. Maybe I was starting to find my people, just like Maisie had said I would. Maybe my days at Imperial Day were going to be good ones. Maybe I was going to be happy.

But I'm barely into the story and I think you already know that isn't what happened because I've never been any good at choosing allies, and nobody should ever take my advice.

"Did Julia break up with Marcus like you suggested?"

"She did. The very next day."

"And what happened then, Claudia?"

"Why does it matter? It doesn't have anything to do with why I'm here talking to you."

"I guess I care because it seems like the next part of the story."

"What happened was exactly what Julia said was going to happen. She moved to a different lunch table. She sat alone. Livia and Augustus and all the Honor Council people stopped talking to her."

"She sat alone? You didn't sit with her?"

"It would have looked odd if I'd left the Honor Council table. I thought it would hurt Maisie's feelings, that I'd seem ungrateful."

"But every once in a while . . . especially right after the break-up. Don't you think Maisie would have understood that, Claudia?"

"Of course, I know what you're getting at. I could have been a better friend. I should have been a better friend. It makes perfect sense now. At the time, I suppose that logic did not present itself to me."

VII

IF YOU'RE HORRIBLY MURDERED, I'LL AVENGE YOU

After Soren's party, I began to notice the disappearances.

The first was Ravi Sejani, a sophomore I'd seen puking in the bushes the night of Soren's party. Unlike Julia, he'd been caught. Unlike Julia, he hadn't had anyone to steer him out of Augustus and Ty's sight. That said, if I'd just stayed home with my history of the Tower of London and never mentioned the party to Maisie, Ravi Sejani probably never would have been suspended in the first place.

I knew that it wasn't my fault that the Honor Council had decided to start policing off-campus parties, and yet, for some reason, I blamed myself.

Honor Council hearings were confidential, but once I started paying attention, I knew exactly what was happening. The people who'd spent Monday high-fiving in the hallway about their weekend exploits were gone by Friday. It didn't take long before a hush fell over Imperial Day. Nobody bragged about their Saturday night plans anymore, people looked over their shoulders before they'd so much as whisper about having a sip of a wine cooler. They were paranoid and mistrustful, wondering whether their friends and partners in mischief would turn around and report them to Augustus the first chance they got. Soon, the only parties that were still happening were ones that made Soren Bieckmann's look like a prayer meeting. They were planned in secret by people who feared nothing and didn't care what happened to them, people like Cal Hurt and Astrid Murray and Chris Gibbons. Obviously, I wasn't invited, but Julia found out about all of them and partied like she was making up for lost time.

"Don't even tell me where you're going," I begged her. "That way, if I'm interrogated by the Honor Council, I won't have to lie to them."

"I should tell someone where I'll be. What if it turns out like an episode of *Criminal Minds?*"

"Julia, if you're getting a *Criminal Minds* vibe from this particular social gathering, maybe you shouldn't go."

I tried to talk her out of it, but the more debauchery was promised, the more impossible it was for Julia to stay away.

"Fine," I'd end up saying. "Write the address on a slip of paper and hide it somewhere in your room. If you're horribly murdered, I'll avenge you."

Meanwhile, things with Maisie had reached an all-time low. It was hard not to look at my sister differently now that I was beginning to see the Honor Council in action.

The power, the secrecy of the meetings, the discipline, the control—none of it fit with the Maisie I knew. *That* Maisie would have been more at home on the Senate. They did all the real work at Imperial Day. They planned the fundraising, field trips, dances, and assemblies. They listened to complaints and settled student grievances. And yet, none of it came with any real power. The Senate merely did the things that everyone expected, the things that made our school a nice place, but that none of us wanted to do ourselves.

They were servants who did our bidding, while the Honor Council representatives ruled us, kept us docile, and made us afraid. And those they couldn't scare, they punished.

I didn't understand why my sister was friends with Livia, and I didn't understand what my sister was doing on the Honor Council, but I felt like those two things were connected, and that what they meant was that what I *really* didn't understand was Maisie.

VIII

AN AFTER-HOURS NUDE SOIREE AT THE ESTHER PICO MEMORIAL THEATRE

I should begin the next part of my story, or testimony, or whatever this is, by explaining to you that the first time I spied on an Honor Council hearing, it was purely accidental.

What happened was, the Honor Council's usual meeting room was going to be painted over the Thanksgiving holiday, so they'd had to convene elsewhere. I was in the storage closet off the Humanities faculty lounge doing extra credit for Ms. Yee to bring up my unspectacular grade in World History. According to Ms. Yee, I would improve as a historian if I learned to focus.

"You start off talking about the Assyrians, then you take a detour into the Shang dynasty and end up writing about Socrates. Try to tell one story at a time, Claudia."

However, because of my enthusiasm for the subject (or because she was trying to get me out of her classroom so she could go home), she'd taken pity on me and offered me a handful of extra-credit points if I agreed to go through the classroom sets of textbooks in the faculty lounge closet after school and weed out the more dilapidated ones.

If Ms. Yee was not precisely a historian, she was at least a very good history teacher. Ms. Yee taught history like she was telling a story. She could reel off dates and the names of ancient capitals and kings without even glancing at her notes, and she always ended her lectures on a cliff-hanger so you spent the rest of the day wondering what was going to happen to old Ashurnasirpal II next. (Spoiler alert: he would kill everybody, then have someone carve into the wall of his palace, "Of the young men's ears I made a heap; of the old men's heads I made a minaret. I exposed their heads as a trophy in front of their city." That's the kind of stuff Ms. Yee told us about in class.)

Okay, and that digression is probably exactly the lack of focus Ms. Yee was complaining about. But suffice it to say, I was perfectly happy to be staying after school on the day before Thanksgiving break, flipping through copies of *The Epic of Gilgamesh* to see if anyone had written "FUCK" in the margin if it meant getting on her good side. I was so engrossed in the task at hand that I didn't hear Augustus and Livia come into the faculty lounge, and it took me a moment longer than that to realize that Soren Bieckmann was with them, and a few seconds more before I figured out that they must have been there on Honor Council business, and by that time I'd been sitting there listening far too long to announce myself.

"Is this it?" I heard Soren say in his affable way. "I thought there'd be more of you. I thought you'd be wearing robes and old-timey wigs or something."

"We only need four for a quorum," Livia said. "Ty's on his way. And your counsel should be here in a moment, too."

"Yeah, about that . . . ," Soren said, sounding doubtful.

"Zelda may be a freshman, but trust me, she's very capable."

Augustus murmured in agreement, but I'm not sure Soren was any more convinced than I was. I didn't even know why Soren was there, but already, the whole thing smelled like an ambush.

If you were accused of an Honor Code violation, you were assigned counsel from someone on the Honor Council itself. That person would conduct the investigation and plead your case. There were eight Honor Council members, so this also guaranteed that there was never a tie when the full Council convened.

That Soren should come to trial on the last day of school before Thanksgiving break, his case heard by the smallest possible assembly of Honor Council members, and that his assigned counsel was not just a freshman, but Zelda Parsons, who followed Livia around like a tail—the whole thing seemed suspicious enough that I decided I owed it to the historical record to stay where I was.

Well, yes, and technically, I was trapped—thank you for pointing that out—but what I'm trying to say is that even before testimony began, I knew it was important that I stay there and witness. Investigate. Eavesdrop. Spy.

There are a lot of ways to say it. Some of them sound nicer than others.

Soon, Ty and Zelda came into the faculty lounge together and I heard some chairs being shuffled around, and then Augustus called to order this session of the Honor Council convened to hear the charges against Soren Bieckmann brought forth by an unnamed party in the name of upholding the Honor Code of the Imperial Day Academy.

Augustus's whole voice changed when he said this. As stuffy and old-fashioned as the words he spoke were, there was no chuckle in his voice, no sardonic humor. It didn't sound like he was reading the words off a page either. He'd memorized them. What's more, you could tell he *believed* them.

"Counselor, please read the charges," Livia said.

Zelda cleared her throat and I could almost see her pushing up the horn-rimmed glasses on her nose.

"That on November 15, Soren Bieckmann did participate in lewd conduct on school grounds, and that on the same evening, he witnessed Honor Code violations perpetrated by others, including trespassing, harassment, and vandalism of school property, but did not come forward to report them."

Immediately, I knew what this hearing was about. Like Ms. Yee, I can also be very good with dates when I have to be. I knew exactly where Soren had been on November 15 and exactly what he'd done because I'd been there, too.

The whole thing was put into motion after the dress rehearsal for *Little Shop of Horrors.* Soren came up to Lola Stephenson, who was playing Audrey, and told her that there was going to be a *thing* after opening night of the show. I was standing right there, and he made no effort to lower his voice. I'd been laying down strips of glow-in-the-dark tape because the idiots on props crew kept wheeling Audrey II out to the wrong spot on the stage.

Lola shot a pointed look in my direction and shushed Soren, who shrugged and said, "It's okay. Claudia's cool."

I shrugged back, like it didn't matter what I'd heard, or whether I was or wasn't cool.

The plan Soren described to Lola was that the cast and crew would sneak back into the school after the show for a party on the stage. And at this party, with each hour that passed, certain items of clothing would become optional.

Lola laughed and told Soren he was insane if he thought

she—or anyone—would go to something like that, but there was something about the way her eyes followed Soren as he walked away that made me wonder if she was thinking about it. As he walked past me, Soren said, "You're invited, too, Claudia."

The tips of my ears turned pink and my cheeks burned at the idea of me, C-C-C-Claudia, attending a party like that.

Of course, Soren was clever. The Honor Council had been keeping an ear out for any rumors of another party at his house, but they would never suspect musical theater dorks of anything as racy as an after-hours nude soiree at the Esther Pico Memorial Theatre. And the musical theater dorks would be so shocked and titillated to receive such an invitation that they wouldn't have dreamed of missing it.

I can see that *you're* shocked. I was, too. Even on the day of opening night, I couldn't believe I was actually going to go through with it. I brought Julia along with me for moral support even though she wasn't part of the cast or crew. She thought the whole thing was hilarious, half because I was so twitchy about it and half because the idea of me engaging in such flagrant rule-breaking blew her mind.

"Soren Bieckmann is a terrible influence on you. Next you'll be sniffing glue in the green room."

Despite Julia's prediction, the whole thing was far less scandalous than you might have expected. Once the idea of disrobing onstage in front of everyone became a reality, people found themselves far less enthusiastic about actually doing it. And like I said, we're talking about musical theater people here. You never saw such an assemblage of virgins in your life.

I never had any evidence that the Naked Cast Party was Soren's idea. All I know is that he spread the word about it. In any case, when the clock struck eleven, the hour at which the first article of clothing was supposed to be removed, nobody except Soren did anything.

Soren put his money where his mouth was and took off his pants, but he was wearing a long button-down shirt that hung to his mid-thigh. Still, he seemed to enjoy himself and took to sliding across the stage in his sock feet, pantsless and carefree. A couple of girls took off their shirts, but they were wearing bathing suits underneath because they planned to break into the Imperial Day swimming pool for a midnight dip. Everybody else went about their business fully clothed and more than a little relieved.

The only person who seemed genuinely upset about the turn of events was Cal (Who had thought inviting *him* was a good idea?), who stormed around the stage in nothing but his boxers and the white dentist's coat that he wore in the play, nagging anyone who would listen to join him. At first, he was sort of funny about it, dancing around and making lascivious faces as he pretended to play with his nipples. But as the evening wore on, he began to sulk, angry that the party hadn't descended into the orgy he'd been hoping for. It was then that his antics became more unpleasant.

"Come on," he whined as he danced up to Lola Stephenson, who had made an appearance after all.

"'Come on' what?" Lola asked with a scowl.

"It's after eleven. Come on. At least unbutton your shirt," he said.

"No."

"If you were going to be such a prude, why'd you even show up?" Cal asked with a snarl.

"I'm not a prude," Lola said, as if *that* was the point that needed debating.

Eventually, Cal left with a freshman from the makeup crew who didn't know any better.

As for the rest of the party, some extras broke into the swimming pool. Two people hooked up inside the giant Audrey II plant. Soren tossed his pants up over a lighting rig, where, for all I know, they may still be to this day. That was the closest thing to vandalism that I saw.

Zelda related this information more or less, though she left out a couple of things I mentioned and added a couple of things I didn't.

"That's all I have," she said at last.

There was a long silence, then I heard Augustus say, "Would you like to add anything on your own behalf, Soren?"

Soren answered in his unperturbable surfer drawl, but there was just a hint of something else in his voice. Was he hurt? Or angry? I couldn't tell.

"Why me?" he asked. "I know you're just doing your job, but is this something personal?"

There was an edge in Augustus's tone when he answered. "You know the Honor Council is never personal."

"Because it *feels* personal," Soren added. "There were lots of other people there. People who did way worse things than me. In fact, I didn't actually do anything wrong."

"It's like a speeding ticket," Livia said, in this super-condescending way. "Even if everybody else was going ninety, you're the one who got pulled over."

In the storage closet, I rolled my eyes.

"But why me?" he asked.

Because you're the most prolific drug dealer at Imperial Day, I thought. *Because the last time you had a party, the Honor Council president and vice president showed up on a surveillance mission.*

Because they've been trying to find something to pin on you since the school year began.

"Is there anything else you'd like to add?" Ty asked. It was the first thing he'd said since the hearing had begun, and it was clear that the answer he most wanted to hear was *No! All done here! Go home and watch young men get concussions on television! Or football! Or whatever you call it!*

"This isn't fair," Soren said.

"Your points have been noted," Augustus said, gently. "Believe me, we're taking everything you said into consideration during our deliberations."

Deliberations, I thought. *Shit*.

It wasn't like they were going to do that in front of Soren. Would they send him out into the hall? Or would they adjourn to the storage room and find me huddled by the door? I pressed myself into a corner behind a bookshelf. It would hide me if someone opened the door and took a quick peek inside, but if anyone came in, they'd find me immediately. And if I was found, I was finished, Maisie or no Maisie.

I heard footsteps, then a click as the faculty lounge door closed. Then Augustus sighed.

"I don't like this," he said.

I felt my heartbeat slow down as I realized that they'd sent Soren out into the hallway. As long as I didn't knock over a stack of books or have an asthma attack, I was safe.

"He confessed," Livia said. "It feels pretty cut-and-dried to me."

"But he's right. Why him? It's not like he went to the party by himself. Why aren't we calling in anyone else?"

"Because he's the name we got, and he confessed," Livia said, her voice full of acid. "Unless you want to track down every single person who was there. Unless you think that would be a good use of Honor Council time."

Augustus might have been in charge of the Honor Council, but I doubted that he made a habit of contradicting Livia.

"How do we even sentence something like this?" he asked.

Ty chimed in right away. This must have been the part of Honor Council he relished most, the part where you got to dole out punishments. "Probation for failing to report. And for the lewd conduct, we could go as high as expulsion."

"He didn't do anything lewd," Augustus said, sounding exasperated.

"He took off his pants," Livia said. "Again, pretty straightforward."

"But was there anything really lewd about it?" said Augustus.

"Does there have to be?" Livia countered.

Ty cleared his throat. "What if we arrived at a compromise?"

I almost snorted. If Ty had come up with that idea—with that *sentence*—on his own, I'd voluntarily live in the storage closet for a week with only yellowed copies of *The Epic of Gilgamesh* for entertainment and nourishment.

The entire hearing was a farce. Lewd conduct? Even Augustus seemed skeptical about that. He was too honorable to go looking for trifling non-offenses to pin on someone he didn't like.

But Livia wasn't.

Livia, I thought. Livia must have told Ty to suggest the compromise.

But why?

Ty continued. "We dismiss the lewd-behavior charge and deliver a more severe sentence than usual for failure to report. Maybe a week's suspension?"

There was a pause before Augustus said, "That seems very harsh. The punishment for failure to report a violation is probation."

"This isn't the first time Soren's violated the Honor Code. It's just the first time we've caught him at it," Livia said, leaping to Ty's defense.

"He's not on trial for his reputation," Augustus said. But he didn't sound in control now. He sounded cornered, two against one. And even if Zelda could have weighed in, I doubted she would have joined his side. "And think about it. If we suspend him for this, and he's brought up on any other charges in the future, he could be expelled, no matter how small the charge."

Livia sighed. "Augustus, he's basically a drug dealer and he doesn't belong at Imperial Day."

Now we came to the truth of it. Livia and Ty were pushing for their so-called "compromise" because they wanted Soren gone. In Livia's mind, there were two kinds of people at Imperial Day: people who deserved to be there, and people who didn't— the right kind of people and the wrong kind of people—and unfortunately for the latter group, Livia actually had the power to carry out her vision, one problem student at a time.

"It sets a dangerous precedent," Augustus said. "I wish the rest of the council was here. This seems like something we should all discuss."

"We can. We should," Livia said, placating him. How could Augustus not see that he was playing right into her hand? I wondered where the other Honor Council members were, if Livia and Ty had even told them about Soren's hearing at all. Where was Maisie in all of this?

"Can we delay the judgment and sentence until all of us can convene?" Augustus asked, sounding hopeful.

"Not a good idea," Ty said.

"Why not?"

"Because of Thanksgiving."

A master orator that one, a regular Winston Churchill.

"We don't want it hanging over his head for the whole holiday break," Livia broke in. "Soren will worry. He'll think he's getting expelled or something. It's cruel. Especially since the sentence isn't that serious."

"You have a point," Augustus said finally. "How about three days' suspension for failing to report the Honor Code violations?"

"I can live with that," Ty said.

"It seems light," Livia said, "but I can live with it, too."

I could hear the triumph in her voice, and I knew then that she'd gotten exactly what she'd wanted.

Like I said, Soren was clever. No one had ever managed to catch him at anything really big, but now that Livia and Ty had gotten him sentenced to a short suspension, they'd never have to. The next time Soren slipped up—and any tiny slip-up would do—he'd be expelled from Imperial Day. He was a hunted man.

They called Soren back in and told him what they'd decided. He seemed to take it in stride, especially when they told him he could serve the suspension immediately after Thanksgiving break, giving him a full week off school. Still, as he was leaving, I heard him pause in the doorway, then ask, "What's up with this, Augustus? I didn't do anything and you know it. Not this time. What'd I ever do to you?"

"Nothing," Augustus said. "But someone turned you in. You know how it works. We have to investigate that shit."

"Who was it?"

"You know I can't tell you that."

As I heard the door close behind Soren, I wondered who *had* reported him to the Honor Council, and why. Was it Lola? She'd seemed leery of the naked party from the start, and I'd heard rumors that she was considering running for the Honor Council in the spring. But why would she report on Soren and not Cal? Or was Cal so pissed off about not getting to see the naked girl parts to which he believed himself entitled that he decided to get someone punished for it?

On top of everything else, where was the rest of the Honor Council? There was no Maisie, no Marcus. There was no sign of the other two non-entities on the Honor Council, a freshman named Jesse Nichols and a sophomore named Rebecca Ibañez, neither of whom seemed likely to win reelection, at least not if Livia had anything to say about it.

Jesse Nichols was a moron, everyone knew that, but Rebecca Ibañez's exclusion from the Honor Council lunch table seemed like a more calculated snub. I knew Rebecca was on scholarship. She wasn't popular exactly, but she was smart and serious and political—she talked about things like fair housing and labor unions and *la raza*, things that most people at Imperial Day didn't know the first thing about. I don't know exactly what Livia had against her, but she rolled her eyes every time Rebecca's name was mentioned. When she made doleful complaints at the lunch table about how the Honor Council "would be able to do so much more if all of us were on the same page," even I knew who she was talking about. It went back to the people who belonged at Imperial Day and the people who didn't. The right kind of people and the wrong kind of people.

Livia never would have pointed to the scholarship or the Latina pride or the political activism as things that made Rebecca the wrong kind of person. She didn't have to. All she had to do was roll her eyes. All she had to do was keep Rebecca out of those lunch table meetings where the Honor Council's core talked business and forged allegiances.

It wasn't hard to guess why Jesse and Rebecca had been iced out of the hearing, but I didn't understand why Maisie and Marcus weren't there. They were Livia and Augustus's best friends, respectively. They were the inner circle.

Then, just when I was sure that Augustus was about to adjourn the Honor Council meeting and leave me alone in the storage closet with my speculations, I heard the door creak open and a familiar voice that made my heart sink.

"Hey, guys, what's going on? Is this some kind of joke?" Julia asked.

"No," said Augustus, and there was no friendliness there, no warmth, no acknowledgment of the fact that Julia had dated his best friend for almost two years.

Shit, I thought, and combed my brain for something, anything, that Julia might have done to be called before the Honor Council. I had my suspicions. There was the flask of bourbon she hid in her locker (one-week suspension). She'd forged excuses for the times she missed first period because she was hung over (two-week suspension). She'd hooked up with Soren Bieckmann in the light booth at the Esther Pico Memorial Theatre naked party, even though I knew she didn't want me to know. (After Soren's sentence, who even knew what kind of punishment they'd decide on for that?)

Julia could have been before the Honor Council for any of those things, but if it was something like that, why did Augustus sound so cold? How hard was it to understand that Julia was going through a rough time, that what she needed most was a little human kindness?

"Ty will be your counsel," Augustus said.

"My counsel for what?" Julia burst out. "What have I done?"

"Julia, please. I know this is hard, but—" Livia started.

Julia laughed her 1940s film star laugh that made her sound like she should be lighting a cigarette while she broke your heart.

"You don't know anything about what this is like, Livia. Maybe you would if you'd spoken to me in the past month."

"Julia, this isn't personal," Augustus said. It was exactly the same thing he'd said to Soren, and I wondered whether he meant it or not.

"Then tell me, what is this? Because I don't even know."

"Ty, why don't you take a minute to go over the charges with her. You can step into the hallway if you'd like some privacy," Livia said, and the smirk in her voice made me wonder if she was enjoying this. I thought back to the day at the Venice boardwalk when she'd only hugged Julia to avoid looking rude. She and Maisie had never included Julia in their plans—that was how she'd ended up with me.

It was like Soren; like Jesse Nichols and Rebecca Ibañez. If you were the wrong kind of person, they'd find a way to put you in your place.

"I don't need to go over anything in private. Just spit it out. What'd I do?"

"This is about the cheating ring, Julia," Livia said.

"I beg your pardon?"

"This is about the research papers you sold, the copies of the tests, all of it. We found everything. We talked to your clients. We'll need to confiscate your laptop," Livia said.

"Wait, are you kidding me?" Julia asked.

Augustus didn't say a word. It was like he'd enlisted Livia to act as his proxy, and clearly, she relished the job.

"You know me," Julia protested. "We sat together at lunch every day. We did things together on the weekend. Do you really think this sounds like something I could pull off? Even if I could, do you really think I'd do that? Do you?"

There was a long silence. The branches of the alder tree rapped against the glass in the wind, and the old Imperial Day furnaces rattled to life, ready to face off against the chill of the fall evening. Ty offered no counsel, Livia no friendship, Zelda no allegiance, Augustus no answer.

"Oh my god," I heard Julia say after a moment. "You *do*."

IX

FUCK YOU EITHER WAY

Dear Claudia,

I'm not supposed to tell you any of this, but I don't think it matters anymore what I signed or what I pledged. They got me. I'm finished, so why shouldn't I tell you anything I want to? What keeps people from doing this? Is it because they're embarrassed? Maybe I'd be too embarrassed to talk if I'd actually done the things they say I did.

I knew that I couldn't just break up with Marcus and have it be easy, but I didn't think they'd punish me for it either.

I guess there were some rumors going around about me, how I turned into some massive slut after Marcus and I broke up. (Also, don't you just love the way everybody talks about it? That we broke up. Not that it matters at this point who ended things with whom, but I guess it bothers me that I can't even get credit for doing that one little thing.) Livia and Maisie never asked me how I felt or offered to take me to the pool at the Standard so we could get umbrella drinks and talk about what a cock my ex-boyfriend was. Livia never liked me— she always thought Marcus deserved someone cuter or more popular or nicer (she was always trying to set him up with this perfect little freshman Esme Kovacs behind my back). But I was surprised Maisie never offered to talk to me about it either. In fact, the only person who ever tried to talk to me about it was you.

The rumors are mostly stupid. Yes, I hooked up with Soren, like, once. We didn't even do that much because while it was happening, I realized how sad I was and that fooling around with Soren wasn't going to make me feel any better. I'm not sad that I broke up with Marcus. Mostly I'm sad that I wasted all that time and I can't ever get it back. I could have had different friends. I could have been a completely different person. So, you may have heard that I was getting blackout drunk every weekend and sleeping my way through Imperial Day, but mostly what I was doing was being sad.

I don't blame Marcus for what happened either. I doubt he had anything to do with it. He's just not a particularly vengeful kind of guy. Besides, he knows I didn't mean to hurt him, just like he probably didn't mean to hurt me. That's just how it happened.

As for what happened to me, Augustus had this list of things he wanted to accomplish while he was Honor Council president. Marcus told me about it. Marcus told me a lot of things about Augustus that no one else knows about, like how he practices making small talk in the mirror and how he always hits on the barista at the Starbucks on Montana Avenue when Livia isn't around. Augustus was convinced there was some huge cheating ring at Imperial Day. He heard so many little cases—copied homework, cheat sheets, plagiarism—and I think it started to get to him. He was like one of those police chiefs on a crime show who thinks that if he busts someone important enough, nobody will ever do anything bad again.

Anyhow, he believed there was somebody out there with a bank of tests and essay prompts. He was a little obsessed about it; he was sure this person would turn up if the Honor Council waited for the right tip. I used to think it was sort of funny, until someone told him that the person he was looking for was me.

They searched my locker, and sure enough, they found a stack of every test given at Imperial Day in the past two years. I'd never seen them before and I don't know the first thing about running a successful cheating ring. But then during the "trial" or whatever that was, Livia points to my clothes and mentions that I'm on scholarship and wonders, how do I always have nice stuff when I'm not supposed to have money, and I must have gotten it somehow.

Marcus recused himself from the hearing, which I get, and your sister wasn't there, which means that the two Honor Council members most inclined to believe me didn't even get to weigh in, and I know that wasn't an accident. I wonder if Maisie or the other two Honor Council representatives even knew they were hearing cases that day. I wouldn't be surprised if Livia never told them about it.

I thought all they had were the tests, which I'd never seen before, but then Ty came forward and produced a written statement from this unnamed mystery witness saying I collected old tests and sold them. Then, he says he wouldn't reveal the person's identity because the witness feared retaliation.

At first I thought it might have been you, Claudia, but it didn't make sense, and I didn't want it to be true. You're not one of them, and you wouldn't do that to me. Would you?

After the "evidence" has all been heard, they send me out and when I come back, I can tell from the look on Livia's face that something's going to happen, but I think, what's the worst they can do to me?

I thought they'd suspend me for a week or two, so when Augustus opened his mouth and said I was expelled from Imperial Day, I thought I'd misheard him. Then he started droning on about the legacy of the school and how I'd threatened the legitimacy of the Honor Council by cozying up to its members and winning their trust, all the while operating a cheating ring under their noses. And I start to realize, He actually believes that I did this.

And then I saw Livia and Ty give each other a look while Augustus was talking, and I knew what was going on, but there was nothing I could do about it. Sure, I can appeal my expulsion to Principal Graves and the Board of Commissioners, but they aren't going to overturn it. They give the Honor Council anything they want.

And what they want now, Claudia, is blood.

My life is kind of over right now. My parents are furious. I tried to tell them my side of things, but they wouldn't listen. They think I'm the mastermind behind the Imperial Day paper mill–test bank–cheating extravaganza, which is hilarious. If I had copies of every single test given at Imperial Day in the past two years, don't you think I might have something over a B average? No wonder the Honor Council can do whatever they want.

The reason I'm telling you all of this is that I want someone to know what happened to me, and when I tried to think of someone who would care, the only person I could think of was you.

Unless it was you who set me up with your secret testimony, in which case, fuck you.

Actually, fuck you either way.

I never should have listened to you. I should have waited it out, been unhappy with Marcus for a few more months, and maybe none of this would have happened. He would have graduated and we would have broken up afterwards, and maybe then I would have been the kind of girl Livia could feel sorry for instead of the kind of girl she wanted to get rid of.

Or maybe it would have happened exactly the same way.

So fuck you, Claudia, and whatever you do, be careful.

Love,

Julia

"How did you feel when Julia was sent away?"

"I was angry."

"With whom were you angry?"

"Livia. Ty. Augustus. Zelda. The people in the room. The people who did it."

"What about the people who weren't in the room, Claudia? What about Maisie?"

X

NO I'M NOT

"What happened to you?" Maisie asked one morning as we were standing in front of the bathroom mirror, getting ready for school. It was the middle of December, three weeks since Julia had become one of the disappearances. "Something's different. I don't even feel like I know you anymore."

"I'm the same as I always was," I said, even though we both knew that wasn't true.

"You never talk to me any more than you have to. You sit there at lunch looking around the cafeteria like you'd rather be at any other table than mine. Did I do something wrong?"

Livia was always over at our house, or Maisie was over at hers. I hated it, and I hated that there were secrets between us. I hadn't seen Maisie do anything wrong, but Livia and the others were her friends. They were the people she chose to be around; the Honor Council was something she chose to do. It was Livia and Cassidy Jones and Mr. Arnold all over again. Was Maisie really so naïve that she didn't see what was going on? Or did she know, and she just didn't care?

It wasn't like I could talk to her about my suspicions either. I couldn't turn to her and ask, *Why didn't you help Julia?* because

I wasn't supposed to know that she hadn't.

"You didn't do anything," I said. "I'm fine. Everything's fine."

Maisie locked eyes with me, stared right into the center of me the way she always could.

"No, it's not."

My heart fluttered, and I noticed a little tremor in my hand, and then all of a sudden, I blurted, "Why are you friends with Livia?"

And then it was out, the great, unspoken topic between my sister and me.

"What do you mean?"

I could tell I'd struck a nerve by the way she stiffened her shoulders at Livia's name. She already knew how I felt, but I'd come this far. I needed to say it.

"I don't think she's a very nice person," I said at last. "I don't know why you're friends with her. And I'm worried about you. You know what she did at the Griffith School, don't you?"

Maisie sighed, then took me by the shoulders and looked at me squarely.

"I think that you don't know Livia as well as I do, and you've never really given her a chance. I know about the Griffith School, but this isn't eighth grade anymore, Claudia. People change."

This was the first time Livia's past crimes had ever come up between us, and now I finally understood what Maisie thought of them. That's the funny thing about history: two people can look at the same set of facts and arrive at different conclusions, depending on their assumptions about human nature. When archaeologists first saw Stone Age cave paintings, they assumed they were forgeries because it was widely accepted that cavemen were violent brutes. Turns out they were wrong about the amount of art and beauty in caveman souls.

Maybe that was the difference between Maisie and me. Maisie knew what Livia had done, but she believed in forgiveness and second chances. She believed that people could change. I believe some things are unforgivable, that there are things a person with art and beauty in their soul would never do, things that a person can never come back from.

"You can go around worrying and being suspicious of everyone if you want to," Maisie continued, "but I can't."

"That's how you get fucked over, Maisie."

"Geez, when did you turn into such a cynic? Is this about Julia?"

"This is about Livia," I said, folding my arms across my chest.

"I will say this much and absolutely not a thing more, but if Julia didn't do it, I promise you, she would still be at Imperial Day. And I know that she's your friend, but, Claudia, maybe I'm not the one with the blind spot this time."

"But you weren't even there!" I said, before I remembered I wasn't supposed to know that.

A little crease formed between Maisie's eyebrows.

"What do you mean I wasn't even there?"

"Nothing. I just meant Julia was my friend, and I know she wouldn't have done something like that."

Maisie went quiet and focused on trimming her bangs with nail scissors, angling the blades so the ends were just a little bit jagged. When she had them just so, she started putting on her eyeliner.

"Are you still looking for your people?" she asked.

I spit a mouthful of toothpaste into the sink and rinsed my toothbrush under the faucet as I considered the question. I'd signed up for another semester of newspaper, and had traded in stage-managing the musical theater kids for equipment-managing the track team. Since there was no history club, I joined Model United Nations, which seemed like the next closest thing. I knew a lot of people. But after what had happened with Julia, I held them at arm's length.

But all I said to Maisie was, "Still looking."

Maisie stopped putting on her makeup and gave me a long, sad look. We used to be each other's people, I realized. Us against the rest of our family. Us against the world. It used to be enough, just the two of us.

"I hope you find them," Maisie said at last. "I miss you, Claudia."

"I'm right here."

"No, you're not."

XI

AUGUSTUS'S MOST LIKELY SUCCESSOR

As I've said before, Maisie tried to make me feel like I belonged at Imperial Day. She invited me to sit with her at lunch, introduced me to her friends, included me in things like that strange trip to the Venice boardwalk. But sometimes I wonder if all of this could have been avoided if she'd cared less. It's possible I never would have appeared on Livia's radar; maybe I never would have found my way into politics at all.

I'm not saying I blame Maisie. I'm just saying it's interesting.

The whole school year, I'd avoided Livia as studiously as I could, considering we ate lunch together most days. I didn't speak directly to her, didn't look her in the eye, didn't try to engage in her conversations, and for the most part, she seemed to appreciate this. So, I was surprised when she turned to me at lunch one day at the end of March and said, "Claudia, you should run for Student Senate."

Ty nearly choked on his Snapple at this suggestion, and Livia gave him a dirty look. I looked down at the table and mumbled that I hadn't thought about it since there was no way I could win.

"Don't run yourself down, Claudia," Maisie said, leaping to my defense. "Why *couldn't* you win? You know everyone, and everyone knows you."

"She's right," Livia said. I took a sip of my milk and tried to calm the nervous feelings swarming in my head. I was not accustomed to having this much attention directed toward me at the lunch table.

"What about Esme Kovacs and Chris Gibbons?" I asked. As far as I knew, my class already had two senators, and it was them. Not that I thought they were doing a bang-up job or anything, but I know enough about history to know that it's difficult to unseat an incumbent, even if that incumbent is a thoughtless clod like Chris Gibbons.

"Esme's giving up her seat on the Senate to run for Honor Council," Livia explained, and everyone at the table nodded in tacit approval because there was a freshman Honor Council representative they very much wanted gone.

You see, there is built into the Imperial Day Academy electoral system, and perhaps all electoral systems, the potential for error. Sometimes, the voters are misled or misinformed. Sometimes they do not have all the facts, and that is how you end up with mistakes.

One of these mistakes was Jesse Nichols, the Honor Council representative Esme Kovacs no doubt hoped to replace. As I mentioned earlier, Jesse Nichols is without doubt the stupidest person I have ever encountered. Teachers avoid calling on him. Entire classes cringe when he opens his mouth. When he approached Augustus—Augustus!—one day and asked if he could join us at lunch, Augustus shook his head sadly and said, "Sorry, dude. No room."

However, since the freshman Honor Council representatives

and senators are elected during the first two weeks of the school year, and it took a solid month for Jesse Nichols to fully reveal the range and depths of his stupidity to us all, he was elected to the Honor Council, and then there was nothing anyone could do about it.

"Is Gibbons actually running for reelection?" Augustus asked, and the entire table groaned in unison.

Chris Gibbons was another electoral mistake, though a different sort of mistake.

I knew him from the Griffith School, where he'd existed on the fringes of popularity, always sitting at the second- or third-most desirable lunch table. He had no discernible faults or quirks, and was mild, pleasant, and generally well thought of, if he was thought of at all. His run for Student Senate at the beginning of freshman year had been a rare show of ambition, and we'd all applauded it, giving him a hefty share of the vote.

But then something had happened to Chris Gibbons. He shed his pleasant demeanor, started dressing all in black, reading Ayn Rand, and scrawling the words LOVE and HATE across his knuckles in Old English lettering.

I fear I have given you the idea that everyone at Imperial Day was some kind of tightly wound, Type-A overachiever, but that wasn't the case. Like any other elite private school, Admissions tried hard to weed out the obvious flight risks, but it did admit its fair share of burnouts, misfits, malcontents, and losers. Some only looked good on paper, some were the grandchildren of people who had given the school so much money they could not be rejected, some had grown weary of playing the game we played at Imperial Day, and some were accidents.

Shortly after his election, Chris Gibbons decided that these people were his constituents, and that what they most wanted from their Senate was for all of its members to be taken down a few pegs.

So, rather than carry out the work of the Imperial Day Senate, Chris became its most vocal critic. He gave blistering interviews to the school paper, and complained to anyone who would listen that the Senate focused all of its energy on the popular people, didn't care about anyone else, and that its entire leadership was dominated by fakes and cowards. When he ran out of things to say about the Senate, he turned his wrath on the Honor Council, loudly criticizing their off-campus surveillance and calling Augustus a dictator.

The students of Imperial Day thought they had elected a mild-mannered public servant, and found themselves instead with a loudmouthed shit-flinger. After a year of ignoring, deflecting, or denouncing his rants, his colleagues on the Senate and Honor Council now simply hoped that Chris Gibbons would not be reelected.

"Please tell me someone else from the sophomore class is running," Maisie said, which was as close as Maisie would ever come to saying something mean about anyone.

"Someone named Hector Estrella," Livia said.

"Who?" asked Augustus and Ty at the same time.

"He's nobody," Livia replied.

"But nobody else?" Maisie asked, a worried look in her eye. If there were only two candidates running for sophomore class senator, Chris and Hector, they were both guaranteed a seat.

"Well . . ." Livia said, cocking her head to the side and looking at me. "That depends."

"You want me to beat Chris Gibbons," I said.

"Which you can," Maisie said.

"We'll help you," Livia added, a coy smile pinching the corners of her mouth. "You're an interesting person, Claudia. Not the usual cookie-cutter type who usually wins these things. That alone will get you votes. And you're not an idiot or a troublemaker. That will help with the people who are tired of watching Chris stir up trouble. Just don't open your mouth too much, C-C-C-Claudia."

She smiled when she used my old middle-school nickname to show that she was kidding, but I knew better. Still, I felt myself bend toward her words and begin to wonder if maybe she was right, if maybe I could win.

Chris Gibbons wasn't interested in making the school a better place, and Esme Kovacs had only used the Senate as a stepping-stone to the Honor Council. Meanwhile, I'd written a successful petition to the Athletic Director to get a new discus cage for the track team, had assistant-stage-managed the best-attended musical theater production Imperial Day had seen in a decade, had opened up what my journalism teacher, Mr. Prettinger, called an "unprecedented" dialogue between the *Weekly Praetor* and the Imperial Day Board of Commissioners, and had gotten the Model United Nations team matching windbreakers that said THIS IS NOT A RESOLUTION. THIS IS A REVOLUTION. on the back because the sad bastards needed to show a little spirit.

And I wasn't even trying that hard.

"She should talk more. Go for the pity vote." I guess that was Ty's cloddish way of showing he was on board with the idea, which of course he was—it was Livia's.

You can probably see what I couldn't then, that once again, I was being used. If I'd read into Livia's words, I would have seen that she wanted me to draw at least some of the freak vote away from Chris. And because I wasn't a troublemaker, she'd ensure that everyone in the freshman class who was the right sort of person—her sort of person—would vote for me to make sure a loose cannon like Chris Gibbons didn't get a second year in the Senate.

But I was momentarily seduced by the idea of power, at being singled out and identified as someone who could be trusted, someone who could be a leader. Even though it was Livia offering, all I could think was, I'll get in, I'll fix things around here, then I'll get out. None of this will touch me.

The moment I nodded my head and said I'd do it was the moment that set me on the path to this chair in your office.

But enough about me. The Honor Council races were where the action was that spring.

With Augustus and Marcus graduating, the Honor Council presidency and vice presidency would be up for grabs, which hadn't happened in some time. Augustus had wielded uncommon power, presiding at the head of the Honor Council for three years, the longest-serving president Imperial Day had ever had. He had changed the shape of it, and now there was a distinctly Augustinian way of doing things.

Sometimes I wonder if Maisie had spent enough time thinking about the political implications of that before she announced to our lunch table that she was running for Honor Council president.

Augustus's smile looked genuine. Ty's didn't, which made sense because as the other junior Council member, it had been a given that he'd run for president. Apparently, it hadn't entered his mind until that moment that Maisie might actually want the job, too. Maybe he thought she was too nice to campaign against him.

"I hope I'm not stepping on your toes," she said. "I think we'd both do a great job."

"Sure, sure," Ty said, his lips pulled tight and thin. "I haven't even decided if I'm going to run yet."

"I wondered if you'd be too busy with football," Augustus said, nodding, and Livia made a face, as if someone had poisoned her egg salad sandwich.

"But you have to run, Ty. Nobody knows the Honor Council as well as you do. Except Augustus," Livia said.

"Hey, I know the Honor Council pretty well, too," Maisie said. She gave Livia a playful shove, but I saw confusion in her eyes that her supposed best friend seemed to have taken Ty's side already. In fact, Livia hadn't even congratulated Maisie or wished her good luck.

I understood it perfectly, though.

Ty *was* too busy with football to be Honor Council president, not to mention he lacked the personality for it. If Livia was his vice president, she'd be running the show in everything but title.

"I think both of you should run," Augustus said. "We don't want it to look like I'm hand-picking somebody—which I'm not."

Augustus might have given his blessing for both Ty and Maisie to run for president, but I knew how he really felt about it. When he'd suggested that Ty might be too busy with football to run, I heard something in his voice that told me Augustus *hoped* Ty would be too busy to run.

And Livia might have been best friends with my sister, but for her to have a chance at any real power on the Honor Council the following year, Ty had to win the election.

So Augustus wanted Maisie to win, but couldn't act like it, and Livia wanted Ty to win, but also couldn't act like it.

Maisie complicated things for Livia. She was smart and nice to everyone. She wasn't just liked; she was loved. And Augustus seemed inclined to support her. If she ran, there was a very good chance she'd win, and I doubted she'd hand over the reins to Livia the way that Ty would.

And so, without meaning to, Maisie had crossed Livia, and when I realized that, I thought about Cassidy and Octavia. I thought about what Maisie had said to me when I confronted her about her friendship with Livia, that I didn't know Livia as well as she did, that people changed.

You're wrong, Maisie, I thought. *And you should watch your back.*

But of course, Maisie wouldn't do that. That was the problem with her. She never saw the worst in people, and I realized that if anyone was going to watch Maisie's back, it was going to have to be me.

XII

THE FEATHER OF TRUTH

It's not that you think that I'm lying exactly, but I can tell from the look on your face that you think I must be mistaken. The stakes were so low—I mean, a high school election, for Christ's sake. What was Livia getting out of this? Weren't she and Maisie friends anyway?

You have trouble believing that this is what happened because your head doesn't work that way. You work with teenagers in crisis, which means you're probably a decent sort of person, and you aren't interested in being powerful, which, believe me, is a good thing.

When Richard Nixon was running for reelection in 1972, he had a whole shadow campaign, a whole team of people who did nothing but sabotage his opponents with dirty tricks that they charmingly called ratfucks. They stole letterhead and used it to send out crazy memos. They broke the air conditioning at a fancy fundraiser so all the potential donors were too hot and crabby to open their wallets. They slipped a fake schedule to one opponent's pilot and had him fly to the wrong city.

You don't just wake up one morning with the audacity to pull something like that in a presidential election. You practice. You practice somewhere it doesn't matter. Nixon's people practiced at the University of Southern California, sabotaging student government elections. Livia practiced at Imperial Day.

Here's the thing: Even if it's not important, winning is winning. And for some people, that's enough.

I wasn't immune to it either. It wasn't just the power, though. It wasn't just the chance to make things better at Imperial Day. It was the way that Livia had pointed her finger at me and said, "You should run, Claudia." It didn't matter that I didn't like her and she didn't like me. In a way, that made it mean even more. There was something about being *chosen* like that, being seen in a way that you'd never seen yourself, that makes it very hard to say no.

It was only after I'd gathered my twenty-five signatures and gotten myself officially on the sophomore class ballot for Senate that I realized what I had done, and immediately thought about trying to get out of it. The fortune-teller at the Venice boardwalk had told me to keep my head down if I wanted to make it out of Imperial Day in one piece, and running for Senate was the exact opposite of that. I was lifting up my head and practically begging somebody to play Whac-a-Mole with it.

But then I thought about Maisie, the look on Livia's face when she announced her run for Honor Council president, and the look on Maisie's face when Livia had all but thrown her support behind Ty. She'd been so happy and excited when she'd told us, and almost immediately, the whole thing had become complicated and thorny and *political*. My sister needed a friend. My sister needed someone to look out for her. My sister needed solidarity. And so halfway back to the main office to have my name stricken from the ballot, I changed my mind. I would risk it. I would run for Maisie.

We could work on our campaigns together, side by side. This was both a nice idea and, for me, a significant advantage, for no one better understood the Imperial Day campaign trail than my sister.

It wasn't just that I needed Maisie's help. I missed her and the way things used to be between us, but how do you have that conversation? I didn't know where to begin. I wanted to tell her I was sorry I'd kept things from her. I wanted to tell her the truth about everything, from sneaking Julia past Augustus and Ty at Soren's party to the Honor Council hearing I'd accidentally spied on. I wanted to explain why I'd acted the way I had, why I'd pulled away.

Instead, I knocked on her bedroom door one night and said, "Maisie, will you help me with my Senate campaign?"

Her face lit up as she jumped up from her bed and ran to the door and put her hands on my shoulders and said, "Of course I will."

We went to the kitchen, where Maisie made a pot of peppermint tea and put out a saucer of shortbread cookies and proceeded to walk me through each stage of election season. We talked about campaign materials, color schemes, slogans, how to hit up people in the art and graphic design classes.

"Don't do jokes on your campaign posters," she warned. "They're funny the first two times you see them, then you're sick of them."

"What happens after that?" I asked, pouring both of us more tea from the little china pot. "Once you have the posters up and everything."

"You campaign. It's two weeks. Of course, you have to be

nice to everybody and talk to everybody, but don't talk about the fact that you're running. Don't come right out and ask people to vote for you. It's gross."

"Then where do you actually talk about getting votes?"

"They do a profile of everyone in the school newspaper, and then on the day of the election, there's an assembly in the auditorium. Everybody gets two minutes to do their stump speech. You can go sincere. You can talk about how much you love Imperial Day and public service. Or you can . . . I don't know . . . perform feats."

"Feats?"

"Play the guitar. Juggle. Saw a woman in half."

"You can't be serious."

"Some people treat it like a talent show," Maisie said, sipping her tea. "It's strange, but sometimes it works."

"Is there anything I should *know*? Anything I should worry about?" I asked.

"Just be yourself, Claudia, and you'll do fine."

Over and over she said that, and every time, all I could think was, *Why would anybody vote for that?*

I looked to Maisie for help, but of course, I also looked to history. There are many ways to run a doomed political campaign, and feeling certain that this was one, I decided that I would at least do it with style. In US presidential races alone, you can find examples of the loser who doesn't know he's a loser; the loser who vastly overestimates his own abilities; the loser who goes negative in so nuclear a way as to make himself sound like an old man who wears black knee socks with shorts and yells at the radio.

But then there are classy losers, ballsy losers, losers who make losing look like winning. For my campaign, I decided to take a page from the playbook of Eugene Debs, five-time presidential candidate of the Socialist Party, who once managed to land almost 4 percent of the popular vote while running his campaign out of a federal prison.

I needed a little bit of that attitude if I was going to very publicly run for Student Senate and very publicly, very probably, lose.

I took a picture of myself in profile sitting on my bed. In black and white, the antique brass headboard looked convincingly like prison bars. After consulting my Imperial Day student ID, I cropped the photo into a circle and ran a ring of text around it that read:

FOR SENATE: STUDENT 1439

People might look at me as Maisie's ugly, limping, stuttering sister, the girl who sat at the lunch table with half the Honor Council because they pitied her. With these buttons and posters, though, I was providing an alternative narrative. I was the girl who went to parties wearing Nixon t-shirts. The girl who knew almost everyone even if she wasn't really friends with anyone. The girl who didn't give a fuck what anyone thought of her. Not an insider. Not someone with an unfair advantage. Not someone to be pitied. It was a good angle, and the best part was, I didn't have to pretend to be anything I wasn't.

I'd just found a way to market the unlovable person I was into something that somebody might want to vote for.

That was the moment I got sucked in. Once I started thinking about How I Appeared as a Candidate, I was a goner, but I didn't see it then. I didn't realize how seriously I was taking it.

Ballots were finalized and campaigning was officially permitted beginning at 3 p.m. on May 1. At 3:05, my posters were up. At 3:07, I was roaming the hallways, studying the work of my competitors.

Based on what I knew of Chris Gibbons, the incumbent freshman senator, I'd expected something punk rock and angry and populist, maybe incorporating some tasteful little anarchy symbols. Instead, he went cute. His posters were a play on his last name and included a picture of an adorable baby monkey nuzzling a blanket.

It was genius.

It didn't matter that Chris Gibbons was abrasive and a loudmouth and a loose cannon, because from now until election day, he'd be Baby Monkey Guy.

I had no chance against Baby Monkey Guy.

When I turned the corner into the main hallway on the first floor, I saw my other competitor. I knew who Hector Estrella was, just barely. He was a freshman, obviously, but had transferred in at the beginning of spring semester, which meant he was either ridiculously rich or important or brilliant, or possibly all three. Imperial Day usually played hard-to-get with transfer students. After all, if they were transfers, it meant they'd chosen some *other* school first. It wouldn't do to look too eager.

When I found him, Hector was on his phone, pacing the hallway with one hand clapped at the back of his neck, his fingers kneading at it as though he was trying to work out a knot in the muscle.

"You're right. Everything looked fine when I picked up the prints. You did a great job. But I'm standing here now looking right at it, and there are two Es and one I," he said. I looked down at the floor and saw what he was talking about.

HECTOR ESTRELLA FOR STUDENT SENATE
VISION & INTEGRETY

Hector stopped pacing, leaned against the row of lockers, and slid to the floor as he listened. He hadn't noticed me yet.

"What I'm saying is that maybe the top one was fine and there was a problem with some of the others." There was a pause, then Hector crushed his forehead into the palm of his hand. "You're saying that's not possible?"

There was another long pause, then I heard him say very quietly, "I know how to spell *integrity*."

I waited until he hung up, then walked over to him, waving to show that I came in peace.

"They ratfucked you," I said.

Hector looked up at me, then down at his misspelled poster, then back at me, and he burst out with some mildly deranged-sounding laughter.

"I'm Claudia," I said. "I'm running against you, actually."

I pointed to the campaign button on my messenger bag.

"I know who you are, Student 1439," he said with a smirk.

"I'm sorry about your sign," I said, taking a seat next to him in the hallway. "And, like, obviously, I didn't do it and all that."

"That's a relief," he said, "because it would be pretty socio-pathic if you sabotaged my posters then came over here to tell me about it."

He really did seem relieved once he knew what had

happened, that he hadn't momentarily lost his mind and his spelling abilities.

I watched as he relaxed his shoulders, leaned his head back against the locker, and closed his eyes. It felt odd sitting that close to him in the otherwise empty hallway. There was all this space, and yet there I was, close enough to smell his cologne or whatever guy thing it was—sandalwood mixed with something green. He wore a plaid shirt with mother-of-pearl snaps, like a cowboy's, only he wore wingtip bowling shoes with it instead of boots.

"You're new here," I said, shaking myself out of a, doubtless, very important and fascinating examination of Hector Estrella's smell and his mother-of-pearl buttons and back to the matter at hand. "I just wanted to tell you not to take it personally. They do it to everyone."

He opened his eyes. "That mysterious *they* again. Who is *they* exactly?"

"I have theories, but no firm leads."

"Chris Gibbons would be the most obvious suspect."

"Baby Monkey Guy."

"Next to you, of course."

"I said I had nothing to do with it," I said holding up my hands.

"Until two minutes ago, I'd never even talked to you. Why should I believe you?"

"Because even if I was the kind of person who would ratfuck somebody's campaign, I wouldn't ratfuck you."

The words were out before I could think about how they sounded, but I meant them. Maybe it was because he was so polite to the person at the print shop, taking the time to tell them they'd done a great job even though he was pretty sure they'd screwed up his posters. Or maybe his sandalwood deodorant had temporarily addled my brain.

"Good luck," I said, pulling myself to my feet as gracefully as I could manage. "I hope you beat Baby Monkey Guy."

"Thanks," he said, looking a little bit puzzled. I wasn't sure if he was touched by the gesture or weirded out by the whole conversation, but I waved and told him I'd see him around.

Hector had been the first target of the ratfucks, but he was far from the last.

A rumor circulated that one of the Honor Council candidates, Cecily Stanwick, had tried to pay someone to take the SAT for her (and it was perhaps no coincidence that she was running against Livia for vice president). Someone drew engorged penises on all of Chris Gibbons's campaign posters and X'ed out the monkey's eyes, a design change that was really far more reflective of the candidate as we knew him. Even Chris Gibbons seemed to think so. He replaced the posters, but kept one of the vandalized copies hanging in his locker.

Rebecca Ibañez, the incumbent sophomore class Honor Council representative, suddenly dropped out of the race, and no one knew why. She hadn't been the most popular elected official, but she was no Jesse Nichols either. What made the decision especially baffling was that she and Livia were the only serious candidates running for their class's seats. She was all but assured reelection, and then suddenly—poof—her posters disappeared from the halls and she had her name stricken from the ballot.

I patrolled the hallways of Imperial Day, watchful for any sign that someone meant harm to my sister's campaign, but of her campaign there was, mysteriously, no sign at all.

"I think they're taking your posters down," I told Maisie

two days into election season. We were sitting at the breakfast table, Maisie sketching in her notebook while I chugged coffee and fretted over answers for my *Weekly Praetor* profile.

"Actually, I haven't put any up yet," she said, tearing a sheet out of her notebook and throwing it in the trash. I snuck a look at it before she tossed it—the page was covered with feathers, daisies, and peace signs. Not her best work.

"I don't want to tell you how to live your life, but shouldn't you get on that? People aren't even sure you're running."

"Trust me," Maisie said. Then she slipped the notebook into her shoulder bag and got up from the table. "Come on, we'll be late for school."

Of course I shouldn't worry. Maisie knew what she was doing, and really, getting a late start was a fairly ingenious strategy. You couldn't ratfuck someone who wasn't campaigning. Maybe that was what Maisie was banking on.

No one ratfucked Jesse Nichols either, but that was because no one had to. His stupidity shone like a beacon warning ships at sea so that they might not crash on the rocks of his dimness.

On the fourth day of election season, the ratfuckers came for me.

I was on my way to eighth period when all of a sudden, Hector appeared at my side, grabbed me by the arm, and dragged me down the hall. I started to tell him that I was going to be late, but when I saw the look on his face, I realized that this almost-stranger would not be dragging me toward the stairwell without a good reason.

It was hanging outside the library, four feet high by three feet wide, glossy paper printed with the words VOTE CLAUDIA McCARTHY FOR SENATE. In the center of the page was a gigantic picture of me, up close and in high definition. The artist had Photoshopped away my pores, evened out my complexion, and significantly thickened my hair. Cheekbones I do not possess had been shaded in, and the bags under my eyes had been removed. Obvious, pathetic levels of Photoshop had been deployed on this picture, and of course, I still wasn't pretty.

That was the joke, I guess.

A good ratfuck needs verisimilitude. Scrawl obscenities and insults on your opponent's poster, and your opponent looks like a victim. Vandalize with subtlety, and your opponent looks however you want them to look.

Anyone who knew me well would know it was a fake. But how many people was that? Maisie, of course. If Julia had been there, she would have known, but Julia was gone. To anyone else, though, it would seem like the obvious: ugly girl wants to be pretty, goes pitifully overboard in the attempt, forgets her classmates see her every day and know what she actually looks like.

"I'm sorry," Hector said as I gaped up at the poster.

Then I wondered, why had Hector shown me? He'd talked to me once. Why had he come to get me?

"I just thought . . ." Hector fumbled for words that wouldn't add to the poster's insult. "I know I don't know you, but after the other day, I just wanted to return the favor."

"Thank you," I said.

Suddenly Maisie was there, breathless, as though she'd come running the moment she'd heard. Her eyes narrowed when she saw the poster up close, then her head whipped around as she looked up and down the hallway, as though she'd be able to use heat-seeking glares to suss out the guilty party. She reached up and tore the poster from the wall, ripping it in half in the process.

"Let's go," Maisie said, storming down the hall. I looked back over my shoulder to see the few people who'd witnessed the whole scene staring after us. Hector picked the tattered poster up off the floor, wadded it up, and threw it into a trash can.

Maisie's fists were balled at her side and she walked with a clear and purposeful intent.

"Where are we going?" I asked.

"To see Principal Graves," she said. "This has to stop."

I stopped in my tracks.

"Maisie, please. No."

I didn't see what good could come of it. Dr. Graves wouldn't stop it. Nothing would change. Word would get around that I'd tattled like a kindergartener. I'd look thin-skinned and weak and like someone who called in her big sister, someone on the Honor Council no less, to fight her battles for her.

Maisie must have been ten feet ahead of me by the time she realized I wasn't following her. She stopped, turned around, and studied my face. There had been a time when Maisie and I couldn't keep anything secret from one another. Without speaking, our faces told everything.

"No?"

"No."

Things like that never go all the way away. Maisie didn't ask for my reasons. Instead, she turned down the hallway that led past the West Gym. The hallway was seldom used during the school day, and the doorway at the end of the hall led directly to the student parking lot. If you wanted to leave campus unseen, this was how you did it. I just couldn't believe that Maisie—rule-abiding, clean-living, Honor Council presidential candidate Maisie—was leading me out the door.

"Where are we going?" I asked.

"Anywhere you want," Maisie said.

Visions of Peet's Coffee and ice cream and pastrami sand-wiches danced in my head for a moment before I realized that I felt too depressed to enjoy any of it.

"Home," I said.

"You've got it," Maisie said. "I just need to make a quick stop first."

It is scientifically impossible to peel out of a parking lot in a Toyota Prius, but Maisie came close. We sped away from the school, winding down Sunset Boulevard until we came to a shopping center. Maisie pulled in and parked.

"Wait here, okay? I'll just be a minute," she said, then cocked her head to the side and asked, "Hey, are you okay?"

I nodded, and motioned for her to go. As soon as I saw her disappear into the shop, I leaned my head up against the passenger-side window and closed my eyes. Grateful as I was for Maisie's rescue, I hadn't said much of anything to her since she'd found me in the hallway. For once, I didn't feel much like talking.

When she got back in the car a few minutes later, she looked at the way I was slumped against the window and said, "You're not okay."

"I told you, I'm over it. Now what's in the package?" I asked, dodging and deflecting her concern.

"I'll show you when we get home," Maisie said, reaching back over the seat and laying the brown paper–wrapped bundle on the backseat.

My thoughts wandered back to the Photoshopped poster. Chris Gibbons was the likeliest suspect in that instance, but with the other cases—Hector's misspelled signs and Cecily's SAT cheating scandal and Rebecca's sudden withdrawal from the election—I couldn't quite shake the idea that somehow Livia was involved.

Ratfucks don't lose elections by themselves. They're minor things, little annoyances. What they do is keep their victims off balance and ill at ease, and that was exactly where Livia wanted all of us—too preoccupied with reacting to really *act*. I wondered what she'd do to throw Maisie off her game.

"Maisie, you need to watch your back," I said.

Maisie laughed at me as she pulled out of the parking lot. "What are you talking about, Claudia?"

"If Ty wins, he'll basically let Livia run the Honor Council, which is exactly what she wants. I was *there* when you announced you were running for president. I saw the look on her face. She didn't even wish you good luck."

Maisie clenched her fists around the steering wheel and took a deep breath.

"You saw a look on her face," Maisie said, her voice steady and deliberate. "And that's how you know that Livia is out to get me?"

That was why I hated talking about Livia with my sister. It was just like the conversation we had after Julia got expelled: I suggested that maybe her friend wasn't a very nice person, and Maisie made me feel like some paranoid conspiracy theorist.

Maisie continued, "Sure, Livia was caught off guard. She was a little hurt that I hadn't told her first, but it's no big deal. We made up. She said she was happy for me."

"Can you at least . . ." I started to say *be careful*, but I knew Maisie would think I was going after Livia again.

"Tell me you'll keep your eyes open," I said.

"My eyes are open, Claudia. I know what I'm getting myself into. Why would I be running for president if I didn't want to change things, if I didn't want to make things better than they are?"

We were home then. Maisie parked the car in the garage and turned to me. "Hey," she said, her voice softening. "Come on inside. There's something I want to show you."

Once we were in the kitchen, Maisie set down the package from the shopping center and ripped off the brown-paper wrapper to reveal her campaign posters.

"Do you like them?" she asked, beaming.

They were black ink on white cardstock, clean and simple. In the center was an old-fashioned line drawing of a feather. Above the feather, MAISIE McCARTHY was spelled out in block letters. Beneath the feather was the word TRUTH.

When your last name is McCarthy and you're involved in politics, even at the high school level, it's hard not to think about your namesakes. On the one side, you had Joseph McCarthy, who lied, pointed fingers, and spread hysteria about the imaginary Communists lurking in our midst. And then on the other, you had Eugene McCarthy, a peace activist who ran for president on the promise to end the Vietnam War. His campaign posters included only his name, a picture of a dove, and the word, PEACE.

He lost.

The ancient Egyptians believed that the hearts of the dead were weighed on a scale against the feather of truth. If the scales didn't balance, the heart was devoured by Ammit, the eater of souls, and the dead, condemned to the underworld. But if the person had lived an honest life, their heart would weigh the same as the feather and they'd pass on into heaven.

I didn't think anyone but me was going to know what it meant, all the history that Maisie had packed into that simple black and white poster. And then I realized why Maisie was smiling, why she'd taken so long getting her posters ready, why she wanted me to be the first person to see them.

The past few months, things had been so strained between us, and now it felt like Maisie was reaching out to me through her 1968 throwback campaign poster and the Egyptian Book of the Dead, saying, *I don't care if people think this is weird. I don't care if they don't get it.*

I made it for you.

"Claudia, what's wrong? Don't you like them?"

I wiped my eyes with the back of my hand and sniffled.

"They're perfect," I said.

XIII

THE REAL, UNVARNISHED ME

To be included in the Weekly Praetor's *Spring Election feature,*
please complete this questionnaire and return it no later than 3 p.m.
on May 5. Answers may be edited for clarity and space.

1. Why are you running for office?
~~Because I was vain and stupid and easily tricked.~~
~~To fix things with my sister.~~
Because I am a student of history, and even though I
shouldn't believe in the democratic process, I do.

2. Why should we vote for you? What kind of asshole question is this?
I am scrupulously honest, hardworking, and will do a good
job. If you don't vote for me, though, I think you should
vote for Hector Estrella. He seems like a decent guy.

3. What makes Imperial Day great?
~~The belief that if we say it enough times, it will be true.~~
~~Nobody has ever set it on fire.~~
Its storied history and legacy of excellence.

4. *Tell us a little bit about yourself. What do you do for fun?*
~~Read presidential biographies.~~
~~Go to museums.~~
~~Cooking show?~~
Think about the past. Worry about the future.

∗∗∗

At first, they looked like easy questions, but when I started trying to answer them, everything sounded either too sincere or too bratty. I agonized over it for hours. They went up on the *Weekly Praetor* website over the weekend. By running for Senate, I avoided the tedious job of having to spellcheck, format, and publish thirty-two candidate profiles, which surely would have been assigned to a freshman. That, in and of itself, probably made the whole thing worth it.

Each profile was more boring than the last. Ty was running for Honor Council president because "it is an honor and a privilege to serve the school that has given me so much." Shocker. And in her spare time, Zelda Parsons volunteered at the children's hospital. I wondered what child would be comforted by the sight of her pinched, disapproving face. Even Chris "Baby Monkey Guy" Gibbons only hoped that his fellow students appreciated the spirit with which he "fought" for them.

I could not imagine the warped soul of the person who would sift through thirty-two of these and read them all.

Before first period on Monday morning, I received a text from Livia:

Meet me in the Honor Council office before lunch. URGENT.

I had no idea what she wanted, and no idea how to get out of going. If I blew her off, she'd know I was afraid of her or she'd be pissed, and either one of those things was worse than just going and seeing what she wanted.

When I arrived at the Honor Council office, Livia was already there, sitting on one of the desks with her legs primly crossed, a kitten-heeled pink pump dangling from her toe.

"We have a problem," Livia said, motioning for me to sit down. The chair she pointed to was low, and I realized I'd have to crane my neck up to make eye contact with her.

"What kind of problem?" I asked. I sat down on top of another desk so we were at the same eye level.

"Better take the chair," she said curtly. "That desk has a wobbly leg."

I took the chair.

"The stats class did some polling, and you're only drawing 25 percent of your class's vote. You're not going to beat Chris Gibbons with 25 percent of the vote, Claudia."

Eugene Debs never polled 25 percent, I thought. If Eugene Debs had polled at 25 percent, he probably would have died from happiness.

"And whatever you were going for with that thing in the *Weekly Praetor* . . ." She rolled her eyes in disgust. "I am here to tell you that is not an effective campaign strategy."

"Okay," I said, because it seemed like this would be over sooner if I agreed with her.

"The assembly on Thursday, do you have something ready for it?"

Writing the speech was even more agonizing than writing the profile for the newspaper, but I nodded.

"Well, stop working on it," Livia said. She picked up two notecards, tapped them twice on the edge of the desk to even out the edges, and handed them to me.

Even before she explained what they were, I knew what she was going to say. This kind of backstage, smoke-filled-room political maneuvering was as old as politics. It was how things got done. It was how the most powerful people got the things they wanted. I was just surprised to find myself a part of it. Why did Livia care if I won? Was it really that she hated Chris Gibbons so much, or did she just think I'd be easier to control than he was?

"Your speech," Livia said as I took the cards. "It's exactly sixty-five seconds long, so you have some wiggle room."

Each candidate got two minutes to speak at the assembly, and most of them used every second of it. To do less would be to deprive us all of their brilliant oration. It was a smart move on Livia's part. To have a candidate get through their remarks uninterrupted by the moderator's 10-second warning would be downright refreshing.

As I scanned the cards, I saw that Livia had included all the usual platitudes about my commitment to service, my love for Imperial Day, but there was some edgier material as well. She'd included a line about how I was tired of watching the same people get elected over and over again, and how I'd represent *everyone*, not just my friends.

I had to hand it to Livia. She was anything but oblivious to the criticisms of her detractors. Augustus would have been horrified. I could almost hear him asking in his naïve way, "Is that *really* what people think of us?"

If he'd known what people thought, who knew? Maybe he would have tried to change things, but Livia was happy to insulate him from criticism. And as for Livia, she knew exactly who didn't like her and why. She just wasn't interested in changing.

Then I flipped the second notecard and read the closing paragraph Livia had written:

It's not easy for me to sit here in front of you, to speak into this microphone and ask for your vote. I don't mean that I'm nervous. I mean that this is physically difficult for me. But I know you can see past all that. You can see a person who will represent you, who will work for YOU in Student Senate.

"You won't have to stand at the podium when you say it," Livia said once I'd looked up. "They'll have a chair for you. I checked."

As I read over the cards again, my cheeks burned. Was this how my classmates saw me? Or how they *needed* to see me if I was going to win their votes? The noble cripple, oh-so-grateful for a seat at the normal-people table? I felt like screaming as I imagined the prospect of standing up on that stage like Livia's puppet. Forgive me. *Sitting.* I meant, *sitting.* Because apparently my mismatched legs wouldn't allow me to stand perfectly still at a podium for sixty-five seconds while I read the words that somebody else had written for me.

And did she have to put so many S's in it?

"So what do you think?" Livia asked, her lips pursed impatiently. She slid down from the desk and crossed to the chair where I sat, resting her fingertips on the desktop and glaring down at me. "Can you do it?"

I skimmed over the notecards again, and my lip curled in distaste as I let what Livia was proposing sink in.

She sensed it, and pounced. "Before you get all self-righteous on me, Claudia, let me ask you this: Do you want to win? Because nine times out of ten, this assembly cannot help you. It can only hurt you. Everybody's already made up their minds before they sit down, and the only way you can change them is against you. You're polling 25 percent. If you want to win, you will need to do something drastic at this assembly. Believe me, I thought about every angle, and this is the one that's going to work. So I'm going to ask you again: Can you do this? Do you want to win?"

There was a friendly lilt in her voice as she spoke, a smile on her lips, but the tendons in her neck strained tight and stood out like a lizard's.

Did I want to win? Not really. Not anymore. I didn't care what happened to me. What I cared about was Maisie, and Maisie had to beat Ty. If she didn't, it would be as good as handing the presidency over to Livia. And then it occurred to me: if I made a fool of myself during my speech, it would hurt Maisie's chances. I was her sister. I was afraid that any tarnish on me would rub off on her.

I thought about my Eugene Debs Socialist prison campaign and my weird newspaper profile. That was real, unvarnished me, and the real, unvarnished me was polling at about 25 percent.

There was one unexpected perk of the insulting speech Livia had written for me: If it made people want to vote for me, maybe it would make them want to vote for Maisie, too. If they pitied me, they'd pity her. Sixty-five soul-crushing seconds. In and out. Probably nobody would be listening anyway.

"Of course I want to win," I said.

"You said you didn't care what happened to you. Why not, Claudia?"

"Because in the scheme of things at Imperial Day, I didn't matter. What mattered was Maisie."

"Let's say you'd run a poor campaign or given a bad speech. Do you think that would have mattered to Maisie? Would she have been ashamed of you or felt that you'd ruined her chances?"

"No, that's not like her."

"Did Maisie ask you to read the speech that Livia wrote for you?"

"Of course not."

"Would she have even wanted you to, Claudia?"

XIV

PUT IT BACK THE WAY IT WAS

On the morning of the assembly the candidates met at school early for a catered breakfast, served to us by the graduating seniors from student government. Marcus and Augustus loaded up our plates with bacon and croissants and cantaloupe slices while the two senior senators poured orange juice and coffee. I picked at my plate, too nervous to eat. I was dressed up, by my standards anyway, in wide-legged black pants and a white button-down shirt that I wore untucked. As a nod to the occasion, I wore a blue and gold striped necktie—Imperial Day colors—tied with a full Windsor knot. Imperious in a gray sleeveless sheath dress, Livia eyed my outfit from across the room, and I did my best to ignore her disapproving stare. Just because I was going along with her plan didn't mean she got to pick my wardrobe. It would be a cold day in hell before anyone got me in a sheath dress.

I was sitting next to Hector at a table with all the other freshman candidates. He looked crisp and senatorial in his charcoal pinstripe pants, cashmere sweater, and shiny black shoes. However, his hands shook so badly he could barely lift the coffee cup to his lips.

"I don't know why I'm trying to drink this," he said. "It'll only make things worse."

It was Hector, Chris Gibbons, and me for sophomore Student Senate, then Zelda Parsons, Esme Kovacs, and two boys I didn't really know for Honor Council. By the end of the day, I realized, three of us would have lost.

"You're going to do fine," I told Hector. "If it makes you feel any better, it's probably going to be me who loses. According to the stats class, I'm polling at 25 percent."

Hector snorted and shook his head. "Who told you that?"

"That's just what I heard," I said, sneaking a look at the table where Livia was chatting politely with her opponents.

"I'm in that stats class," Hector said, "and the people who ran those numbers did *not* get a good grade. I think they surveyed, like, five guys who sit with Chris Gibbons at lunch. Not exactly a representative sample."

"Oh."

"I don't know what you're polling, Claudia, but it's not 25 percent."

After Hector's revelation, I was too rattled to answer. This changed everything. Maybe I didn't need to resort to desperate measures to save my campaign and help my sister look good. Maybe I already looked good. The problem was, I didn't have a backup plan: all I had was Livia's speech. I read over the note-cards and thought about what she'd said: *Everybody's already made up their minds before they sit down in the auditorium.* Maybe I could just read the boring parts and cut out the pathetic part about how difficult it all was for me. And I'd read it standing up, that was for sure.

"Are you okay, Claudia?" Hector asked. "You sound disappointed."

A smile played at the corner of my lips, and I discovered my appetite had returned.

"I'm fine," I said, stuffing half a croissant into my mouth. "Great, actually. Hector, you have revived my political career."

"But I didn't do anything," he said.

The first-period bell rang, and Augustus set down his bacon-serving tongs and said, "Everyone to the auditorium. It's showtime."

We lined up backstage, the upperclassmen claiming the folding chairs along the wall, leaving the underclassmen to stand. The freshmen went first because we were less important, but the way Hector spoke, you never would have guessed this was the case. The moment he stepped in front of the microphone his nerves vanished and he looked genuinely happy to be up there. He even got a laugh for a self-deprecating joke about the correct spelling of the word *integrity*. When he left the stage, the applause sounded sincere.

Next was Chris Gibbons, who took the stage looking like he'd just rolled out of bed. As he spoke about his past year of service, about how he wasn't afraid to speak up when he saw hypocrisy and laziness and poor governance, I thought about what Hector had said. It was hard to know what would happen. Hector had charisma, but he was new, so it was possible that not enough people knew him to elect him. Chris had his troubled past with the Senate, but had run a clean, clever campaign with no missteps. And then there was me.

"Claudia, you're up."

The voice shook me from my thoughts, and I realized that Chris Gibbons had finished his speech and a freshman stagehand in a black turtleneck was nudging me out onto the stage. I'd worked with him on *Little Shop of Horrors*. His name was Daniel, and he had that impeccable stagehand quality of being completely invisible until you needed him. He walked alongside me onto the stage where I saw someone had moved a wooden chair. Daniel lowered the microphone down toward it, then offered me his arm—so I could sit down, I guess.

I didn't know what the real numbers were. I didn't know how many votes I really had, but when I imagined myself reading the speech that Livia had written for me, sitting in a chair because I was supposedly too crippled to stand, I knew I couldn't go through with it. It would have been one thing if the chair and the microphone and Daniel's arm were there because people were being nice, but the whole thing was a manipulation, and I wanted no part of it. I tapped Daniel on the arm.

"Could you put it back the way it was?" I whispered.

My mind was made up.

Daniel moved the microphone as I took Livia's notecards out of my pocket and placed them on the podium. I cleared my throat, adjusted my Windsor knot, and began to read:

"I might not be the typical or ideal Imperial Day student, but that doesn't mean I haven't felt welcomed here. At the beginning of the year, you were mostly strangers, and now, I call many of you my friends. That's one of the most special things about Imperial Day and one of the reasons I'm so eager to serve as your sophomore senator. However, I won't just represent the interests of my friends. It is my pledge to listen to the concerns of every—"

Then a voice called out from the back of the darkened auditorium.

"P-P-P-PLEDGE."

I froze in the spotlight, unable to believe what I'd just heard.

"S-S-SENATOR."

It was a different voice that time, a different corner of the auditorium. A gasp and a few nervous titters rolled through the crowd as they waited to see what was going to happen next. I waited, too. Somebody knew who had done this. Somebody had been sitting next to them or behind them or in front of them when it had happened. I waited for a third voice to chime in, to denounce what had just happened, but after a few seconds, it began to dawn on me that this was not going to happen. The whispering and giggling died down, the room fell silent, and I realized that the voice they were waiting for was mine. Nobody was going to defend me. Everybody was too interested in seeing how I was going to respond, what I was going to do next.

I looked down at the words on Livia's notecards and wondered if I should have listened to her. If I'd been sitting down in the chair, would that have made a difference? Is that what they wanted me to be? But I didn't have the stomach to finish reading that speech now. I couldn't stand to say one more nice thing about Imperial Day or its students. No one was going to stop this and no one was going to be punished, so the only thing I could do was to get off the stage with some dignity.

I would not run away. I would not let them see me get angry. I would not let them see me cry.

I would not give them the satisfaction.

Instead I stood at the podium and looked out into the crowd, keeping my expression as neutral as possible. I met people's eyes and forced them to look at me. I refused to look away first. One face after another. I did this until the moderator said, "Ten seconds, Miss McCarthy."

I took a deep breath and let it out slowly until I was sure I could get the words out without stuttering or bursting into tears. As I leaned toward the mic, my necktie fell against the podium, and I clamped my fingers down on it, stroking the silk. The audience looked restless as they waited to see what I'd do next. Some looked downright hostile, like it was my fault they'd spent sixty seconds feeling uncomfortable, but I didn't care. I'd spent a year trying to fit in, becoming involved, meeting people, and after a year of that, the student body of Imperial Day had responded with a resounding *Fuck you*.

"Thank you for your time and, I hope, for your vote," I said at last before walking off the stage. I left Livia's notecards on the podium.

The audience was quiet, but the moment I was behind the curtain, I heard the chattering begin as everyone began to talk about what they'd just seen. Backstage, all the other candidates stared at me in horror. Maybe a few were stunned that it had happened in the first place, but they seemed more scandalized that I'd chosen to stand there, absorbing it in silence.

What would you have done if it was you? I wanted to ask. *Because if it was you, I like to think I would have done something.*

Suddenly, Mrs. Lester, the AP Government teacher who was ostensibly coordinating this thing, was standing by my side and clutching my arms in her hands.

"I'm so sorry, Claudia," she said, exhaling her coffee breath in my face. With each word, she gave me a little shake that I suppose I was meant to find emphatic and reassuring. "I will find out who did this."

"Okay," I said, though I did not think Mrs. Lester would find the culprits. I mean, what was she going to do? Drop everything and question the whole student body? She had an assembly to run. There were thirty-six candidates, each with two minutes to speak, and I'm sure Mrs. Lester knew that a freshman with hurt feelings was a less volatile situation than an auditorium packed like a powder keg with bored, restless people.

She did stand there with me long enough to make sure that I was not about to fall to pieces outside the green room. Once she saw that I was more or less all right, she let go of my arms and swept past me. A moment later, she was standing at the podium trying to hush the crowd so she could introduce the people running for the junior class seats on the Senate and Honor Council. The show had to go on.

Rather than face the stares of my fellow candidates in the green room, I returned to the wings where I had a good view of the stage, and watched Mrs. Lester tap impotently on the microphone.

"Attention, please. May I have your attention, please?"

I almost felt bad for her. It wasn't fair expecting a teacher like that to stand up for me when she was outmatched herself. The buzz of conversation grew even louder and Mrs. Lester began to look desperate. The lull in the program had lasted a minute too long, and now disorder had spread over the auditorium like kudzu. I saw her crane her neck, looking out into the audience for some other teacher or administrator to come to her aid.

It wasn't a teacher who rescued her, though. It certainly wasn't Principal Graves. It wasn't even Augustus.

It was Cal, psycho-eyed creep and sexual harasser of theater girls, who appeared from the far side of the stage. I was used to seeing him in his white dentist's coat, terrorizing the cast and crew of *Little Shop of Horrors*. Now, he wore a navy blue suit and a red striped tie. His hair was slicked back and there was a pocket square folded in his breast pocket. He glided up to the microphone, nudged Mrs. Lester aside, and said, "Please show this woman some respect," which was ironic, considering the source.

A hush fell over the room as Cal, who had never come to a teacher's defense in his life, stood there before them looking like JFK.

"Are you ready, Calvin?" Mrs. Lester asked.

Cal nodded, and Mrs. Lester smiled. Order restored, she leaned over and said, "I am pleased to introduce the candidates for junior class Honor Council representative."

"Thank you," Cal said as Mrs. Lester made her exit. He rested his forearms on the podium and leaned forward like this was just a casual conversation between friends. "Before I begin, I wanted to say how surprised and how disappointed I am about what just happened up here a moment ago. According to the Honor Code, we're not supposed to lie, cheat, or steal, but if that's all there is to it, so what? It has to mean more than that. The Honor Code has to function in our lives in such a way that when one of our classmates is bullied, we refuse to tolerate it. That's why right now, I want to ask if anyone knows who made fun of Claudia McCarthy during her speech. Or maybe those people want to confess themselves?"

As if things were not already bad enough, Cal was about to drag out the agony that was my public humiliation by outing the guilty parties right here during the assembly. I wanted to hide under the stage.

At first, all I could think was, *When did this happen?* Cal must have collected the twenty-five signatures needed to get himself on the ballot, but he hadn't campaigned, hadn't done a newspaper profile. He hadn't even made an appearance at the candidates' breakfast. Until now, as far as anybody knew, there were only two people running for the junior class seats on the Honor Council, Livia and Cecily Stanwick, who'd been dogged throughout the campaign by rumors of an SAT cheating scandal. Livia had barely campaigned, and why should she have? She was guaranteed a seat, and the vice presidency was all but a formality. The other incumbent, Rebecca Ibañez, had dropped out for no reason, but seeing Cal at the podium in his suit, I began to suspect there had been a reason after all.

It was not difficult for me to picture Cal approaching Rebecca with intimidation or threats. That would be entirely in keeping with what I knew of his character. But neither was it difficult for me to imagine that Rebecca simply might have reached her limit. For a year, the rest of the Honor Council had treated her like she scarcely counted, like she was a mistake. The sight of a ballot that included all those names again—Livia, Ty, Maisie, Zelda—might have made Rebecca Ibañez decide she'd be better off enacting change somewhere her talents were appreciated.

I felt a tap on my shoulder, and when I turned around, Maisie was there, a stricken look on her face.

"I've been looking everywhere for you," she said. "Are you okay?"

"I'm okay," I said, then gestured toward Cal, who was still scanning the audience for the guilty parties. "But this? This is not okay."

"I can't believe he's running for Honor Council," Maisie said, a distinctly un-Maisie-like sneer on her lips that vanished as she turned to face me. "Is there anything I can do, Claudia? Anything you want me to say in my speech?"

"Please don't," I said, my eyes widening in horror. It didn't matter that Maisie's intentions were good. If she did it, every other candidate who followed her would do it, and the thought of my humiliation becoming the prevailing theme of the entire election made my face burn with shame.

"Don't even mention it, Maisie," I said. "Act like it never happened. This is bad enough."

"I wouldn't do what Cal's doing. You know that, right?"

"I know," I said. "But still."

There was something else Maisie didn't understand. When I told her that I was okay, I meant it. I mean, I won't lie. The scene unfolding in the Esther Pico Memorial Theatre had hurt me, and hurt badly. However, what Maisie didn't get was that I was used to it. I'd been excluded from birthdays, picked last for teams, and laughed at for a very long time. People had been mocking my limp, my looks, my stutter since first grade, and no matter what any teacher promised to do about it, I had realized early on that it would never stop, and that I could either absorb every last hurt my classmates inflicted, or I could choose to do something else.

People could still hurt me, but I would never be surprised by it, and that made all the difference.

Running for office had certainly brought out a kind of overt, blunt cruelty, but the only difference was in its scale. At its core, it was the same thing I'd been dealing with for the past ten years. I'd learned that the best way to keep it from sinking into the vulnerable nooks and crannies of my brain was to move on and not to dwell.

"Just give the speech you were going to give," I said. "Please just don't call any more attention to it."

Out on the stage, Cal had spotted a raised hand in the audience.

"Petra," he called out. "Did you have something to say?"

From the darkened auditorium, I heard a voice call out, "I know who said it."

A triumphant, malevolent grin oozed onto Cal's face. Quickly, he tempered it into something a bit more befitting the occasion.

"Thank you, Petra. Thank you for speaking up. I know you'll report that to an Honor Council representative after the assembly."

Cal turned back to the mic, addressing the whole room once again. He seemed as much at home on the stage as he had a few months before doing musical theater.

"*That* is the kind of accountability and transparency I am offering you. No more party-crashing. No more lurking around your extracurricular activities, waiting for you to step out of line. The Honor Council should be where you need it: here at Imperial Day, not in your private lives. The Honor Council should make your time at school easier, not harder. It should protect you, not expose you. It should make your life better, not worse. Thank you for your vote."

Maisie's face went slack as Cal finished his speech and the auditorium erupted in enthusiastic applause. Cal nodded his head, taking it all in as though we owed him this, that we were finally dishing out the acclaim and respect he'd deserved all along.

Under her breath, I heard Maisie whisper, "He set the whole thing up."

"Maisie . . ." I started to speak, but Maisie would not be interrupted.

"He probably paid them to heckle during your speech so he could come to your rescue during his own. Or maybe he didn't pay them. Maybe he just threatened them instead."

My sister is a very sane and well-adjusted and reasonable person, so I was not quite sure what to make of the unhinged look in her eyes, the grim smile that played across her lips.

After everything I've said about ratfucks and Nixon and winning at any cost, you'd think it would have been easy for me to accept Maisie's theory. But all I could think about was the audacity of the thing. Who would *do* something like that? It was too risky, there were too many uncontrollable variables. If any piece of the plan had failed, the results would have been catastrophic for Cal. Besides, was it more likely that Cal enlisted ringers to heckle me during my campaign speech in front of dozens of witnesses so that he could then swoop in and pretend to save the day? Or that a couple of people at Imperial Day were insensitive jerks?

"Do you have any evidence?" I asked.

"I have the evidence of knowing him."

"I don't know, Maisie," I said, shaking my head.

And then it occurred to me that if it had been Livia up there, I would have believed the worst in a heartbeat. In fact, even as Maisie's shoulders slumped and she leaned back against the wall with a defeated sigh, I found myself wondering if Livia had had something to do with it, if this was retaliation because I hadn't delivered my speech the way she'd told me to.

I chased theories down rabbit holes through the rest of the candidate speeches, including Livia's. All the while, Maisie stood against the wall, silent and brooding, until Mrs. Lester took the stage once more. There were only a handful of speeches left to go, but these were the big ones.

"It's my pleasure to introduce our first candidate for Honor Council president, Ty Berman."

Ty walked to the podium like he was getting in the lunch

line. Actually, no. On omelet bar day, I'd actually seen him do that with something like enthusiasm. His speech was like elevator music or wallpaper, and even though it was right there in front of me, I couldn't bring myself to notice it. The words crumbled and blew away like dust the second they landed on my ears. Even when I really tried to pay attention, other thoughts kept jumping to the forefront: What was Maisie going to do? She seemed more upset about all of this than I was.

I turned to Maisie and whispered, "You can beat this guy. A giraffe puppet on the end of a rake could beat this guy."

Maisie smiled, but didn't say anything. I watched as she closed her eyes and rubbed her temples, mentally preparing to take the stage.

"Are you ready?" I asked, but Maisie didn't answer me, and then Ty was done and Maisie's name was being called. I caught a whiff of rosemary mint shampoo as she brushed past me, squeezing my arm, and then she was standing at the podium, her voice clear and her eyes fierce. I'd never been nervous for Maisie before. Whenever she did something, it was confident and considered and reliably solid, but the look on her face before she'd taken the stage made me worry that Maisie was—for the first time in her life—about to do something ill-considered.

"Ever since I was a freshman, I've wanted to be Honor Council president," she said. "I had a pretty great one for a role model. When I looked at Augustus, I saw an honorable person, a natural leader, and a person with vision. Augustus had a vision of what the Honor Council could be and do, and it's one I admire. I spent the last three years admiring Augustus, but what I realize now is that I'm not him and neither is my opponent, and no matter which of us you elect, things are going to be different next year.

"You can have a leader who will try to pretend that things are the same, and we are good people, and this school is a nice place, or you can have me.

"I'm going to do things my way if you elect me, and I'm not entirely sure what that is. But I promise you three things:

"I will be fair. I will do what is right. I will tell the truth. Thank you."

Maisie stalked off the stage without waiting for applause. When it came, it sounded confused and was quickly drowned out by chatter from the audience. Even from where I stood, I could make out the gist of it because I was thinking it, too.

"What was that?" I asked, stepping in front of Maisie before she continued on, possibly through a wall.

Maisie's eyes softened as they focused on me. She blew out a deep breath and covered her face with her hands for a moment. When they dropped back down to her sides, she was herself again.

"I'm glad that's done," she said, smiling at me.

"But what did you *do*?" I asked.

"I did what you asked me to. I didn't say anything about you. I gave the speech I wrote last night. I said what I wanted to say."

Maisie's smile crumpled then, and she went silent and looked down at the floor, and I knew that there was something she wasn't telling me.

"Maisie, what's wrong?" I asked.

"I'm not going to win," she said with a shrug. "I looked out into the auditorium during my speech and I saw it in their eyes. They don't want me."

"That's insane," I said. "You've been going to school with these people for three years. They know you, and they know

Ty, and if they don't vote for you because they didn't like a 30-second speech you gave, then they're idiots."

Maisie shushed me, and when I looked over my shoulder, I saw Oberlin St. James, one of the candidates for Senate president, shooting us a poisonous look. Maisie took me by the arm and led me through the backstage area and into the green room, where most of the candidates had retired after giving their speeches.

When we opened the door, people turned to stare at us and conversations stopped mid-sentence, and even if I hadn't heard the last thing Zelda Parsons said before clamping her mouth shut like a lantern fish, I would have known they'd all been talking about us.

"Her own sister, and she didn't even say anything."

I glared at Zelda, then looked around the room until I found a quiet corner and pointed it out to Maisie.

"Over there," I said, and we went over and took a seat on some risers, and then I asked, "What's going on, Maisie?"

She looked down at the riser. Long ago, someone had written I FARTED HERE in Sharpie. Even though the residue of the act had doubtless evaporated, we caught ourselves moving away from it at the same time and laughed a little harder than the moment warranted.

When we couldn't pretend it was funny anymore, Maisie looked up at me and said, "Claudia, there's something I need to tell you."

So I was right. There had been something Maisie wasn't telling me.

She started off looking me in the eye, but within a few words, she'd turned her head and was staring out the window, weighing each word with the precision of a coke dealer.

"This thing came up, Claudia, this art and language immersion program. It's in Rome, and you spend your senior year studying there. Livia gave me the application—I guess her dad knows someone on the board—and I got in. I just found out last Monday."

There was a buzzing in my ears and Maisie's voice sounded like it was coming from underwater. *She'd known for over a week*, I thought. *She'd known before she even started campaigning. And Livia had given her the application.*

I'd thought the ratfuck on Maisie would come in the form of sabotage or humiliation, but Livia was too smart for that. She'd delivered it in the form of a one-way ticket to Rome, exactly the thing to keep Maisie too distracted to run a proper campaign.

"I would have told you sooner, but I promised myself that I'd stay if I won the election. And until today, I thought, well, maybe there'd be nothing to tell."

"So you blew your campaign on purpose?" I snapped at her.

"No, Claudia."

"Then what was all that stuff with the feather and the Egyptian Book of the Dead and not even starting your campaign until a week in and practically calling Ty out in front of the whole student body?"

"You inspired me, Claudia. I'm tired of the way things are. If I win, things are going to change around here."

"And if you don't?"

"Then I don't want to stay here and pretend I'm doing anybody any good. You're right. All those people voting for us have known me for three years. They know what I stand for. I'm tired of watching people pat themselves on the back for how virtuous and honorable they are when it's a lie," she said, then added, "If I lose, I'm leaving."

"Do Mom and Dad know about Rome?"

"Of course they know," Maisie said. "They had to sign a waiver. I made them promise to let me tell you myself though."

"But you're going to win," I said, hating the desperate whine that crept into my voice.

"I hope so."

The idea of Imperial Day without Maisie, of our parents' house without Maisie, days and weeks without her like she'd been ripped out of my life—it hurt, and it hadn't even happened yet. I wanted to bury my head in Maisie's shoulder and beg her to stay. I wanted to tell her how much I needed her.

So instead, of course, I yelled at her.

"No, you don't!" I said. "If you really wanted to win, you would have tried. You would have made normal posters and said the things you were supposed to say. You wouldn't have sabotaged yourself."

The bell sounded, and Mrs. Lester's voice came over the loudspeaker in the green room.

"Thank you for your attention and your participation in the democratic process. It's all just so exciting. Please return to homeroom at this time to cast your ballots."

Maisie got up from the risers and held out her hand to help me up.

"I have faith in people, Claudia. If they look at me and decide they trust me to be in charge of the Honor Council, then I want to stay here and do that. But if what they want is something else, if they want to elect someone who's just trying to add a line to his extracurriculars like Ty, or someone who's just running to mess with us like Cal, then I don't want to be here. I don't want to serve alongside them like I think everything is fine, because nothing good is going to come of it."

The one-minute bell sounded and Maisie eyed the clock, ever the perfect student.

"We'll talk more at home," she said. "I promise."

"Aren't you going to be at lunch today?"

"Library. I didn't do my calculus homework last night because I was working on my speech." She looked at the clock again, then back at me with an apologetic look on her face. "I have to go now, Claudia. But if I don't see you again today, good luck."

"Maisie—"

I wasn't even sure what I wanted to say. All I knew was that I didn't want this conversation to end. I wanted it to be always the moment before I had to go cast my ballot, my sister by my side. I wanted us to stay where we were, to never vote, to never find out the end result of the Imperial Day Student Elections because either way, everything from here on out was going to be different. This was the end of something, the beginning of something else, and I knew in my heart that—

"What is it, Claudia?"

"Good luck to you, too, Maisie."

XV

My Sincere Respect To All Who Ran

It was later that day, during seventh period, when the election results came in.

By then, I'd sweated through my dress shirt, and my necktie felt too tight, and I was wishing that I'd brought a t-shirt to change into. I put my head down on the desk, daring Mr. Woolf to say anything about it. I wanted to get through the next forty-five minutes, go home, crawl into bed, and stay there for the next two days. I hadn't spoken to a soul since the assembly. During lunch, I had gone to the Humanities faculty lounge and hidden in the book storage room where I'd eavesdropped on the Honor Council hearing the previous fall. I sat in the corner with my knees drawn up to my chest, and with each breath I took I thought, *I will not cry, I will not cry, I will not cry.*

I put on my armor, I hardened my heart, and after half an hour, I was ready to come out of the storage room, ready to endure three more hours of stares and whispers without lashing out. That I did not ask a single person what the fuck they were looking at should have qualified me for some kind of medal.

Now, with my head down on the desk in Mr. Woolf's class, I imagined that the medal was real, that they held another assembly just so they could loop it over my head while Mrs. Lester told me how brave I'd been and how sorry they all were and the entire student body stood up one by one and begged for my forgiveness.

We were wrong, Claudia.

We are sorry, Claudia.

Nobody has ever suffered the way you have suffered, Claudia.

It was self-indulgent and pathetic, and it felt excellent.

I was deep into enjoying the public groveling segment of my fantasy when the bell rang, which caused me to jolt upright in my chair and knock my tablet and books onto the floor. There were a few giggles as I flailed and blinked myself back to consciousness. It seemed too early for the bell, I thought. Or maybe I'd been asleep much longer than I'd thought. I picked up my notebook and was inspecting it for drool when the seldom-heard voice of Dr. Graves crackled through the loudspeaker. It sounded as though it had traveled a great distance to be there, possibly from the 1900s and through a Victrola.

"Good afternoon to you all." There came a little cough, a rustling of papers, and the creaking of a leather chair before he continued. "I offer my most heartfelt congratulations to the winners of this year's elections and my sincere respect to all who ran. To participate in the Senate and the Honor Council elections is to embody the very spirit and soul of the Imperial Day Academy, and it is one of the noblest things you can do during your time here."

I thought about what Maisie had said about how much people at Imperial Day liked to pat themselves on the back. There was nothing noble about what I'd done. I'd gotten some signatures on a petition, made some posters, given a speech, and I wasn't even sure why I was running anymore.

Dr. Graves continued. "Without further ado, then, I am pleased to announce that your new Honor Council president is Ty Berman. Honor Council vice president is Livia Drusus . . ."

He went on announcing each seat, class by class, but I didn't hear a word of it. All I knew was that Ty was president and Maisie wasn't. When I closed my eyes, I could almost see Livia beaming, nodding graciously as she accepted congratulations from the people in her class. I could almost see the glint in her eye as everything unfolded exactly as she'd planned. I wondered how long it would take for Ty to all but turn over the Honor Council to her. Maisie would be in art class right now, I thought. I wondered what she was feeling. Was she relieved? Was she already dancing on the tables that now she was absolved of trying to make Imperial Day a better place? She could go to Rome and study Italian and art with a clear conscience. There was nothing holding her back now except me.

I felt a tap on my shoulder and turned around, eyes narrowed, and said, "What?" with unmasked hostility.

Tabitha Lyons pulled back her hand as though I'd bitten it, and I immediately felt bad. Tabitha was sweet and timid and not at all a bad sort of person. I had a hard time believing that she would have giggled behind her hand while some clod shouted "P-P-P-PLEDGE" in the middle of the auditorium. If she wasn't so cripplingly shy, maybe she would even have done something to stop it.

"I'm sorry, Tabitha," I said, my face softening. "It's been a shitty day."

"But you won," she said.

"I did?"

I searched her face for something to suggest she was joking. Even if she was making fun of me, that would have been all right, but her eyes were as wide and brown and sincere as a dairy cow's.

"You did," she said. "You and Hector Estrella. Congratulations."

Instead of thanking her, I turned around and put my head back down on the desk.

IMPERIAL DAY ACADEMY BOARD OF COMMISSIONERS v. CLAUDIA McCARTHY

OFFICIAL HEARING TRANSCRIPT

MR. CARSON QUENTIN MATHERS, PRESIDENT OF THE IMPERIAL DAY ACADEMY BOARD OF COMMISSIONERS: Isn't it possible that the Honor Council had been overzealous under its previous leadership, and these changes under Ms. McCarthy's leadership merely signified a regression to the norm?

CHRISTOPHER GIBBONS: I don't think it's possible. I've gone to school here for three years. There's no way people aren't lying and cheating as much as they ever did. People don't change that much.

MR. MATHERS: Then what are you suggesting, Mr. Gibbons?

CHRISTOPHER GIBBONS: I'm suggesting that Claudia got everything she wanted, just like she always does. She can act like it's an accident or like she's some dork with a limp and a stutter, her whole little "poor me" routine, but I promise you, everything that girl does is on purpose. None of it is an accident.

PART II
THE REIGN OF TY

THE HONOR COUNCIL

SENIOR CLASS REPRESENTATIVES:
Ty Berman, President
~~Maisie McCarthy~~ (RESIGNED)
Lola Stephenson (RUNNER-UP)

JUNIOR CLASS REPRESENTATIVES:
Livia Drusus, Vice President
Cal Hurt

SOPHOMORE CLASS REPRESENTATIVES:
Esme Kovacs
Zelda Parsons

THE SENATE

SENIOR CLASS REPRESENTATIVES:
OBERLIN ST. JAMES, PRESIDENT
JASMINE PARK, VICE PRESIDENT

JUNIOR CLASS REPRESENTATIVES:
ERNEST COLLINGSWOOD
MORGAN PETERSON

SOPHOMORE CLASS REPRESENTATIVES:
HECTOR ESTRELLA
CLAUDIA MCCARTHY

TWO FRESHMAN REPRESENTATIVES FOR BOTH THE HONOR COUNCIL AND THE SENATE WILL BE ELECTED DURING THE FIRST TWO WEEKS OF FALL SEMESTER.

XVI

CORPORATE YOGA

In case you cared, the summer before sophomore year was the best one of my life. It was the last gasp of my old life before politics reeled me in. It was my last real summer with Maisie before Rome took her away from me.

Maisie didn't spend much time with her old friends once she'd resigned her seat on the Honor Council. At the lunch table, Augustus was disappointed and constantly trying to talk her out of it. Ty was as taciturn and graceless in victory as he was in everything else. Marcus was checked out, his thoughts already three thousand miles away at NYU, and Livia could hardly contain her glee that things had turned out just like she'd hoped they would. It was, overall, not an environment that was conducive to friendship, and when school was over, I noticed that Maisie never seemed to return any of their texts, seeming instead to prefer my company.

She taught me to drive that summer. We practiced in the parking garage at our parents' office. They'd long ago sold their interest in DeliverMe, which had weathered the storm of the security breach and the Melinda Incident and was eventually absorbed into Amazon. Following that crisis (and, of course, the crisis of my birth), our parents had really gotten into What Really Matters and Giving Back to the Community and An Ethical Corporate Model and things like that. They wound up starting InVigor, a network of charitable ventures that allowed people to make low-interest loans to poor people or fund installation art projects and basically feel very good about themselves by doing very little. Maybe they were trying to be better people, but it was hard to take any of that seriously when they operated out of a beachfront office building in Santa Monica and brought in an instructor for staff yoga classes on the beach at 8 a.m. and noon.

All summer, Maisie and I drove to InVigor to do corporate yoga. We went out for coffee. I sat on the beach and read history books while she ran on the bike path. We cooked. We talked. We were inseparable, but it wasn't until the Fourth of July that Maisie finally brought up the thing that nobody had been saying all summer. We were parked on the roof at InVigor so we could watch the fireworks at the Santa Monica Pier without actually having to deal with the crowds.

"Are you mad at me for leaving?" she asked.

I could tell she'd been wanting to ask me for a long time. I could tell it was hard for her to ask it, and I didn't know what to say back. I was upset. Maisie was abandoning me, abandoning Imperial Day, abandoning all the things the two of us could have done together to make it a better place. And of course, I missed her already.

"I'm not mad," I said at last, turning over the words I wanted to say next, making sure they were the right ones. "I just don't know how I'm going to get through the next year without you."

"You'll get through the same way you got through your freshman year," Maisie said. "You didn't need me then."

There was the tiniest shred of hurt in her voice, and I felt guilty all over again as I remembered the ways I'd tried to distance myself from Maisie when I'd been keeping secrets from her.

"I'm sorry," I said. "I was an idiot."

I didn't want to let on that I'd ever doubted her. The dirty tricks, the shady expulsions, the power plays—those things were the opposite of everything Maisie was about.

"That's not why I'm leaving. You know that, don't you, Claudia?"

I nodded, but it was still nice to be reassured.

"Do you think less of me now, Maisie?" I asked. She gave me a puzzled look, so I clarified. "I mean, do you think I'm one of them now?"

Maisie took a pull on her bottle of sparkling water, then twisted the lid back on the glass bottle and set it in the Prius's cup holder.

"You don't have control over any of this," she said, gesturing toward the parking garage, the night sky, the beach, all of it. "The only thing you can control is the way you act. Whatever kind of person you are or aren't is up to you, Claudia."

And that brought me right back to the place our conversation had started.

"I don't know if I can do it without you, Maisie."

"You know I'll be here if you need me."

"It's not the same."

"I know that, but it's not nothing either."

XVII

ELEGANT SOLUTIONS

As President Oberlin St. James called to order the first session of the 116th Imperial Day Senate, ingloriously gathered in Mr. Samson's chemistry classroom, I couldn't shake the feeling that my fellow senators were surprised to see me there. Like they didn't think I'd go through with it, like my victory was such an obvious sham that I should have done the decent thing and resigned like Maisie had.

"Our first order of business is to welcome our new senators, Hector Estrella and Claudia McCarthy." Oberlin St. James nodded in our direction as we lifted our hands to wave to our new colleagues.

"Okay, then. Moving on to the next thing: special elections to fill the freshman seats."

Between Ty and Oberlin St. James, Imperial Day had not elected especially personable leadership. Ty wouldn't talk to you at all, whereas Oberlin St. James wouldn't talk to you until he'd decided that you weren't an idiot, and Oberlin St. James thought almost everyone was an idiot.

"Claudia and Hector, we expect you to attend the orientation for all freshmen wishing to run for Senate, but you are not to speak to any of the candidates or answer their questions or breathe a word of advice to them. Please leave that to those of us who know what we're doing."

Oberlin St. James gave a cloying smile to his vice president, Jasmine Park, and to the other upperclassman senators, but there were no smiles for Hector and me. We were still on probation.

I noticed that Hector was writing down everything Oberlin St. James said as he laid out the itinerary for the freshman election orientation.

Shit, I thought, *I should be taking this more seriously*, and I reached into my bag for a notebook. When I leaned over, though, my eyes fell on Hector's paper and I saw that he'd written in blocky, draftsman letters along the margin:

THANK YOU TO OBERLIN ST. JAMES FOR THAT WARM WELCOME

and beneath that:

WHAT SHOULD WE TELL THE FRESHMEN IF THEY ASK US WHAT IT'S LIKE TO BE A SENATOR?

He hadn't nudged me or made a thing of it. He'd just been sitting there waiting for me to notice.

I opened my notebook and pretended to write down the date and time of the assembly, but what I really wrote was:

LET'S TELL THEM IT'S A CULT.

"Moving on to Homecoming," Oberlin St. James said, and without meaning to, I let out a small sigh. It was a reflex, a momentary forgetfulness on my part. After all, it was only a year ago that I'd been the kind of person who studiously avoided all Homecoming-related activities, and now I had been put in charge of them. But momentary lapse or not, Oberlin St. James was not amused.

"Is this beneath you, Claudia?"

I'd assumed it was a rhetorical question, but after an excruciating silence, it became clear that Oberlin St. James was waiting for a response.

"No," I said at last.

"Because this is what we do. We hear student grievances. We intercede on their behalf. And we plan and we organize and we raise money for the events that make life here at Imperial Day something other than a desolate wasteland of interminable sameness, punctuated by nothing but tests and lunch. Do you understand, Claudia?"

"Yes," I said, more quickly this time.

But what I was thinking as Oberlin St. James glared at me, probably wondering if I was another Chris Gibbons, and as Jasmine Park rolled her eyes at the junior class senators, Morgan Peterson and Ernest Collingswood, was, *Can't we do better than that? Can't we do more?*

Having put me in my place, Oberlin St. James carried on with the Homecoming plans.

"The feedback we got last year indicated that people preferred to have the dance off-site rather than in the gym. Jasmine and I have been going over possible venues, and so far the frontrunners are the Queen Mary, the Getty, and the Skirball. I'm going to turn things over to Jasmine to discuss what we need to do for any of this to come close to happening. It won't be easy, but I think Jasmine has figured out a few elegant solutions to our fundraising situation."

My eyes darted over to Hector's paper, and I saw that he'd written:

OH MY GOD HE LOVES HER.

Happily, I hadn't alienated all of my Senate colleagues. I snuffled out a laugh in the back of my hand and jotted back:

ELEGANT FUNDRAISING SKILLS = VERY HOT

Jasmine flipped her highlighted hair over one shoulder and ran us through the price for each venue, what people were willing to pay for tickets, and how we'd make up the difference. She explained the kinds of fundraising that Imperial Day students were resistant to and those they could often be tricked into doing. She showed us her spreadsheets. I'd joked about it, but I had to admit that the whole thing was, in fact, sort of hot.

For Homecoming, the most lucrative fundraiser was the teacher car wash. Senate members sweet-talked ten teachers into volunteering, and then people would pay obscene amounts of money to have Mr. Woolf or Mrs. DiVincenzo or whoever scrub their cars.

It struck me as a little tone-deaf and possibly cruel in the extreme when you considered the financial situation of most Imperial Day teachers compared with that of the typical student. Asking them to take a rag to the wheel well of Lexus after student-owned Lexus seemed a little too close to saying outright the thing that was silently implied in our dealings: You serve at *our pleasure*.

Jasmine Park licked her lips and reported that the Senate had $5000 in the account set aside for Homecoming expenses, and I saw Oberlin St. James's prodigious eyebrows knit together.

"Are you sure that's all we have?" he asked. "I could have sworn there was $10,000 in that account."

Jasmine looked down at her papers, then shook her head. "According to the bank statement, it's $5000."

"Huh, remind me to look into that," said Oberlin St. James in a distracted way that made me fairly sure he was never going to look into it. "Anyhow, Claudia and Hector, for your first assignment as senators, I put it to you to find ten teachers for the car wash. And don't come back without Yee."

I felt immediately defensive of my brilliant history teacher. "Why do you want Ms. Yee?"

"She gives more Cs than anyone at Imperial Day. Our constituents will find it most gratifying to see her washing our cars."

I resisted the urge to roll my eyes. A C at Imperial Day was like an F anywhere else.

"At our next meeting, we'll open up for public comment from the student body. Brace yourselves. The first one is always long. Until then, Claudia and Hector will organize the car wash. Jasmine will book the Homecoming venue. Get the Queen Mary if you can, Jasmine, and I want everyone to come up with at least three ideas for Homecoming week activities. See you Thursday."

I looked at the clock. With the nine-hour time difference, I'd missed my chance to Skype with Maisie. I sent her a quick text apologizing and asking if she was free the next night instead.

Everyone else left the second Oberlin St. James dismissed us, but Hector waited for me to finish my text before getting up to go.

"Are there ten teachers we can persuade to do the car wash?"

He kept his tone light, but I could tell the ethical implications had occurred to him as well, and he was troubled, torn between offending our teachers by asking or invoking the wrath of Oberlin St. James by failing.

"Oh, there are ten teachers. That's not the problem."

"Then what is?"

Hector had transferred in last year. He only had four and a half months of Imperial Day under his belt. I had a full year, plus an older sister, which translated to fairly reliable intel on who would be flattered to be asked, who would agree under duress, and who should not be approached under any circumstances. But it wasn't that easy.

"They're all going to want something," I said.

We were walking toward the journalism classroom where my old newspaper advisor, Mr. Prettinger, sat at his desk eating a Cobb salad and reading the sports section of the *Los Angeles Times*.

"Hi, Mr. Prettinger," I said, sticking my head through the door.

"Claudia," he said, raising his hand in greeting and folding up the paper, "you are just the person I wanted to see. There's a Board of Commissioners meeting tonight and nobody can cover it. Can you go?"

"What's on the agenda?"

"Donations. New hires." He mimed a yawn. "But you know how it is. Gotta keep an eye on the bastards."

"Sure, I'll do it," I said, hoping I didn't sound too eager. Maybe Jasmine Park could have found an elegant way to maneuver the conversation toward my next point, but Mr. Prettinger was a journalism teacher. I figured a man who worked on deadlines would appreciate bluntness. "Mr. Prettinger, are you familiar with the Senate car wash fundraiser for Homecoming?"

"I am," he said cagily.

"Is there any chance I might prevail upon you to volunteer two hours of your time washing the cars of ungrateful children for a good cause?"

"Since when is Homecoming a good cause?" he asked, though before I could answer, he scrunched up his face in disbelief and said, "Wait, you're a senator now?"

"I thought you knew," I said, then sensing his disapproving tone, I added, "It's not like I'm selling heroin or something."

"It's just that once a person crosses the line from journalism to politics, they rarely cross back," he said, regarding his Cobb salad as though it had disappointed him, instead of me.

"You haven't totally lost me, Mr. Prettinger. I could be persuaded to cover the next three school board meetings for the *Weekly Praetor*."

"If I wash cars," Mr. Prettinger said.

"If you wash cars."

Mr. Prettinger weighed the unpleasantness of this prospect with trying to wrangle unwilling student journalists into dull meetings for the next three months, then nodded when he'd made up his mind.

"You might actually make a very good politician, Claudia," he said, then looked over my shoulder at Hector, who was pretending to read Mr. Prettinger's bulletin board on AP Style, a faraway look in his eyes. "Who's your friend? I don't suppose you're a writer, are you?"

The moment he found himself on Mr. Prettinger's radar, I saw Hector snap to attention and turn into himself. Or rather, turn into the version of himself that did so well at Imperial Day. The warm eyes and easy smile, the confidence tempered by respectful deference, whether he was talking to a teacher or a student.

"Hector Estrella," he said, stepping forward to shake Mr. Prettinger's hand. "Nice to meet you, though I'm afraid I'm not much of a writer."

Mr. Prettinger persisted. "Photography?"

"A little."

"Cover three board meetings, your friend shoots the field hockey match on Friday, and you've got yourself a deal, Claudia."

I turned to Hector before accepting his offer, wanting to make sure that I hadn't roped him into anything too onerous—but then I thought about all those smooth, strong field hockey player legs, and judging by the smile on Hector's face, he was thinking about the same thing.

"Done," he said.

Mr. Prettinger saluted me before turning back to his dinner and baseball scores and said, "Pleasure doing business with you, McCarthy."

"Likewise, sir."

As Hector and I walked down the hall, I said, "Now we just have to do that nine more times."

"Next time we split up," Hector said. "No more of this two favors for the price of one nonsense."

I had four and a half months of Imperial Day experience on Hector, and an older sister, but he was catching on fast.

XVIII

A PILE OF BRICKS ON YOUR CHEST

Dear Maisie,

Don't get me wrong, I'm not going to say that being on the Honor Council was an easy job or anything, but when people came to you, all you had to do was decide their fates.

I have to listen to their problems.

Oh, Maisie, their problems . . . There are the people who complain that the vegetarian hotdog is not also gluten free (Hint: because the main ingredient is gluten!), and the people who are upset that our parking lot is not covered, and what are we going to do if their precious Range Rover is exposed to the elements? (Oh my god, it is southern California, there are no elements.)

And if I want to keep my job and avoid being a one-term wonder like Chris Gibbons, I have to act like I care what these people have to say, and like I might be inclined to do something about it.

You might ask, Why is this a job you actually want to keep? To which I would reply, Because then there are the other kinds of problems.

There are the people on scholarship who can't pay for their stupid required gym uniforms, which cost $200 including shoes, because whoever picked them out sure as shit wasn't thinking about the scholarship *kids when they did it. And there is the person who asked why we have two dedicated college and career counselors, yet no one who can really help you if, say, you have a panic attack in the middle of Calculus that makes you feel like there's a pile of bricks on your chest. There is the person who wants to know why we don't have an anti-bullying policy like every other school.*

The Honor Council can't protect people from things like that. And as long as the Senate is happy to be a glorified party-planning committee, neither can we.

Once upon a time, some smart person created the fiction that the Honor Council was where the wisest and the most promising and the best went, and that the work of the Senate was carried out by those of us who fell just a little bit short. I'm sure you never thought of it that way, but that's what everyone else thinks.

But I think that a different kind of smart person would figure out a way to make people see that real power should live in the open, not in secret, that their lives should be ruled by hope that things could be better, not fear that they could lose everything if they made the wrong move.

Maisie, I have so much work to do.

But I know what I'm doing.

I really really miss you, Maisie.

XX,

Claudia

Of the last three things I told Maisie, two of them happened to be true.

XIX

WHAT WE'D SECRETLY WANTED ALL ALONG

I'd never been so lonely in my life. As it turned out, you could fill up your days with all the theater practice and newspaper meetings and Senate hearings you wanted to and it didn't make you any less lonely. I thought all the time about the conversation I'd had with Maisie before she left for Rome.

Am I one of them now?

That depends on you.

Of course, sitting at the old Honor Council lunch table without Maisie was out of the question now, so I spent lunch in the library, catching up on the homework I was increasingly neglecting, writing the newspaper stories I owed Mr. Prettinger, and going through the minutes of old Senate meetings. If I learned from the mistakes of the past, I reasoned, I might avoid them. Maybe I could actually make things better around here.

It was a pair of freshman girls named Lucy Lin and Veronica Ollenbeck who emerged victorious from the Senate elections. They did everything together, had known each other since the first grade, and Oberlin St. James could scarcely hide his contempt for them. They came from a world where being in student government meant that you got your picture in the yearbook and nothing more was expected of you. They had no idea they'd signed themselves up to be yelled at by their class-mates each Tuesday during public hearing, then bossed around by the unappreciative Oberlin St. James and Jasmine Park each Thursday during our closed sessions. Hector and I took pity on them and even tried to include them in our surreptitious note-passing, but they were too terrified to respond.

Halfway through September, Hector and I had collected four teachers for the car wash, though I had not yet worked up the guts to approach Ms. Yee. Oberlin St. James gave us a stern look during our Thursday meeting while exacting a promise that it would be done by the next meeting, but I was too frus-trated to care. What I wanted to be doing was drawing up some impactful policy and petitioning the Board of Commission-ers to make changes and create a fund for people who couldn't afford to buy a stupid required gym uniform, but instead, Ober-lin St. James and Jasmine Park had me bothering overworked educators and pricing balloon arches for a pep rally.

When we came to her part of the agenda, Jasmine Park made a pouting face and said, "I'm just going to come right out and say it: The Queen Mary is already booked for the night we want and they can't squeeze us in. Same with the Skirball and the Getty."

A collective gasp and groan went up in the room, and Oberlin St. James actually said, "How can this be?" like he was a 19th-century farmer who'd just lost his crop to a swarm of locusts.

Jasmine continued, "How would you guys feel if we had the dance here instead? The Queen Mary is so far away any-how. What if we did it here in the gym, but really made it nice?

152

More underclassmen would be able to attend. Would everyone be okay with that?"

I am sure it never once crossed Jasmine's mind that we would not be okay with it. She had no backup plan, unless her backup plan was to subtly convince us that having Homecoming in the gym was what we'd secretly wanted all along. However, not even the freshmen, Lucy Lin and Veronica Ollenbeck, seemed to appreciate the decision that Jasmine had allegedly made on their behalf. The fact was, Imperial Day students expected to be spoiled and fussed over to a certain extent, and no amount of foil fringe and paper lanterns could make the idea of spending Saturday night dancing in our gym seem glamorous.

Oberlin St. James sighed and said, "This isn't what we'd hoped to hear, obviously, but let's not decide anything about the venue today. I propose we hold a special meeting next Monday and come to a final decision then."

We all agreed to this and moved on to the next order of business. This was the point at which I should have left well enough alone, but I couldn't help thinking that just because Jasmine Park couldn't get a reservation at the Queen Mary, that didn't mean that no one could. I wanted to prove that I deserved to be part of the Senate, that even though I was a mistake and a fluke and a person who should not have been elected, I was not without my uses.

I was only trying to be helpful.

XX

WOODWARD & BERNSTEIN

Other people leveraged their famous families all the time. Livia's dad had gotten her that internship at Google when she was a freshman, and Astrid Murray was always surrounded by people angling for a visit to a set, or a studio internship, or an invitation to one of the star-studded parties her parents threw at their house during awards season. My parents may not have been the richest or the most famous at Imperial Day, but still, InVigor was a name that got people's attention.

The problem was that in order to exploit it, I had to call the Queen Mary, and my stuttering on the phone is a miserable experience for everyone. Even if the person on the other end of the line had the patience to understand me, nobody would believe I was legitimately affiliated with a major corporation. That was why I brought Hector in on the plan. He'd make the call for me, on behalf of Tessa McCarthy, CEO of InVigor, to inquire about availability for a little something she'd like to arrange for the students at her daughter's school.

At first, Hector hated the idea.

"It's shady, Claudia. It might even be an Honor Code violation."

"What if I told my mom what we were doing? Would that make you feel better?"

"You're going to say, 'Mom, is it okay if we impersonate your assistant in order to book the Queen Mary for Homecoming?'"

"That is exactly what I'm going to say."

What my relationship with my parents lacks in warmth, it does at least make up for in honesty.

Hector considered this. I could tell what he wanted to say because I have known third graders who possessed better poker faces. He wanted me to let it go. He wanted us to keep our mouths shut and have Homecoming in the gym, but instead he said, "Okay, I'll do it, but only if you talk to your mom and she says it's okay."

He sounded crabby about it, and that was how I realized that Hector Estrella was my friend. The rest of them could have polite, respectful, warm, smiling Hector, but crabby Hector was all mine.

"Then I'll do it right now," I said, pulling out my phone and sending a text. A few seconds later, my phone buzzed. "She says it's fine."

Hector sighed. "Let's get this over with."

I entered the number for the Queen Mary corporate reservations line and put the phone on speaker.

"What should I say?" Hector asked while I was ringing, and I realized that maybe we'd underprepared.

I only had time to jot down my mother's name and the name of her company before a woman's voice came on the line and asked how she could assist us.

"This is Hector Estrella," he said, cringing as his real name slipped out. I poked him in the arm and motioned for him to keep talking.

Hector recovered and gave the representative his false credentials.

"What date were you looking for?" the woman asked, adding, "And you said you were calling from InVigor?"

I could almost hear her straighten up in her chair when Hector said yes.

"On behalf of Tessa McCarthy," he repeated. "We were hoping for October 15. She's trying to organize something for her daughter's school."

"Very good. Let me just check the calendar," the woman said. I could hear her fingers clicking on the keyboard. "And what school is this for?"

"The Imperial Day Academy."

There was some more clicking, then a long pause, and then the woman said, "Huh. There's already a reservation for the Imperial Day Academy here. For the 16th of October, actually, not the 15th."

"That's odd. What name is it under?" Hector asked, his voice blandly cheerful so that it didn't even sound like he was asking for information that was none of his business and that the woman on the reservations line should not have been giving out to him.

"Oberlin St. James is what it says here," the woman said.

Hector didn't miss a beat.

"That makes sense. Oberlin is one of Tessa's daughter's friends. He must have taken care of it already."

He was proving himself to be a far more accomplished liar than I'd expected. While he carried on his pleasant back-and-forth with the reservation lady, he and I locked eyes, the implications of this phone call dawning on us.

"And it's for three hundred?" Hector asked.

That was how many students were expected at Homecoming. There was more keyboard clicking.

"No, it's only for forty." I let out a gasp, and the woman asked, "Is something wrong?"

Hector maintained his composure. "Everything's fine. Maybe there's been a change of plans. I will have Tessa's daughter check with Oberlin and we'll get back to you if there are any changes."

"Very good," the woman said. "And what was your name again?"

Hector hung up without answering her. We sat there, both of us staring at the phone on the table between us, absolutely still and silent.

"Come on," I said.

I got up from the table and headed down the hall to the classroom where the Senate met. Hector followed behind me. We didn't speak the whole way there even though the halls were deserted. This was too big to say out loud anywhere public. Once we were inside, I locked the classroom door behind us, turned out the lights, and sat down at the classroom computer.

Hector and I didn't talk about what we were doing. We didn't have to. I logged in with the Senate password and opened up the folder labeled BUDGET. One by one, we read every document that had been opened in the past week, then looked through the other files, even the ones with names that made them sound unrelated. People at Imperial Day didn't succeed at deception, fraud, and embezzlement by going around naming files things like "Secret Homecoming Dance" or "My Plan to Defraud the Imperial Day Academy and Throw a Giant Party for My Friends."

Because that was what this was, right?

I couldn't think of any other possible explanation. The officers of the Senate had lied and told us that we couldn't have Homecoming at the Queen Mary because it was already booked when, in fact, they'd already booked it for themselves. Only a fraction of the student body would be able to attend because, presumably, only a fraction of the student body would even know about it. The rest would go to Homecoming in the gym like suckers.

"Maybe it's not what it looks like," Hector said. So sweet of him to go looking for the best in people.

"Maybe," I said, but I had a tight feeling in my throat. My hands shook as I moved the mouse and opened file after file. As the light from the screen bathed our faces in an icy blue glow, I wondered if *Washington Post* journalists Bob Woodward and Carl Bernstein had felt this way back in 1972. One minute, they're investigating a little break-in at Democratic Party headquarters, the next they're finding out that President Nixon's reelection committee cut the burglars a check for $25,000 the week before.

"Check the downloads," Hector said. I clicked on the folder, sorted the files by date, and opened the most recent one, a file named REFNO6379. It had been downloaded right before the last Senate meeting.

When I saw what it was, I covered my mouth with my hand.

"Oh my god," I said.

"Print it," Hector said. "Print five of them."

Hector and I shut down the computer, shut the classroom door behind us, and headed for the nearest exit. It took every ounce of self-control I had not to break into a limping run. We couldn't stay here. We needed to be somewhere we could talk freely, and I wanted to be there as soon as possible.

We left campus and crossed the street to the corner bus stop, which no one from Imperial Day ever used. As meeting places went, we could hardly have found anything safer this close. This being west LA, the likelihood that a bus would materialize was next to nothing.

The secret vibrated between us as we sat on the bus stop bench. In our bags, we each carried copies of a receipt for a deposit for a party at the Queen Mary paid out of the Imperial Day Academy Senate bank account. I doubted it was a coincidence that it was for $5000, the exact amount of the discrepancy between what OSJ thought the Senate had to spend on the Homecoming dance and how much Jasmine Park claimed was actually in the bank.

"How do you want to play this?" I asked.

"We should report it to Dr. Graves," Hector said, looking at me like I was insane, like the appropriate course of action was self-evident, and I remembered that Hector wasn't the type of person who considered the angles. Hector would always do the simple, right thing.

"Nobody reports anything to Dr. Graves."

"Then we'll report it to the Honor Council."

I hesitated here as well.

"Hector, no one would do something like this, something that involved this many people, unless they thought they could get away with it. Inviting a few Honor Council representatives to a party seems like a decent way to give the whole thing a veneer of legitimacy. They wouldn't even have to know the party had been paid for with stolen money."

You would have thought I'd told Hector that JFK was assassinated by CIA goons hiding out on the grassy knoll.

"Which is why we would *tell* them, Claudia," he explained patiently.

Hector's logic made sense, until you thought about the people who would be involved.

"Hector, think about it. Who is going to be invited to this party? Forty of the most popular, high-achieving, ambitious students at Imperial Day. The faces of the franchise. Do you think they're going to go quietly if they get in trouble?"

I paused to allow him a second to imagine Oberlin St. James, Jasmine Park, and thirty-eight of their closest Ivy League–bound friends facing expulsion for theft and assorted treachery.

"Do you think Imperial Day is really going to let that happen? The school's reputation would be ruined. No, they're going to find a convenient way to pin this on a couple of convenient people. You haven't been here as long as I have, Hector, but trust me when I say that the two of us look awfully convenient."

"But we're the ones who *found out* about it! Why would we turn *ourselves* in?" Hector said, eyeing me like he suddenly wasn't so sure I was on his side.

"Hector, we don't even know who's involved. Until we know that much, trust me, we shouldn't say anything."

Hector shook his head, no doubt asking himself what collection of poor choices had lured him into this nest of snakes that was the Imperial Day Academy. I didn't want to see him hurt by any of this. After all, he hadn't asked for it.

He'd been minding his own business, trying to be a good senator, when I talked him into impersonating my mother's assistant on the phone and we uncovered this whole mess. If there was a way I could protect him from whatever came next, I resolved to do it.

"We could pretend we never found it," I suggested. I had to try.

"No, we can't," Hector said, thumbing the invoices we'd printed. "You know that."

"Can we take the weekend before we decide who to talk to?" I asked.

"Can we investigate?"

"We should," I said, though I didn't trust anyone but myself to do the real digging. Not because Hector wasn't trustworthy—in fact, the opposite. I wanted to keep him as far away from the people who were likely to be involved as possible. They'd sniff out his naïveté in a second and exploit it. "Can you try to find out who paid the deposit on the Queen Mary?"

"It was in Oberlin St. James's name."

"That doesn't mean anything," I said. Oberlin St. James was the sort of person who attended Homecoming because it was his job, not because he enjoyed it. The idea of him master-minding an extra, unnecessary, illegal party struck me as odd.

Hector got up from the bus stop bench and tucked the invoices into the side pocket of his shoulder bag.

"What about you?" he asked.

"I'm going to very subtly, very carefully see if I can find out who knows about this."

"How are you going to do that?" Hector asked.

"I'll think of something."

I could tell that he didn't quite trust me, that he thought it was more likely I'd spend the weekend acting like the whole thing had never happened.

And he was right not to trust me. I had no intention of being subtle or careful, and when we said goodbye that day, I already knew what I was going to do.

On Saturday, I went to see Livia.

"You went to Livia? After everything you've told me, after what happened at the Griffith School and what happened with your sister, not to mention how much you seem to dislike her, why would Livia be the person you decided to trust with this?"

"Trust had nothing to do with it."

"Then what was it?"

"I was aware of my own shortcomings as a politician. There were so many things to think about: who to hold responsible, who to protect, knowing that they would owe you a favor at some point, how to keep the school's reputation—and by extension, our own—intact. Hector wouldn't think to exploit a situation like that. He wouldn't think to play it in a way where it might do him some good."

"Was going to Livia a way to ensure that she might owe you a favor at some point?"

"It wasn't like that exactly. I wanted to watch her in action. I wanted to see what she would do."

"You mean you wanted to learn from her?"

"She was the only person I could think of who would really understand the nuances of the situation."

XXI

BEFORE THEY CAN'T TAKE IT BACK

Under the reign of Sulla and the purges of the Roman ruling class that followed, one senator begged the bloodthirsty dictator, "We are not asking you to pardon those you have decided to kill; all we ask is that you free from suspense those you have decided not to kill."

Standing in Livia's hallway that Saturday afternoon, waiting in silence as she sized me up, trying to decide whether I was worth squashing or keeping around, I felt like that senator.

"Who told you to call the Queen Mary?" Livia snapped.

"No one," I said, truthfully. In fact, I'd told her the truth about everything. The only part of the story I left out was Hector. It was safer for him, I reasoned, if Livia didn't know he'd had anything to do with it.

I continued. "But I found out about it and I wasn't even looking."

"You know this probably involves half the Senate," Livia said.

And half the Honor Council. And the rest of your friends, too, I thought.

Livia examined her reflection in the enormous oval mirror in the hallway. She picked a morsel out from between her front teeth, then abruptly turned and walked down the hallway, as if she'd forgotten I was standing there. She was a fast walker. By the time I worked up the nerve to follow her into the house, lurching across the slick ceramic floors, dragging my bad leg behind me, she was already standing at the kitchen counter, a highball glass full of ice in her hand.

"Even if it turns out to be true, how's it going to look if I bring charges against them?" Livia asked, picking up our conversation as if she hadn't just walked away from it. She opened the refrigerator, poured herself a glass of water from a pitcher, and took a sip.

She didn't wait for me to answer her question. She also didn't offer me a glass of water.

"It's going to look like a power grab. A vendetta. It will undermine trust in both institutions."

She set the glass down on the countertop, then picked it up again, then put it down, and repeated this until she'd left a row of interlocking condensation circles on the granite.

"This is huge. They can't just get away with it," she said at last. She was pretending to think it over, to change her mind, even though I felt sure she'd known what she wanted to do from the beginning. "Maybe the important thing isn't to catch everyone in the act and punish them. Maybe it's to give them the opportunity to do the right thing before it's too late. Before they can't take it back."

I was beginning to see what she was driving at. Blackmailing the guilty parties was an option I hadn't even considered.

"It's still a month until Homecoming," I said.

"Exactly," Livia said. "Nothing's been done yet that can't be undone."

They must have been reading *Macbeth* in her Honors English class.

"So, what are you going to do?" I asked.

"None of your business," Livia snapped before realizing that maybe it was to her advantage to be just a little bit nicer to me given the information I had. Her voice softened. "What I mean is, it's confidential. Like everything the Honor Council does. But, Claudia, I want you to know that you did the right thing coming to me."

I had no idea how Livia was going to use this information, but it was clear she had options. She could wield it like a machete and clean house at Imperial Day. She could bury it and protect Jasmine Park and Oberlin St. James and whoever else was involved. Or she could use it to blackmail them into doing whatever she wanted as long as they were all at Imperial Day.

One thing was certain, though: it was out of my hands. All I had to do was sit back, watch to see what happened next, and, as you put it, *learn*.

XXII

LOOKING FOR FIFTEEN PEOPLE
TO MAKE OUT WITH

I excused myself, leaving Livia to her Saturday night scheming, and returned home, where I planned to spend the night watching a documentary about the construction of the Duomo in Florence (one of the great architectural marvels of the Renaissance—and the guy who figured out how to build it was a goldsmith who'd never even designed a building before, if you can believe that). I had really been looking forward to it, so I was actually a little disappointed when Hector texted, asking me to meet him downtown.

Downtown?!? I texted back. *Why on earth would I do that?*

I was a Westside Angeleno and did not venture east of La Cienega if I could help it.

After a minute, Hector texted back:

You'll like it. It's very historical.

Curiosity won out. I changed clothes and got an Uber, thinking only a little bit wistfully about my comfy bed and sweatpants and television.

The place Hector wanted to meet was called The Last Bookstore, and it was in a building that looked like it must have been a haberdashery or a bank a hundred years ago. Hardly anything in LA looks like it's been there for a hundred years, so that alone was worth noting.

Most used bookstores look like they defeated their owners at some point. Maybe once upon a time, the collection was carefully curated, but eventually fatigue set in and the place was overrun, one dog-eared copy of *Cold Sassy Tree* at a time. If a used bookstore could feel new, this one did. Every title seemed like it was there on purpose, like a person had touched it with their hand and thought, Yes, *this*, as they placed it on the shelf.

I found Hector standing in the local history section, leafing through a book of maps.

"Did you know people used to live where Dodger Stadium is now?" he asked, showing me the map of Chavez Ravine he'd been looking at.

"No," I said.

"The city had it declared a slum and evicted all the families who lived there. They got away with it because they claimed they were going to build public housing on the land, but as soon as the last Mexican was out, they turned around and sold it to the Dodgers."

I hadn't heard that before, but I didn't doubt it. I knew enough about history to know that anytime it seems like some noble, virtuous, powerful person should have stood up and said, *This is wrong! It must be stopped!* they almost never did.

What I said to Hector, though, was, "I didn't know you were into history."

The brown jacket he was wearing looked so soft, I had to stop myself from reaching out to touch it as Hector put the book back on the shelf.

"I just think it's important," he said. "So, did you think any more about what we should do?"

I was about to say that some ice cream sounded nice, when I realized what he was talking about.

"About the Queen Mary thing?" I asked. Hector gave me a patient look that said, *Yes. Obviously.*

I'd unburdened myself to Livia, but Hector hadn't. I'd put the situation out of my mind almost entirely, but Hector was the kind of person who couldn't even wait until Monday morning to do the right thing.

"I think it's taken care of," I said.

Hector's eyes widened. He took me by the sleeve and led me toward the leather couch in the center of the store. A scraggly-bearded hipster in red jeans sat at one end of it reading a filmmaking book that I was sure he'd never buy. Hector sat down at the other end, pulling me with him.

"What did you *do*, Claudia?" There was an edge to his voice I'd never heard before, and his nostrils flared when he spoke.

"I took care of it," I said, suddenly defensive. "I did what needed to be done."

Weird Beard had stopped dog-earing the pages of his filmmaking book and was now listening avidly to everything we said. I could see his sordid little imagination trying to work out what we were talking about, what a guy who looked like Hector was doing with a girl who looked like me. I decided to help him out.

"G-g-get fucked," I said, and even though he lifted his hand to his mouth to cover a giggle, at least he took his stupid book and went somewhere else.

"Look," I said, turning back to Hector. I felt calmer after

working out some of my aggression on Weird Beard. Now I just had to get Hector to calm down, too. "I went to someone on the Honor Council."

I saw his shoulders relax as I told him. After all, that was one of the things he'd suggested we do. He could hardly get mad at me for that. The confused look hadn't left his face, though.

"I thought you said we couldn't go to them."

"I did it in a sort of . . . unofficial capacity."

"What did this unofficial Honor Council person have to say? Unofficially."

"That it was still a month until Homecoming. That there was still time for whoever was responsible to do the right thing," I said, remembering the look on Livia's face as she'd said it. Right this minute, on the other side of town, she was probably trying to figure out what to do with the information, who to tell, how to play it.

"So the Honor Council is going to make sure they cancel the party?"

"I think so?"

Hector's nostrils flared again. "You mean this person didn't actually *tell* you what they're going to do?"

"It's the Honor Council," I said. "It's confidential."

"And did this person happen to mention how they knew who to talk to when we don't even know?"

I swallowed and looked away, knowing that what I said next was going to send Hector flying into a whole different kind of rage.

"I did sort of get the feeling that this person might have already known about it," I said.

Hector looked as though he wanted to knock over a bookshelf. He balled his fists at his sides and glared at me.

"So you gave them a warning, and now they can do whatever they want. What were you thinking, Claudia?"

Now I felt *my* hackles go up. It wasn't like I was the one who'd stolen the money. It wasn't like I'd done anything wrong.

"What did you *think* was going to happen, Hector? That we were going to make them pay? That they'd all be expelled and a glorious new reign would come to power, and nothing like this would ever happen again?"

I could feel my cheeks color as I stumbled over my words. It was always harder to keep from stuttering when my emotions were stirred up.

"I saved our asses, Hector. I kept the most powerful people in school from getting to do whatever they wanted, and I think that's pretty good. At least the best I think we can hope for, so give me a little credit."

After I'd finished making my speech, Hector was quiet. I couldn't tell if he believed me or not.

"Was it Ty?" he said at last. "Was that who you went to?"

"No," I said, probably a little too quickly.

I thought about telling him everything about my visit with Livia, but before I could, I got the distinct feeling that Hector and I were being watched. I turned my head and saw Cal Hurt standing by the True Crime shelves, staring at us as he paged through a copy of *Helter Skelter: The True Story of the Manson Murders*. By his side was Kian Sarkosian, one of the new Honor Council representatives, a gawky puppy of a freshman. He wore a daily uniform of plain white button-down shirts and dark, stiff jeans, though I couldn't tell if he was trying to look like a nerd from the 1950s, or if he just lacked imagination. The Honor Council was supposed to attract the best, the most charismatic, the most ambitious. If Kian Sarkosian was the most suitable representative they could elect, it did not bode well for the current freshman class at Imperial Day, especially if Cal had already managed to recruit him as a disciple.

"Shit," I muttered under my breath, and then probably just to piss me off, Hector got up from the couch and strolled over to him.

"Hey, Cal," Hector said, his voice so cheerful you would have thought they were actually happy to see each other.

Cal nodded, and then the two of them shook hands, then Hector and Kian shook hands. This is a dude thing at Imperial Day. Instead of fist bumps or one-armed bro hugs, when they see each other outside of school, the men of Imperial Day always shake hands like they are diplomats or Southern gentlemen. The legacy of Paul Chudnuff, Imperial Day founder, homophobic tit, strikes again.

As I reluctantly limped over to join the group, Cal nodded in my direction and said, "C-C-C-Claudia." He reeked of weed and gin.

I wished that all the people who'd voted him onto the Honor Council after he'd rushed to my defense during the campaign assembly could see him now.

As he smiled at me—you know, to show it was just a joke— I could feel myself go somewhere else. I was still standing in the middle of the bookstore, a sneer on my lips, but that was just my outsides. My insides were curled up in a ball, my head tucked under one arm, waiting for the moment to be over.

"What are you two doing downtown?" Hector asked coolly. "Not exactly your neighborhood."

"Maddie Urrea's quinceañera after-party is somewhere around here. Are you guys going?" Before Hector could answer, though, Cal kept talking. "I mean, if you weren't invited, I don't think anyone's going to kick you out."

"Quinceañera *after-party*?" Now Hector had a sneer on his lips to match mine, but Cal was oblivious—or didn't care. He brushed his sun-streaked surfer hair off of his forehead and flipped through the pages of *Helter Skelter*.

"Yeah, you know how Maddie is. I think she's looking for fifteen people to make out with, and the later it gets, the less discriminating she might be."

I didn't know how Maddie was. I didn't even know her well enough to get invited to her party, but what I knew did not align with Cal's hopes and dreams for the night.

"At least you've got that going for you," Hector muttered.

"I hate it when there are no good pictures in these things," he said, slipping the book into the breast pocket of his coat. Kian's eyes got big and darted back and forth, looking for any sales clerks who might have seen. I wondered if Kian was beginning to have second thoughts about his Saturday night plans, and found myself hoping that Cal wouldn't do anything to get him arrested. He was a freshman. Maybe he didn't know any better yet.

"And now, it is my intention to get drunk as a lord," Cal said, "and high as a viscount."

"That expression seems about as plausible as a quinceañera after-party." Hector's voice dripped with contempt as he stared at the pocket where Cal had hidden the Manson family book.

The look on Cal's face reminded me of that night at the Venice Pier when Julia insinuated he couldn't actually use the skateboard he was carrying around. *Back off, Hector*, I thought. *Retreat.* That was the look Cal got on his face right before he made you sorry you'd pushed him at all.

"I mean, if your dad can hook me up with a few of his horny interns, I could be persuaded to change my plans," Cal said.

Hector's face went still and blank. He had no snappy comeback, not even the barest of responses for whatever it was that Cal had just shoveled his way.

Cal, of course, took advantage of the dead air to strike a cheesy bodybuilder's pose. At least that's what I thought it was at first. He flexed a bicep in front of his abs, bit his lower lip, and gritted his teeth, his face grotesque and straining with effort. Then he pulled out his phone and pretended to take a selfie.

That was when it clicked. The disgraced state senator. The sad, shirtless bathroom selfies that had been plastered on every clickbait news-aggregating website and every political talk show for a week last year. Apparently there had been other photos too obscene to show on television.

"I see the two of you don't have the same taste in women," Cal said, gesturing toward me.

"What's that supposed to mean?" Hector asked, still rattled.

"I mean, if Claudia is, like, your gateway drug to making out with dudes, I get it."

He doubled over giggling at this, loudly and for much too long. I wanted to run away. I wanted to find the two most obscure shelves in the store and hide between them for the rest of the night. But all I could do was stand there, my cheeks flushed, my eyes locked on the floor so I didn't have to look at Hector. My throat tightened as I willed myself not to cry.

Hector didn't move either, but he did take my hand. When Cal finally pulled himself upright and wiped the tears from his eyes and patted the book in his breast pocket, Hector gave my fingers a squeeze and let go.

Kian fiddled with the buttons on the sleeve of his white

button-down shirt, his eyes trained on the floor, like as long as he did that, he wasn't there and it wasn't happening.

"Anyhow, toodles," Cal said, waving over his shoulder as he breezed past the register and toward the door. Kian tried to meet our eyes, mumbled an apology, then shuffled after Cal.

"You know, I don't believe he's going to pay for that book," Hector said.

My chest felt hollow, my throat raw from holding back tears, but it was over. My insides uncurled. I lifted my head, and I made myself look at Hector like everything was okay and whatever had just happened, I was over it.

"You know, I believe you're right," I said as I watched Cal leave the store, jumping up to slap the top of the doorframe on his way out. He missed.

"Do you want a ride home?" Hector asked, his voice softer now.

"Yeah."

We were quiet as Hector pulled out of the parking garage and drove through the streets of downtown Los Angeles. Since he was doing me the courtesy of acting like the conversation with Cal had never happened, I thought I'd do the same.

Still, it hung in the air between us, the difference between talking about it and not talking about it, and the kind of friends Hector Estrella and I were going to be depended on what happened in the next ten minutes.

I didn't want to be the one to ask, and Hector didn't want to talk about it, but at the same time, we came out with it.

"What Cal said back there . . . ," he started, but I was already talking.

"You can talk to me," I said. "I mean, I never talk to anyone, so if you ever want to talk about it, you can talk to me."

I saw Hector's face relax and his shoulders go slack. Under the downtown streetlights, his skin glowed, soft and warm and peaceful.

"It's true," Hector said. "What Cal said. That's my dad. He sent a bunch of dick pics to some of the interns in his office and they got leaked and he got caught, and it was gross and embarrassing, and that's why I'm at Imperial Day."

He let out a mortified sigh after he'd finished talking, and gripped the steering wheel.

"I thought you were there because you were some kind of multibillionaire legacy genius," I said, and Hector burst out laughing.

"Sorry to disappoint."

"You kind of are, though," I said. "You must be. They hardly ever take transfers."

Hector's cheeks reddened. "I was at Harvard-Westlake last year when it happened, and things got mean in a hurry. I'd hear people whispering the things he texted to these girls when I walked past. It was embarrassing, but the part I couldn't deal with was that to so many people—not just students, but teachers, too—it was like I was disgusting by association. It changed the way they looked at me. My mom ended up meeting with Dr. Graves and getting him to agree to take me in. I go by her last name now, not my dad's."

I thought about what Maisie had said to me in the InVigor parking garage that summer.

"You don't have control over what other people do. The only thing you can control is the way you act. Whatever kind of person you are or aren't, it doesn't have anything to do with him, Hector."

"I know."

"And you are definitely not disgusting by association."

Hector released his death grip on the steering wheel.

"That means a lot, Claudia," he said. "Now, what about you? Is there anything you want to talk about?"

"What do you mean?"

"I mean, I could tell you were upset back there, that Cal hurt your feelings. Do you want to talk about it?"

"I don't need to talk about it," I said.

Cal was a jerk and a bad person, and I didn't care what he thought of me. On the other hand, when he turned all that contempt in my direction and focused it, all I could think was, *Am I really that hideous and pathetic?*

"You sure?"

I gave Hector a smile that I hoped had at least a little verisimilitude in it. "I'm over it. I'm good."

A few minutes later we were sitting in my driveway. Hector gave me a hug. We said good night. I went inside and went straight to bed without watching my Duomo documentary.

"Do you think talking to Hector would have helped?"

"How so?"

"After Hector opened up to you about his father, he said that your words meant a lot to him. I'm just wondering if you might have felt the same way."

"My situation was totally different. Those things that Cal said about me . . . talking about them with Hector would only have given them time and attention and psychic real estate they did not deserve."

"You're telling me about them now. Is it possible that they've been in there taking up psychic real estate all this time?"

"They're part of the historical record now. Part of the story. Just neutral information."

"Since when do you believe history is neutral information, Claudia?"

XXIII

A CRIMINAL, A COLLABORATOR, OR A RAT

TO: cmccarthy@imperialday.org
FROM: hc@imperialday.org
SUBJECT: Official Summons

You are summoned to appear before the Honor Council on Monday, October 1, at 7:30 a.m. At this time, you will be called upon to give witness testimony in an ongoing investigation.

If you are unable to appear, you must provide written documentation at least 24 hours in advance. Failure to do so may result in disciplinary action. Please note that extracurricular activities are not excused absences.

✳✳✳

The email had been sent exactly thirty hours before I was scheduled to appear, so technically, I'd had six hours to feign some wasting illness and produce a doctor's note. As it was, I hadn't even seen the message until the night before. I didn't even know the Honor Council had hearings before school started. The first thing I did was text Hector, but after a fitful night of sleep, a miserable shower, and an anxious commute, I still hadn't heard from him.

"What's the matter with you this morning?" my father asked as I twitched in the passenger seat.

I could have told him nothing was wrong, but I've never seen the point in spinning elaborate lies to tell my parents when a truthful answer would end the conversation more quickly.

"I have to testify before the Honor Council this morning," I said.

"What'd you do?"

"I found out that some people embezzled $5000 and were going to use it to throw themselves a party."

"Did you do anything wrong?"

"No."

As the Chief Operating Officer at InVigor, my father organized his day into various piles of tasks and interactions that varied in priority. I saw him consider his reply, as well as the pile upon which this particular story belonged. If I had to guess, I would have said, "Noncritical, but Requires Follow-Up."

"Then you have nothing to worry about," he said. "Don't let them intimidate you."

Though I remained largely mysterious to him, he had endured a science-nerd adolescence and had some sympathy for my position.

"Okay."

"Walk into that room with your head up and tell yourself, 'They can't touch me.'"

If only it were that simple, I thought as I got out of the car and

180

walked through the doors of Imperial Day to find out what the Honor Council was going to do to me.

I wouldn't have put a blindsiding past Livia, but still, it seemed low to do something like this to me without warning when I'd had the decency to rat to her in the first place.

Whether Livia was behind it or not, the suddenness of the hearing had to be on purpose. I wouldn't have time to think. I wouldn't have time to weasel out of it, and most importantly, I wouldn't have much time to get a story straight with Hector. Lying to the Honor Council was an automatic suspension, but lying to Hector felt almost as careless. I could explain that I'd left out his part in the story to protect him, but I doubted Hector would see it that way.

I took the elevator to the top floor, then rounded a corner and made my way to the end of the hall and the classroom where the Honor Council held their meetings. The Senate met on the first floor in the main hallway where anyone could—and did—wander in. If you didn't have business in the Honor Council hallway, though, you didn't go there. People didn't even like to be seen heading in the direction of Room 305 because it meant that you were a person under suspicion: a criminal, a collaborator, or a rat.

I still hadn't heard from Hector, and I half-wondered if he was sitting before the Honor Council right then. I put my ear to the door and heard a murmur of voices too low to make out. Then I knocked on the door and the voices hushed, and after a moment, Zelda Parsons appeared.

"We'll be ready for you in a moment," she said, gesturing toward a small room just inside Room 305. "You can wait here."

It might have been a storage closet at one point, but now it was the Honor Council's holding cell for the people it wished to question, and it was not designed to make one feel at home. A single light bulb in a cage shone weakly over the cinder block walls, and the room was empty except for a wooden desk and chair shoved in one corner.

"Have a seat," Zelda said, smoothing the prim Peter Pan collar on her dress. Over the summer, she'd started to dress like Livia, wearing the same kitten heels and gold hoop earrings. She'd held on to her horn-rimmed glasses, though. "Someone will come get you when we're ready."

Not *who* would come to get me. Not when. She shut the door behind her. I didn't feel like sitting so I paced. I understood the purpose of this room. It kept witnesses confidential. It protected the accused and the accusers from one another, but I understood its implicit purpose as well. When you were in this room, you were on trial, no matter who you were or why you were there. Off-kilter and on edge was exactly how they wanted you.

It was only because I was standing and pacing from one side of the sparse room to the other that I saw the scrap of paper stuck underneath one of the desk legs. If I'd been sitting, like Zelda had told me to, I'd have missed it. It stuck out just the tiniest bit, blending in with the white tile floor, but it had been folded into quarters, and someone had definitely put it there on purpose. I knelt down quickly and pulled it free, looking over my shoulder in case Zelda suddenly came back.

I sat down in the chair and unfolded the paper, the blocky letters so precise and regular that they could have been printed by anyone:

THEY'RE GOING TO ASK YOU TO BE PRESIDENT.

I was glad I was sitting.

So much for all of Livia's talk about it not being too late, about nothing having been done that couldn't be undone.

In 1440, the Earl of Douglas and his brother were invited to dine with the King of Scotland, with whom they'd been having a power struggle. The food was good, the conversation was lively, everyone was having a blast, and it looked like they were about to patch things up. Then, all of a sudden, someone dropped a severed bull's head on the table in front of the Earl of Douglas, which, in case you didn't know, is a pretty clear indicator that your dinner party is about to go tits up, and he and his brother were dragged out of the castle and beheaded.

This was how Livia had decided to play it: it was going to be an ambush against every upperclassman on the Senate.

I heard the sound of chair legs sliding across linoleum, then footsteps. I folded the note back up and slipped it into my shoe. Then the door opened and Zelda Parsons was there.

"We're ready for you, Claudia," she said.

She walked me out of the holding cell and around the corner into a room where the seven other members of the Honor Council were seated in a semi-circle, all of them facing one lonely chair in the middle—mine. Ty and Livia sat in the center. To their left were Cal and the two freshman representatives, Kian Sarkosian, the spineless bystander who'd been with Cal at the bookstore, and a girl I didn't know. To their right sat Lola Stephenson, the senior who'd taken Maisie's place, and Esme Kovacs. Zelda took her place next to Esme, and then everyone turned their attention to me.

"Claudia, what can you tell us about Oberlin St. James?" Ty asked. For once, I almost appreciated his lack of social graces. The sooner we got down to business, the sooner I would know where I stood.

"What do you mean?"

I didn't know what they wanted out of me. My knowledge was long on the whats and the hows, but short on the whos. What did Ty want to know about Oberlin St. James? That he was a pompous tool? Or that out of all the upperclassman senators, he was the one I suspected *least*?

"Livia told us that you came to her and what you told her. Since then, we've independently verified those details," Ty said. "The reason you're here is because it's serious. A lot of people may be involved. If you know anything else about this, now's the time to tell us. Holding back information will not only be detrimental to this case; it will also be detrimental to you."

Ty had an extra-stiff and -formal way of talking when he was in Honor Council mode. I think he was trying to sound like Augustus, but mostly, he just sounded like he didn't quite understand the words he was throwing around.

"Does anyone else know about this?" Cal asked, his piggy eyes dancing at the sight of me in the interrogation chair. I thought about the vile things he'd said to me at the bookstore, and I realized that out of all of them, Cal was the one I was most afraid of lying to. He'd seen Hector and me together. Maybe he already suspected.

THEY'RE GOING TO ASK YOU TO BE PRESIDENT.

Livia had written the note, I was sure. She was the only one on the Honor Council who'd have any reason to tip me off at all.

But Ty said they'd verified the details of my story. Maybe they'd turned up more. Maybe they already knew about Hector and this was one final test of my honesty before offering me the presidency.

"I don't kn-kn-kn-kn-kn—" It was the worst, when a word completely eluded me like that, when I could feel it in my mouth, hear myself saying it, but just couldn't coax it out. I blamed Cal. In cases like these, I'd found the best course of action was usually to abort the sentence and start over. "The reservation was for forty people. I guess someone knows."

"Claudia," Livia said, and her voice sounded like a warning. "What Cal's asking is, did you find all of this out by yourself?"

Ty gave Livia a dirty look, before turning to me. "Before we move on to anything else, you still haven't answered my question. What kind of Senate president is Oberlin St. James?"

"Sorry, Ty," Livia said, demure in her pink cap-sleeve dress. "You lead the questioning."

The others nodded.

"I will," Ty huffed.

It couldn't have been easy being Ty, being the leader in name only, knowing that every time you made a statement, people would look to Livia to see if she agreed with it.

It must have been frustrating.

"What kind of president is he?" Ty asked petulantly.

Before I could answer his question, Cal stood up and walked out of the room, like he had better things to do than wait around for me to stammer out another sentence. Livia's eyes looked like they might shoot twin rays of butane flame, and Ty scowled and muttered something under his breath, but nobody else really looked all that surprised.

"Oberlin St. James seems like a good president," I said. "I don't really know him."

Ty heaved a sigh. He spoke slowly, like he was explaining something to a child. "Does he seem to be in control? Do the other officers respect him?"

"I think so," I said.

"Does he seem to know what's going on?"

I thought about the unaccounted-for $5000 and wondered if that was what they were talking about.

"Jasmine Park handles most of the money," I said.

They all exchanged knowing glances.

"And you don't know who booked the Queen Mary with Imperial Day Academy funds?"

"No," I said.

"Whose name was on the reservation?" Ty asked, a triumphant, told-you-so tone in his voice, like he'd just caught me in a lie.

"Oberlin St. James," I said, "but anyone could have said that."

"But why would they?" Livia asked.

Livia leaned over and whispered something in Ty's ear. He nodded, then turned to me and said, "We need a minute to discuss. Kian, could you take Claudia back to the waiting room? And check the hallway for Cal. He should be here for this."

Kian had gotten a bad buzz cut since the night I'd seen him hanging out with Cal at The Last Bookstore, but he was wearing the same outfit, the Kian Sarkosian uniform—white button-down shirt, dark jeans, black lace-up shoes. As he walked me back to the cinder block holding cell, I wondered which type of electoral mistake he'd been, something of the Jesse Nichols variety, or more of a Chris Gibbons.

"I'll be back in a few minutes," Kian said, holding the door open for me.

"You realize this whole thing is a shit show," I said. I never would have talked that way to Ty or Cal or even Zelda Parsons, but Kian was just a freshman. I thought a little intimidation might play well with someone who'd stood idly by while Cal drunkenly mocked Hector and me.

"I'm sorry you feel that way," he said, gesturing for me to go into the holding cell, "but I don't know what you're talking about, Claudia."

I hadn't rattled him in the slightest, and that was when I saw the first clue to whatever it was that Kian Sarkosian was doing on the Honor Council. For all his gawky weirdness, Kian had a steely, decidedly un-freshman-like confidence that made me wonder what it would feel like to know that someday you were going to grow out of all the things that were wrong with you.

"Stick around and maybe you will," I said. Kian didn't reply. He just closed the holding cell door behind me as I sank down into the wooden chair, leaned my elbows on the desktop, and bowed my head. I had no idea whether my testimony had made things better or worse for me, much less anyone else. Mouthing off to a freshman at this point profited me nothing.

I sat in the dank little room considering my next move. Livia had spun that beautiful line of bullshit about stopping things before it was too late when her intention all along was to use the scandal to get rid of as many people as possible. After a show of power like that, no one would take the Senate seriously and no one would dare cross the Honor Council again.

Livia had said what she needed to say to keep me calm, to keep me from telling Hector.

It was a good maneuver.

A few minutes later, Kian came to the door, knocking first like it was a doctor's office and he wanted to make sure I had my paper gown on.

"Still here," I said, and he opened the door and took me back.

They were all there, even Cal, and there was an uneasiness in the room. Half of them looked like they'd gotten their way, and the other half were still stewing about it.

"There's something else we'd like to go over with you, Claudia," Livia said, but then turned to Ty and nodded her head in a show of deference. "Why don't you lead the discussion, Ty."

Ty cleared his throat. "This is all strictly confidential, Claudia. None of it leaves this room. But we need to know, in the event that Senate officers have to step down, would you be willing to lead in an acting capacity?"

Whistleblowing seems like it would feel noble and righteous, but mostly it makes you feel awful. This is especially true when one of the governing bodies at your school decides to hand you the presidency like it's a reward for your snitching.

I remembered the moment when Livia had singled me out at the lunch table and said, "You should run for Senate."

I didn't want anything else she had to give me. I didn't want to owe Livia Drusus anything, ever.

"No," I said to Ty, probably much too quickly. "I'm not the right person for it."

Relief washed over Ty's face.

"Suit yourself," he said, but the look Livia gave me told another story. I hadn't done the thing she expected me to do, the thing she wanted me to do, the thing she'd probably made Ty ask me to do, the thing she would have done if she'd been in my shoes.

And I could tell she'd never forgive me for it.

XXIV

THE WAY HE LOOKED

Hector wasn't getting books out of his locker in the science hallway, or in the library, or any of the other places I usually ran into him during the day. It wasn't until the last bell rang that I finally got a text from him.

Meet me at the pond. I'll get there as soon as I can.

Imperial Day had three stories, four long hallways that formed a square and a boxed-in garden courtyard with a fountain and a wishing bridge and a little pond with turtles in it.

That was where I waited for Hector, realizing I hadn't seen him since Saturday night when he drove me home after our run-in with Cal.

I took a seat on one of the benches and went through the motions of reading a Civil War history, but mostly I watched the turtles. Some of them swam, one made its way from one side of the wishing bridge to the other. Two babies had climbed out of the water and were adorably sunning themselves on a rock. They looked like they had a very nice life.

People at Imperial Day would do the worst things to each other, but we all agreed: nobody fucked with the turtles.

When Hector sat down next to me on the bench, I jumped,

partly because he'd approached so quietly, partly because of the way he looked. His skin was wan, there were dark circles under his eyes, and a whiff of stale sweat mingled with his usual sandalwood smell. "You look awful," I said.

He gave me a sad smile, then asked, "But do I look presidential?"

✳✳✳

Dear Maisie,
I know you told me you wanted an Imperial Day gossip blackout, but this is not gossip. This made the news.

TWENTY SUSPENDED, FOUR EXPELLED FOLLOWING EMBEZZLEMENT INVESTIGATION AT LOCAL SCHOOL

Four students at the Imperial Day Academy, all of them members of the school's student government, were expelled Tuesday in the wake of an investigation that revealed they spent thousands of dollars in school funds to throw a private party for themselves and their friends aboard the Queen Mary in Long Beach.

A spokesperson confirmed that school officials had become aware of the party after a receipt for a deposit was leaked anonymously to Imperial Day administrators as well as to officers in the school's Honor Council.

"They stole from the very people they'd been elected to represent," said Imperial Day sophomore and former senator Chris Gibbons. "It's despicable."

The twenty students who confessed they had been invited to the party were suspended for one week. All of them maintained that they did not know the party at the Queen Mary was funded with stolen money.

Imperial Day is known for its Honor Code, a pledge signed by students upon admittance to the school promising that they will not lie, cheat, or steal while they are enrolled. Asked whether this incident undermines the Honor Code, Imperial Day Academy head Dr. Bob Graves said, "If anything, this affirms that the Honor Code works. Our student body is composed of young men and women of integrity who speak up when they hear about wrongdoing."

Ty Berman, President of the Honor Council, could not speak about the investigation, but said that new Senate leadership had been appointed. "We are confident that those responsible are no longer representing the student body," he said.

"Everything is crazy right now," said junior Soren Bieckmann. "These were the people who were supposed to be going to Harvard, and now they might be going to jail."

School sources would not comment on whether the accused would face criminal charges.

So that's what's going on here. Also, I am vice president of the Senate now.

How's Rome?

Ciao, bella,

XX,

Claudia

"You turned down the Senate presidency but accepted the vice presidency?"

"Just so we're clear, I turned down the job Livia offered me. The one Hector Estrella offered me, I took."

XXV

THE THING WHERE WE HAVE THIS CONVERSATION AND I END UP THINKING LESS OF YOU

Of course I agreed to be Hector's vice president. I couldn't just leave him out there all by himself. It was not a great time to be a senator. At our first public hearing after the purge, people were spilling out of the room. Ty and Livia came to lend some air of legitimacy to the proceedings, but the students were out for our blood.

"How do we know you weren't involved in this?"

That was from one of the asshole freshmen who'd run and lost his Senate race just a few weeks before, one of those rare cases that restore my faith in the democratic process.

"I think that the entire Senate should be disbanded," said Chris Gibbons, smug in his faux retro Hot Topic t-shirt. "The whole thing is illegitimate."

"*You're* illegitimate," someone jeered from the back of the room, and the tips of Chris Gibbons's ears turned red.

While the underclassmen seemed to want our heads on pikes alongside Oberlin St. James's and Jasmine Park's, the upperclassmen wanted our jobs.

"No offense, but do you know what you're doing? Are either of you even qualified to lead the Senate?" asked a girl with corkscrew curls and a narrow nose, whom I recognized as the worst backup singer from *Little Shop of Horrors*.

Another girl standing next to her nodded in agreement. "Can't we have a new election or something?"

There was a buzz of approval in the room, and that was when I realized that half the students in the room weren't there to complain. They were hoping we'd cave in and hand over our titles, or that we'd prove ourselves to be so incompetent that we'd be immediately forced to resign.

I looked nervously at Hector, who absorbed it all stoically.

Ty stood up and said, "The investigation is closed. If Hector and Claudia had anything to do with what happened, they wouldn't be here now."

"And you haven't even given them a chance," Livia said.

The room went silent for a moment, during which someone coughed the word "SNITCH" into the back of their hand.

Livia's eyes widened, and I saw her open her mouth to lay into the guilty party when Hector raised his hand and said, "You can have a school governed by an Honor Code or you can have a school where you call each other snitches, but you can't have both. Nobody's happy about why we're here or why I'm your president, but that's all in the past now. I plan to work hard and listen to what you have to say and do a good job. So, that said, does anyone else have something to ask, other than whether or not we deserve to be here?"

After a long pause, a sophomore raised her hand and asked, "What about the money?"

"Homecoming's supposed to be next week!" another voice

called out plaintively, as though he thought that perhaps we'd all forgotten.

"I know," said Hector. His voice was level, but his eyes were shining with excitement. "And I have a plan."

Oberlin St. James always got pompous when he was speechifying, but Hector sounded natural, like he was looking right at each person in the room and speaking only to them. He belonged up there.

Off to the side, I saw Livia's jaw tighten as she turned and whispered something to Ty. That probably meant she knew as much about Hector's plan as I did, which is to say, nothing.

Hector forged ahead. "No car wash, none of the other fundraisers. We don't have enough time or people, and to be honest, I hate the idea of asking our teachers to wash our cars."

A murmur went up in the room. I couldn't make out what anyone said specifically, but the general gist seemed to be, *Look at the sophomore, having opinions.*

"Instead of Homecoming Week, we'll have Honor Week. People will pledge to do one honorable thing a day and get their friends and family to sponsor them. You help an old lady cross the street, you collect a dollar from each of your sponsors. You read stories to the little kids at the library, collect another round from your sponsors. Take pictures of all of it. And at the end of the week—" Hector paused for a moment and took a deep breath. "We take the money we would have spent on the dance, and we donate it to the Union Rescue Mission."

At this, the murmur turned into a roar, and I saw Livia smirk behind her hand. A sophomore didn't just waltz into the Senate presidency in the wake of a scandal and tell his constituents, *Oh, and by the way, Homecoming is canceled*. From the hostile faces in the room, I wondered if Hector's presidency was going to be even shorter than Oberlin St. James's.

Hector's cheeks reddened, but he stood his ground. His gaze traveled across the room, and one by one, he stared down every angry person until, at last, they fell silent, waiting to hear what he was going to say next. Livia looked surprised by this, then annoyed.

"I know you're angry, and I know it isn't fair. You didn't steal any money, so why shouldn't you get to have a normal Homecoming? The answer is, we can't just go on like nothing happened. We have to do something radical and public and loud to let them know that's not what Imperial Day is.

"I transferred here because I want to go to Harvard or Berkeley or Yale someday. Probably a lot of you do, too. And if we do nothing, the admissions people are going to look at our applications and say, 'Wasn't that the school where the students stole thousands of dollars?' And it won't matter that you didn't have anything to do with it.

"But if we do something different, people will think of something positive when they hear about Imperial Day. I am really sorry that there won't be a Homecoming dance this year, I'm sorry you're being asked to fix something that wasn't your fault, but I think this is worth it."

Looking out at the students, I could see that Hector had won more than a few people in the room over to his plan. Still, I could also see people grumbling to one another. I heard one girl complain that she'd already bought her dress. Hector had tried appealing to the better angels of their nature, but for some students at Imperial Day, that was never going to be the best point of entry.

Five minutes ago, I hadn't known anything about Hector's plan, but even with minimal preparation, I could see that it had its more venal charms as well. That was the angle I'd take.

"This week, we'll be contacting all the news channels," I said. "We'll have pieces on Buzzfeed and the *Huffington Post* and the *LA Times*. We have a call in to *The Ellen DeGeneres Show*."

I didn't know whether I was making things better or worse—I was talking too fast—but still, I had a feeling that I was onto something. I could see it dawn on all of their faces that this could be *huge*, and they could be a part of it.

Before I could go on, Hector jumped in. "Obviously, I still need to talk it over with the other senators and get some feedback from the Honor Council, but more details are coming this week."

That was smart, I thought, mentioning the Honor Council like that. If there was one thing Livia loved, it was being asked for her opinion. It might even have been enough to make her forgive Hector for publicly sharing his plan without running it by her first.

"I think it's brilliant."

Livia's voice cut through the chatter, and everyone turned to see her beaming at Hector. Once he knew what he was supposed to think, Ty beamed at Hector, too, and then I knew that it was only a matter of time before everyone else fell in line.

He'd done the impossible. Hector Estrella had reestablished the legitimacy of the Imperial Day Senate with one speech. People gave him approving nods as they filed out of the room. A few smiled on their way past, and one came up to the front of the room to shake his hand: Chris Gibbons.

Hector still had to pull it off, of course, but people wanted to believe in him. They wanted his plan to succeed.

Ty and Livia waited until everyone else had left to approach Hector.

"Let us know what you need to make this happen," Ty said, shaking Hector's hand, while looking to Livia for approval.

"Yes, you have our full support," Livia said.

As long as we make you look good, I thought. Even though she'd spoken up in favor of Hector's plan, I had no doubt it was more political maneuvering on her part. Livia liked being on winning sides, and suddenly, nobody-sophomore that he was, Hector Estrella looked like a winner.

Hector seemed dazed, but he mumbled his thanks and said that he'd be in touch, and eventually they left and we were alone. That was when I looked down at the desktop where Hector's hands rested, and I saw that they were shaking.

"You did a great job," I said. I put my hand on top of his on the desk and gave it a squeeze. This was a thing we were doing now, I thought. We were hand-squeezing buddies. "How did you think up Honor Week?"

"I couldn't fall asleep last night," Hector started. "I was lying in bed, wishing that everything with the Senate and the money and the Queen Mary had never happened, and I was trying to think of a way to make up for it."

Suddenly, I was flooded with relief that I'd turned down the presidency when Livia had offered it to me. Why did they even ask me first? I never would have thought of something like Honor Week.

"I'm going to assume you don't actually have a call in to *The Ellen DeGeneres Show*?"

"No, but I will. I had to think on my feet," I said. Maybe I wouldn't have thought of Honor Week, but I certainly knew how to sell it.

I'd also lied in front of two Honor Council officers and thirty other people, so my vice presidency was off to an excellent start.

"So, now you know what it feels like," Hector said with a smirk. "When I do something important without telling you about it first."

Ah, there was Crabby Hector. I'd been missing him.

"You're still mad at me for going to the Honor Council?"

I knew what he was going to say before he said it because I was thinking the same thing.

"No," he said. "But you can't do something like that again. Neither one of us can. You saw what people were like today. They'll turn on us in a second."

"I'm sorry the meeting was so awful," I said. "You were brilliant, though. It was very Obama circa 2008. Or maybe JFK."

"Thanks," he said. "I was expecting it, so it wasn't so bad."

"If we were juniors, nobody would have said anything about it."

Hector shook his head. "If I was less brown, nobody would have said anything about it."

"Really?" I asked, cocking my head to the side. If you'd asked anyone at Imperial Day their attitudes on race, they probably would have told you that it was the 21st century, we were all equal, and they didn't even *see* color.

Hector looked surprised that I'd question it, but then also not really surprised at all.

"Like, how can you tell it's *that*?" I asked.

"Could we not do this?" Hector asked. He looked uncomfortable. He looked like he wanted to flee the room.

"Do what?"

"The thing where we have this conversation and I end up thinking less of you."

"I don't see why it's a big deal. You could just explain," I said.

Hector sighed, then headed for the door. As he opened it, he turned and looked back over his shoulder at me.

"Or you could just believe me, Claudia," he said.

By the time I made it to the door, he had already whipped around the corner and out of sight.

"Hector!" I called out after him. I heard the squeaking of his shoes on the tile floor slow, then stop, but he didn't reply.

Of course I believed him.

Hector was exactly what his campaign posters had promised: vision and integrity. I was a meddling, foul-mouthed, duplicitous white girl, and which one of us had the Honor Council tapped for the job first?

Hector's footsteps started up again, growing fainter until the sound faded away altogether, and I stood there wondering why I couldn't bring myself to lift my voice and call "I believe you" down the hallway.

Was it that hard to admit I was wrong?

Was I that much of an asshole?

Apparently, yes.

XXVI

HONOR WEEK

Honor is a maddeningly subjective word, and most of the other words that can be used to define it are similarly vague: *upright-ness; virtue; nobility; righteousness.* Things I suspected that I was not, at least not in the way Hector was.

I think he did the smart thing by keeping things loose and letting people decide for themselves what constituted an act worthy of Honor Week. A few people grumbled about the dance, but word got around about what Hector had said during the Senate meeting and people also grumbled that he was right. Some people fell in line because Ty and Livia and all of their friends seemed to be so excited about it. And others got into it because there was just something about Hector.

He inspired them. He gave them a way to feel like *they* were the ones who'd stopped corruption, enacted justice, and ushered in a bright and promising future. And the polit-ical genius of Hector was that he *let* them feel that way. He wasn't interested in looking good or taking the credit for himself.

Behind every idealist, though, is a realist. Behind every lofty intention is the person who's tethering them to the ground.

Behind the person cheering, "This is right!" is the person asking, "But will it sell?"

Hector could handle the ideas all by himself, but he needed me to manage the public relations component of his plan to resurrect Imperial Day from its shameful scandal. Honor Week was something Hector wanted to do for its own sake. If the ways in which it could be marketed to our advantage had occurred to him, he would have felt too guilty to properly exploit them.

Which is not to say he wouldn't let me do it for him.

✳✳✳

To KTLA Channel 5 News, I sent word of the following:

- Maddie Urrea's book drive for the local juvenile detention facility
- Kian Sarkosian's trash clean-up effort at the Venice boardwalk
- Zelda Parsons's care packages of toiletries and snacks for homeless people on Skid Row

I wrote a piece for the *Huffington Post* about how:

- Ravi Sejani prepared and delivered meals to all of his elderly neighbors
- Lola Stephenson played improv theater games with the patients at Children's Hospital
- Ty and Livia held a canned goods drive for the local food bank
- Trixie Pappadou came out. She said it was the most honest thing she could think of to do during Honor Week.

Other stories I shared more selectively or decided not to share at all.

I was effusive in my praise of freshman senators Lucy Lin and Veronica Ollenbeck, who managed to capture fifteen feral cats, transport them to the local veterinary clinic, and have them spayed or neutered. I just left out the part where they both contracted some sort of bacterial infection and spent the rest of Honor Week out of school recovering from it.

I left out of my reports that Chris Gibbons made cupcakes for every teacher with a little flag stuck in them that said, "You make Imperial Day great," which was a nice gesture, only everyone was afraid to eat them.

Known asshole Astrid Murray bought a round for everyone at a local coffee shop, which at first Ty tried to argue wasn't strictly "honorable," even if it was generous, but Astrid stood her ground and argued that she'd supported a local business and made a lot of uncaffeinated people very happy, which was certainly a public service.

Octavia Resnick and Cal teamed up to give free guitar lessons to kids in an after-school program. Had it been anyone else, I would have included it in my press releases, but I didn't want Cal getting anywhere near a reporter. Not when Hector's reputation was on the line. And mine, too, I suppose.

To the surprise of all, it was Soren Bieckmann who got us on *The Ellen DeGeneres Show*. One of his parents was on the board at LA County Hospital, and he somehow got a list of every cancer patient without insurance. Then he set up a campaign on InVigor to pay for all of their chemotherapy and radiation, and charmed celebrities on as many social media platforms as he could think of until he got it to go viral in less than forty-eight hours. I think he wound up raising something like half a million dollars for these people.

✷✷✷

What did *I* do for Honor Week?

Why do you want to know that? Like I told you, I wrote copy and press releases. I applied many hashtags to many pictures. I asked my parents to make Soren's fundraiser a featured campaign on InVigor, which may or may not have been ethical, but considering the cause was people with cancer, I decided the scales of justice were tipped in my favor. I put in a call to *The Ellen DeGeneres Show*. But you want to know what honorable thing I did?

It was almost two years ago.

I don't even remember now.

I don't care if you think I'm lying.

XXVII

AFTER YOU EXPLAIN THAT IT IS IN MY BEST INTEREST TO COOPERATE FULLY

During Honor Week, I didn't take any pictures of myself doing any good deeds. I did not collect any sponsors or raise a single dollar for the Imperial Day Academy.

Every morning that week, I came to school early. I made sure no one was watching.

I ripped a sheet of paper out of my notebook, wrote I BELIEVE YOU on it, folded it up, and stuck it in Hector's locker.

We never talked about it.

XXVIII

VALENTINE'S DAY

During the first one hundred days of his presidency, Franklin Delano Roosevelt stabilized the banks, provided emergency relief to starving families, regulated the stock market, put more than eight million people to work through the WPA work-relief program, and set the bar for presidential dynamism so high that no president since has matched it.

"This is what I want to do," Hector said. He never hit you over the head with it, but in some ways, he was every bit the student of history that I was.

"Then let's make FDR proud," I replied.

There were no banks to stabilize, but Honor Week raised so much money that even after the Union Rescue Mission donation, there was enough left over to create a fund to buy school supplies for scholarship students. The financial reform we enacted made all student organization spending public and transparent so that nothing like the Queen Mary debacle would ever happen again. We set to work creating a model for mental health services and drafted an anti-bullying policy. When Soren Bieckmann came to us about forming a drug and alcohol addiction support group, we helped him do it. Hector and

Esme Kovacs and Lucy Lin started a mentoring program to encourage students of color to take leadership roles in the disproportionately lily-white student government at Imperial Day.

Franklin D. Roosevelt was our role model, our inspiration, and we wielded him like a talisman. Hector got me an FDR action figure for Christmas, and I got him a key chain that said, THE ONLY THING WE HAVE TO FEAR IS FEAR ITSELF.

After Hector Estrella's first one hundred days, nobody at Imperial Day was asking whether he deserved to be president.

We made a lot of changes to the way the Senate did things at Imperial Day, but we didn't dare touch the Valentine's Day flower sale. If we'd messed with that, they would have killed us.

Hector, Veronica, Lucy, and I were excused from all of our morning classes to collect money and sort order forms into piles. It was so busy, I didn't have time to glance at the sappy notes people wrote to each other or to think about the fact that none of them was for me.

Cal had a way of making you pay attention to him, though, whether you wanted to or not.

Each bouquet was $15. He handed me a $100 bill and a stack of order forms. I wondered what kinds of lurid notes Cal had written to his would-be conquests, but knew better than to peek.

"Don't worry, Claudia," he said, running his tongue across his upper lip. "One of these is for you."

When I shuddered and gave him his change, he handed the $10 bill to Hector.

"So you can get something nice for your lady," he said, pressing the bill into Hector's palm, then patting him on the back of the hand like he was somebody's grandmother. "I insist."

Hector said nothing as Cal walked away chuckling to himself, but he crumpled the $10 bill up in his fist, then set it on the table between us. As he sat there quaking with rage, I picked up the bill, smoothed it flat, then folded it into the shape of an elephant. My mom had taught me this trick. When Maisie and I were little, she had a habit of taking us to fussy lunch places where children were about as welcome as hepatitis C, and the dollar bill elephant trick usually shut us up for fifteen minutes or so.

I put the $10-bill elephant down on a sheet of notebook paper, scribbled on the page and passed it over to Hector:

That at least got a smile out of him.

After lunch, we retreated to Senate headquarters, where it was every man on deck. For the next two hours, we tucked heartfelt messages into the bouquets, then delivered them just before eighth period, consulting the seating charts that the teachers had grudgingly left for us.

It was hard enough for eight senators to do it, and now there were only four of us. No one had the stomach for special elections after the Homecoming scandal, and Hector and I swung into action so quickly that no one seemed to miss the extra bodies except for us. Lucy and Veronica recruited four freshman girls to help, which probably didn't take much arm-twisting. Once they found out they'd get to spend the afternoon sorting Valentine's Day flowers with Hector Estrella, they were probably falling over themselves to volunteer.

Eighth period I had Art History, which was both ideal and horrible. Looking at pretty pictures in a dim room at the end of a long day was extremely Zen, but it was also a recipe for narcolepsy, no matter how interesting Mrs. Castaneda's lecture was. Fortunately, it was also a small class, and not terribly full of the kind of people who were likely to get a lot of flowers, so that was a relief. Mine wouldn't be the only empty desk.

In fact, there was only one bouquet in the whole classroom, and it was on Trixie Pappadou's desk. As the bell rang, the rest of my classmates trickled in and took their seats, and Mrs. Castaneda dimmed the lights. After saying a few words about the 1940s and late period realists, she pulled up a slide of a girl crawling through a field of dried brown grass toward a house that seemed much too far away.

"*Christina's World* by Andrew Wyeth," said Mrs. Castaneda. "The model for this painting was stricken with polio, and as Wyeth described it, his challenge was 'to do justice to her extraordinary conquest of a life which most people would consider hopeless.' Some people consider it to be sentimental. An art columnist for the *New York Times* called it a dorm room poster. If you are a jaded sort of person, I suppose that this painting does not have much to offer you."

As Mrs. Castaneda went on to the next slide, there was a knock on the door, which then inched open to reveal Kian Sarkosian and his prison haircut.

"May I help you?" Mrs. Castaneda asked.

"I'm sorry to interrupt, but I have a flower delivery that ended up in the wrong classroom," he said. Then, much to my surprise, he turned to me and said, "I think these are yours, Claudia."

I started to get up from my desk, but I think he realized the distraction and embarrassment watching me hobble up to the door would create for everyone, so instead, he dashed into the classroom, his long legs carrying him to my desk in three paces. He set the bouquet down on my desk, gave me a stern nod, and was gone just as suddenly as he'd appeared.

I took the flowers, not caring about the cellophane crinkle that made Mrs. Castaneda break off her lecture mid-sentence and glare at me. There was a note taped to the bouquet wrapping that read:

TO CLAUDIA—YOU ARE A FORCE FOR GOOD IN THE UNIVERSE.

It wasn't signed, but that was almost beside the point. For a moment, it was enough to know that somebody—at least somebody on this continent anyway—felt that way about me. You know how, when somebody likes you for exactly the reason you most want to be liked, it makes you like them even more? If they'd written that I was nice or funny or smart, it wouldn't have hit me so hard, and all of the feelings that I usually kept shoved down wouldn't have threatened to come leaking out right there in Art History class.

At least it was dark. At least it was because I was happy.

I'm sure Andrew Wyeth is a terrific artist and very important, and I promise to read a book about him someday to make up for the amount of attention I paid to Mrs. Castaneda for the next forty minutes. As the slides faded in and out, all dark landscapes and lonely people, a different series of images played in my brain like something out of a movie. There was a soaring soundtrack as I ran in slow motion down the hallway, then a dramatic cut and a zoom in for a close-up of our faces as I said, "It was you," and then a long kiss and fade to black.

The bell rang, and I jumped up from my seat, gathering up my books and flowers, and I limped down the hallway as fast as I could, past the gym, turning down the long hallway where the auditorium was, and finally rounding the corner to the science hallway. I caught the wall and stood there a moment to gather up my courage and breath. The noise in the hallway faded as I zeroed in on Hector standing at his locker, loading up his backpack with books for the weekend. The hallway was filled with people kissing, people crying, people holding hands, making plans, saying that they loved each other. I felt like all of it was a beautiful backdrop to the scene that was playing out as I fought through the crowd of people to get to Hector, not wanting to wait one second longer than necessary to reach him.

And then I was there, and he was there. His face lit up when he saw me, and he gave me a hug, crushing me to his shoulder. My cheek rested on the gray cashmere sweater he wore.

"Happy Valentine's Day, Claudia," he said. "Who are the flowers from?"

Everything stopped.

The noise in the hallway, the kissing, the smiles, were all swallowed up by a roaring of white noise in my ears, the world around me suddenly reduced to Hector's shoulder, the collar of his shirt, the hollow of his throat.

"I don't know," I said, realizing that if they weren't from Hector, I didn't care who they were from. "I'm sorry. I have to go."

I pushed through the crowd of happy couples who were too lost in one another's eyes to notice an elbow in the side or a shove in the back.

"See you Monday?" I heard Hector call after me. He sounded a little hurt by my sudden departure, but I didn't stop and I didn't look back.

Stupid, pathetic, self-pitying tears began to well up in my eyes as I turned the corner, and I considered whether I'd be less likely to humiliate myself if I ran straight home or if I stopped by the restroom first and found a stall to cry in.

Instead, I almost ran into Cal, who didn't notice me because he had his tongue down Octavia Resnick's throat. Five bouquets of flowers dangled from her fingers, their cellophane wrapping brushing the ground. Her other hand disappeared up the back of Cal's shirt.

As if I hadn't already felt ill.

I limped as fast as I could toward the nearest exit, then went tearing across the parking lot. Someone almost hit me with their BMW and honked their horn angrily. I flipped the driver off without looking to see who it was and ran to the bus stop, tossing my bouquet of flowers into the first trash can I saw, like they'd never happened and nobody thought I was a force for good in the universe.

XXIX

BETTER THAN THE ALTERNATIVE

Stupid, stupid, stupid.

If there had been one small mercy in any of it, at least I hadn't had a chance to embarrass myself by leaning in for a kiss.

Even weeks later, the thought of what I'd almost done would make me cringe. However, in the immediate aftermath, the weekend after Valentine's Day, I stayed in my room. I consumed nothing but grilled cheese sandwiches and ginger ale and watched one Ken Burns documentary after another. As I drifted off to sleep, I reminded myself, *This is who you are, this is what you do.*

On Monday, I went back to school, my thoughts about love and romance and Hector Estrella shoved back down good and deep where they belonged.

✳✳✳

There were other things to keep me busy, too. Hector organized a club to keep Honor Week going year round, kind of a pep club for good deeds. We commissioned a mural for the band hallway. However, our most important achievement was the creation of the Imperial Day Clean Elections Initiative. We got the Honor Council and the Board and Principal Graves to sign off on it, and what it meant was that if you were participating in the spring elections, you pledged not to sabotage anyone else's campaign. No dirty tricks, no ratfucks.

It wasn't perfect. The pledge only applied to candidates. There was nothing to stop anyone else from messing with campaigns, and as long as the candidate could make a case that they hadn't known about, encouraged, or endorsed the ratfuck, there was nothing we could really do to them.

But still, it was something. For years, the bullying that had gone on during election season had been regarded as part of the game, and if you wanted to play, it was on you to toughen up. Now, at least we were calling it what it was. At least we were saying it was the ratfuckers who needed to change, not the rest of us.

Baby steps.

Hector and I still hung out. He dragged me out of the Westside, and made me do things like ride the subway and stand in line for food trucks, and most of the time, I was able to make myself forget that I was half in love with him.

Stupid, stupid, stupid.

And then, before I knew it, it was spring and we were up for reelection.

"Are you sure you want to do this again?" I asked Hector as we sat at Starbucks filling out our applications.

Hector looked at me like I was crazy, like the previous Senate president's life hadn't been totally ruined by the job.

"Of course I want to do it again," he said.

All he could see was the good work he'd done, the better work he was going to do, but as a student of history, I knew where his blind spot was: Hector never thought about the people who might be gunning for him.

In the space of a few months, the two of us had transformed the Senate from a glorified party-planning committee into an engine for change. Meanwhile, the Honor Council had become almost an afterthought. The purge of the Senate had been their one great show of power, and following that—nothing. I wondered if it was driving Livia crazy to have been eclipsed by underclassmen.

And if it was, I worried what she might do about it.

"Think about what happened to Oberlin St. James," I said, trying to get Hector to at least consider the darker possibilities.

"Well, as long as I manage not to steal a few thousand dollars, I should be fine."

I remembered how Oberlin St. James had mentioned the missing $5000 in the middle of a Senate meeting, like that was the first he'd ever heard of it. A few months ago, the story had been complicated, but now, the only version of it was that "Oberlin St. James stole a bunch of money."

Maybe, maybe not. If I'd held on to what Hector and I had known, maybe he and I could have answered some of those questions ourselves instead of taking the Honor Council at its word when they said that justice had been served. There was nothing we could do about it now except keep running.

"Any other candidates for president?" I asked.

"Not that I've heard of yet."

The lines of succession seemed to be cycling along very quietly this year. As far as anyone knew, Livia was running unopposed for Honor Council president with Zelda Parsons as her vice president. Hector for Senate president. The only race where there were significant challengers so far was mine.

"There are three juniors running for Senate VP," I said. "That's just the ones I know about."

"They want to add a line to their college applications, and Imperial Day Senate was in the news, so it's all sexy, but they don't know what they're doing and you do. Besides, the only one I'll endorse is you. You're too good at it not to win," Hector said. He took a sip of his latte, then frowned like the milk had gone bad. "Are *you* sure you want to do this again?"

I didn't answer. I wanted to be there for Hector. I liked being in charge and making things better. I liked being good at my job, but sometimes, when I really thought about it, I felt exhausted. As soon as you fixed one thing, another thing popped up to claim your attention. No one appreciated what you did; no one said "thank you." They just came to you over and over again, needing something. It was never over. Nothing ever got better, not really.

And when I thought about another year of that, I felt like getting on the next train out of Union Station, dyeing my hair with shoe polish, changing my name, and starting a new life anywhere but here.

✳✳✳

But look, whatever. Obviously I ran. Obviously I won because I'm sitting in your office and we're having this conversation. So what does it matter if I had a moment of doubt about it? Hector was right: I was good at the job. I knew what I was doing, and as long as I was running on Hector's ticket, my reelection was in the bag.

Things in the Honor Council became less clear-cut, though.

The trouble started during spring break when Livia had gone for her Ivy League tours and interviews, and while she was making the Princeton-Harvard-Yale circuit, she and Augustus broke up. She'd left for the East Coast like it was a victory lap on her junior year and returned in a state of shock.

Word spread fast, the way it always does when something bad happens to someone important, and yes, some people seemed to enjoy it. Believe it or not, I wasn't one of them. Watching Livia get dumped wasn't the same thing as watching her get justice, and while the latter would have been enormously satisfying, the former was just sad.

It was in this state that she came to me for help. I was eating lunch in the library, trying to keep up with the homework I never seemed to have any time to do anymore, when Livia came through the double doors. I saw her before she saw me. The girl working at the checkout desk gave her a wave and a shy hello, but Livia ignored her as she brushed past, Kate Spade bag bouncing off her hip. She scanned the library until her eyes fell on me, and she marched up to the table where I sat eating my orange and pretzels.

"Who did your sister's campaign posters last year?" she asked.

No "hello," no "how have you been."

I shrugged. "You should probably ask her."

"She hasn't written back."

While I may not have taken any pleasure in Livia's breakup, I was secretly pleased to learn that Maisie was still ignoring her texts.

"What do you have planned so far?" I asked.

I could tell that she didn't want to talk to me about it, so just for fun, I added, "VP to VP."

Livia curled her lip at the reminder that, technically, we were on the same level. Still, she sighed and sat down, sliding a sheet of paper across the table.

KEEPING YOU SAFE
BACK TO BASICS
PROVEN LEADERSHIP

"These are . . ." I struggled to find the right word.

"Shit."

I nodded in agreement, and Livia leaned across the table, her eyes darting left and right to make sure no one was watching us.

"Cal's running against me," she whispered.

She said it like she couldn't imagine a universe where such an outcome was possible, but she must have been worried or else she wouldn't have been talking to me.

I hadn't seen much of Cal since his Valentine's Day make-out session with Octavia Resnick in the middle of the science hall. That romance—such as it was—lasted about as long as you'd expect. By the end of February, Octavia went back to her quiet, black-wearing, poetry-writing skulking ways and Cal went back to dry-humping the legs of freshman girls he cornered in the lunch line.

"Why are you telling me?"

"Because we can't let him win," Livia said.

"Does he still walk out of the room in the middle of hearings?" I asked.

"It's gotten worse," Livia said. "He wears headphones and sings to himself. Or he sleeps. We've had to start using secret ballots to reach verdicts because he just votes the opposite way I do."

Then I realized Livia didn't care who did Maisie's campaign posters last year. That was the excuse she'd manufactured to talk to me. She was here because there was nowhere else she could go, no one else who would understand the nuances of the situation.

Augustus was gone, Ty was useless. Zelda Parsons worshipped her, but I *knew* her.

"Why don't you and Ty just kick him out?" I asked.

"I tried. Why do you think he decided to run against me?"

To my consternation, I found myself rolling my eyes in solidarity with Livia Drusus. Only Cal would run for Honor Council president in retaliation and out of spite.

"So are you going to help me or aren't you, Claudia? How do I beat him?"

I would never have presumed to speak for Maisie, but I thought about what she would say right now if she were here and if she and Livia were still friends like Livia wished they were.

"Be your best self," I said. "Remind the voters that they know what they're getting with you and that Cal's a wild card, but don't leave it at that. It's not just that you're better than the alternative."

I stopped short of paying her an actual compliment like Maisie would have done because I found myself wondering, what *was* Livia's best self? Was it any better than Cal's?

"You know who Cal really is, Livia. If anyone knows how to destroy him, it's you."

Whether or not you agreed with it or had moral qualms about it, there was no question that when it came to that kind of politics, Livia was a master.

Just to be clear, though, I never told her to *do* anything. I didn't want Cal to be president any more than she did. But I had no advice for her, no words of wisdom. She acted alone.

It Stops Here

Two days later, there was a sign hanging in a stall in the second-floor girls' bathroom that read:

If Cal Hurt has ever harassed you, harmed you, or made you feel unsafe and you need a place to talk about it, email itstopsherecal@gmail.com. All inquiries kept strictly confidential.

IT STOPS HERE

It was gone by lunchtime, but by then, all the girls were already talking about it, and from the things I heard whispered, I knew that my handful of creepy run-ins with him had been mild by comparison.

I could only imagine the horror stories that people were writing in to the email address. Of course, if Livia was really the one who set it up, those stories would find their way out into the open *en masse* within a few days and Cal's presidential campaign would be as good as through—one hoped.

As a historian, I can't say with certainty that it was Livia who was behind it. I can only say that she and I talked in the library, and within two days, I found the sign in the bathroom. Those are the facts. The rest are only theories.

The stories never made it out, though.

If this was Livia's plan to destroy Cal, she should have moved a hell of a lot faster.

The day the sign went up in the second-floor girls' bathroom, everybody was talking about Cal.

The day after that, everyone was talking about Livia.

✳✳✳

"When I told you the story about what Livia did at the Griffith School, I was telling you to explain why I hated her and why I hated that my sister was friends with her and why I mistrusted everything she did.

"But I also told you so that when I got to this part of the story, you'd understand that she deserved it."

✳✳✳

On Friday, the leaflets went up, one stuck on every bulletin board and bathroom stall door:

IS THIS THE HONOR COUNCIL PRESIDENT **YOU** WANT?

Beneath it was Livia's picture, then a bullet-point-by-bullet-point account of how Mr. Arnold had caught her cheating and punished her for it, so she'd written a letter claiming that he'd seduced one of his eighth-grade students. How she'd forged poems in his handwriting and stuffed them into the locker of a girl she didn't like.

The poster omitted some key points. There was no mention of the girl Mr. Arnold really *had* seduced, and Octavia's name didn't come up once.

Between the front entrance and the Honor Council room, the hallways were electric with gossip. A semi-circle of bodies four deep stood in front of every copy of the poster, reading and snapping pictures for posterity. Even if the posters were down by first period, every word written on them was going to be splattered across the digital universe within hours. And one thing was sure—Livia's campaign for presidency was over.

✳✳✳

"Were you glad it happened, Claudia?"

"Are you kidding? Of course not."

"There's something I have to ask . . ."

"You want to know if I had anything to do with it."

"The thought did cross my mind that you might have."

✳✳✳

This is how I think it happened.

Like most of the students at Imperial Day, Cal hadn't gone to the Griffith School. He'd never known Cassidy Jones or Mr. Arnold. By the time he met Livia, she was on the Honor Council and dating Augustus, and Octavia Resnick was a freshman nobody with bangs that covered half her face.

I hadn't thought about Octavia in three years, not until I saw her making out with Cal in the hallway on Valentine's Day.

It was entirely possible that she didn't need to be persuaded with flowers and love letters. Maybe she'd been waiting since the eighth grade to show somebody the poems that Livia had forged in Mr. Arnold's handwriting.

Eventually, it came out that the morning the posters about Livia went up, Cal had been doing volunteer work at a suicide hotline. It was an airtight alibi, but all that means is that he had help. Chris Gibbons ended up on the Honor Council eventually, so if you're looking for accomplices, that's my guess.

I cannot verify this story. It's the best I have been able to piece together with the facts at hand, and it makes just as much—if not more—sense than to arrive at the conclusion that I had something to do with it.

But if my alternate narrative doesn't satisfy your suspicions, consider this: I hated Livia, but do you really believe I hated her enough to turn the school over to Cal?

XXXI

IT WASN'T BLEEDING AND NONE OF IT WOULD SHOW

A few minutes after Livia's presidential hopes were crushed, my phone buzzed.

Honor Council room. Now.

Well, good morning to you, too, Livia.

The Honor Council room was unlocked. I walked past the holding cell and rounded the corner to find Livia sitting at her desk with her hands wrapped around a steaming KEEP CALM AND CARRY ON mug.

"Did you do this?" she asked, her voice scary-calm.

"No," I said.

The coffee mug went sailing past my ear. As it shattered against the wall, tea and milk streaming down the wall, Livia sprang to her feet, her eyes shining with hate. In three steps, she was across the room and holding a hank of my hair in her fist.

"Don't lie to me, you fucking worm," she said, giving it a tug.

"It wasn't me!" I shrieked in pain, and then Livia hit me in the face.

For a moment she froze, her breathing heavy, her eyes wide, like maybe she'd never hit anyone before. And then something wild came over her face, as if she'd just realized that maybe she'd like to do it again.

Her hands flew, guided more by rage and frustration than precision. She shoved me, pulled my hair, pushed me toward the wall, slapped at my face, punched my stomach. She missed as often as she made contact, but eventually I stopped keeping track. I squeezed my eyes shut and held up my hands to shield my face as I sank down to the floor and curled up in the fetal position. Livia kicked me in the thigh, but lost her balance and staggered toward the wall, catching herself on a desk before dropping to her knees.

I heard the catch in her breath as she hit the floor, then a low moan that gave way to ragged sobbing. I lifted my head and leaned back against the radiator with my legs stretched out in front of me, and I watched Livia cry.

There were only a few places that really hurt. I'd have a bruise on my thigh and another on my shoulder, but I wasn't bleeding and none of it would show.

The first-period bell rang, but neither of us moved.

"Are you going to hide in here all day?" I asked, gasping for breath.

"Fuck you," she said.

She was still on her knees, clinging to the desktop and sobbing, but not because she was sorry.

I could have screamed. I could have gone running down the hall saying that she'd thrown a mug at my head and beaten me up. Someone might even have believed me.

But what was the point?

"I didn't do it," I said, as if saying it one more time was going to make a difference. "If I did, why would I come running up here the second you called me?"

Livia stopped crying and wiped her nose with the back of her hand.

"Why *did* you come?" she asked. Her eyes were swollen to slits.

"I thought you needed help," I said, but that wasn't the whole truth.

I came because I wanted to see her like this, ruined and disgraced.

I went because I *hoped* she needed my help. I wanted to hear her ask for it, and I wanted to tell her no.

Livia pulled herself to her feet and glared down at me.

"You act like you're still the same sad little worm you were at the Griffith School with your limp and your stutter and your wheezing, but you're not. You have everything, and you don't deserve any of it. I *gave* it to you."

"I never asked you to give me anything," I said, craning my neck to look up at her.

Livia kicked me in the side. Then she kicked me in the stomach so hard that it took my breath away.

"Get out of here," she said, kicking me once again, this time in the ribs.

I could already feel my airways closing up as I crawled for the door, staggering to my feet before I stepped out into the empty hallway. Once I was out in the open again and safe, I reached for my inhaler, but my shoulder bag was still sitting next to the radiator in the Honor Council room and I didn't want to go back in there. I hugged the wall and closed my eyes and struggled to catch my breath as my chest tightened up. My guts and ribs ached where Livia had kicked me, and it made it hurt even more to breathe. Suddenly, I realized that I was too far gone and I couldn't make it back to the Honor Council room for my bag before I collapsed. I couldn't call out, so I banged my fist against the row of lockers as I slumped over to the floor and wheezed.

Then I heard a soft thump near my knees and looked up to see my bag sitting next to me. I clawed at the zipper, then dipped my hand inside the bag, pulled out my inhaler, and breathed.

As I fell back against the lockers, I watched Livia walk down the hallway, her heels clicking on the linoleum. When she reached the end, she shoved open the double doors, one with each hand, and let them slam shut behind her.

***

Livia didn't come back to school on Monday, and she was out the rest of the week. She missed the assembly and the speeches. The day of the election, rumors began to circulate that she was taking a leave of absence from Imperial Day, but by then it was too late to change the ballots.

So she got some votes, even if it wasn't nearly enough.

Some people still preferred her to Cal.

"What did you tell Maisie about all of this?"

"The night Maisie got back from Rome, we went to the roof of the parking garage at InVigor again. There, I told her the whole story, from the Queen Mary to the Valentine's Day flowers to the Senate presidential election results to Livia's foot in my ribcage and her subsequent leave of absence from Imperial Day. When it was all over, I felt wrung out, just like I do now, only about a hundred times worse because it was the first time I'd ever said it all out loud at once."

"What did your sister have to say?"

"She said, 'You made a great friend, exposed corruption, enacted change, got a secret admirer, won your Senate reelection, and on top of everything, someone you've always disliked is gone and probably never coming back to Imperial Day. It sounds to me like you got everything you wanted.'

"I was less surprised when Livia hit me in the face. I couldn't answer. All I could do was stare at my sister and think, Were you even listening? How could you think that any of this was what I wanted?"

IMPERIAL DAY ACADEMY BOARD OF COMMISSIONERS v. CLAUDIA McCARTHY

OFFICIAL HEARING TRANSCRIPT

ZELDA PARSONS, HONOR COUNCIL REPRESENTATIVE: Livia and I wanted the same things. That's why she was grooming me to be the president, not Claudia or Esme or any of the other underclassmen.

MR. MATHERS: Did she tell you that?

ZELDA PARSONS: She told me that she admired my work. During election season.

MR. MATHERS: What about your work did Ms. Drusus admire?

ZELDA PARSONS: Elections are not just about convincing voters that you're the best candidate. They are about convincing them that their worst fears about your opponents are all true.

And that can be accomplished by . . .

MR. MATHERS: Ratfucking.

Apologies for the language. It's a term that came up in Ms. McCarthy's testimony.

ZELDA PARSONS: That's a strange word for it. I always thought of what I did more as . . . massaging an election.

Rat massage.

MR. MATHERS: According to Ms. McCarthy, you and she were involved in a physical altercation after this story got out.

LIVIA DRUSUS, FORMER HONOR COUNCIL VICE PRESIDENT: That is a lie. I never even spoke to her. She came into the Honor Council room after the lies about me went up all over the school. I don't know why Claudia came to me. Maybe she wanted to gloat. I was upset. I threw a coffee mug on the floor and some of the shards might have bounced over near where she was standing, but I didn't lay a hand on her.

PART III
THE REIGN OF CAL

THE HONOR COUNCIL

SENIOR CLASS REPRESENTATIVES:
Cal Hurt, President
Rebecca Ibañez

JUNIOR CLASS REPRESENTATIVES:
Esme Kovacs
Zelda Parsons, Vice President

SOPHOMORE CLASS REPRESENTATIVES:
Kian Sarkosian
Maddie Urrea

THE SENATE

SENIOR CLASS REPRESENTATIVES:
Trixie Pappadou
Sarah Reisman

JUNIOR CLASS REPRESENTATIVES:
Hector Estrella, President
Claudia McCarthy, Vice President

SOPHOMORE CLASS REPRESENTATIVES:
Lucy Lin
Veronica Ollenbeck

Two freshman representatives for both the Honor Council and the Senate will be elected during the first two weeks of fall semester.

XXXII

NATURE ABHORS A VACUUM

Those first days back after summer vacation, all anyone could talk about was Livia. Not only had she not finished out the school year; as far as anyone knew, she wasn't coming back for her senior year at all. It was college application suicide, not the kind of thing any Imperial Day student would have done. The fact that it was Livia who had gone and done it was the most shocking thing of all.

People claimed to know all kinds of things about what had happened to her: They said that she'd enrolled in a boarding school back east or fled the country for the same language immersion program Maisie had done. There were alleged sightings at the Grove, the Arclight, the Trader Joe's, but as no one actually claimed to have spoken to her, I disbelieved them all.

Besides, Livia was gone, and I had two very real, very immediate problems that I needed to solve if I was to survive another year at Imperial Day.

The first problem was that I needed not to be in love with Hector Estrella.

"Where the hell have you been for the past two weeks?"

Hector asked, bouncing up to my locker on our first day back. "I missed you."

"Family stuff," I said. "Maisie got back from Rome."

I tried to look casual as I closed my locker door, but my heart was sproinging around my ribcage and my cheeks were flushed and my hands were trembling because Hector had said that he missed me. *He missed me, he missed me, he missed me.*

This situation was untenable. I could not go around love-stricken and sweaty-palmed, threatening to make a fool out of myself every time Hector talked to me. I had work to do. We had a school to run. Something had to be done immediately.

I would be Hector Estrella's vice president, his right-hand woman, and his political manager. I would be his friend, but I'd shove the rest of those feelings down until I'd crushed them to dust.

So a few days later, when I saw Esme Kovacs gazing longingly across the cafeteria in Hector's direction, the way that every other girl with half a brain in her head at Imperial Day did, I said, "She likes you."

Hector reddened, like this was the first time he'd ever realized such a thing was possible. In the year and a half I'd known him, I'd never heard him talk about a girl he liked. I'd never heard rumors about him hooking up with anyone. I'd walked down the halls with Hector enough times, heard the underclassmen shriek and giggle as he went past if he happened to wave or look in their direction.

Sometimes I wondered if Hector's indifference was an act, if he was awkward around girls or pretended not to notice when they swooned over him because he thought it would keep him from turning into his dad. I never asked him, though. Except for that night with Cal at The Last Bookstore, he never talked about his dad at all, and I got the sense that it was a conversational no-fly zone.

Out of all of the girls who batted their eyes in Hector's direction, Esme Kovacs seemed possibly worthy of him. She was smart, pretty, together. She was a former senator, a current Honor Council member. She was nice to everyone. On top of that, I found her to be so boring that I knew I wouldn't be jealous if Hector started dating her.

I mean, look, I knew that I couldn't *make* Hector date anyone, but I thought I could at least give him a nudge in the right direction. Anyway, it was time.

"How do you know she likes me?"

"Because she's looking at you."

"You're looking at me."

"I'm sitting next to you. Where the hell else am I supposed to look?" I said brusquely. "Esme Kovacs has options, though. There are lots of things Esme Kovacs could be looking at, but every time, she picks you. God knows why."

Hector turned pink again and looked down at the cafeteria table, obviously pleased with this information.

So that was one problem taken care of. My second problem was very different.

My second problem was that I needed to figure out how to run the school in close proximity to a raging psychopath without attracting his attention or displeasure.

With Cal, I thought, the trick was to stay out of his way and let him do whatever he wanted. He might make things difficult for us at first, but sooner or later, he'd get bored or distracted and move on to something else. If I could keep Hector and me off of his radar until Christmas, we'd be fine.

What I observed quickly was that Cal didn't do things like Augustus and Ty did. He didn't associate with Honor Council people outside their meeting room on the third floor. At lunch, he sat with rabble-rousers like Chris Gibbons and Astrid Murray, but one or two days a week, he'd pick some random, unsuspecting table and join them. During these forced and terrifying affairs, everyone's sphincters would clench so tightly I'm surprised the effect did not create a black hole in the center of the Imperial Day Academy cafeteria.

The weird thing was, people still liked him. He was always surrounded by people who were drawn to his confidence and swagger and the way he did whatever he wanted. And if he put his hand on your thigh in chemistry lab and wouldn't move it, or pulled your deodorant out of your gym bag, swiped it on his armpits in front of everyone, then handed it back to you, that was just Cal being himself.

At the beginning of the school year, when Cal assumed the Honor Council presidency, we all held our breath, waiting to see what he was going to do with that kind of power.

As it happened, there was a controlled-substance vacuum at Imperial Day at this time. Soren Bieckmann, who had raised tens of thousands of dollars for cancer patients during the previous year's Honor Week, had surprised everyone by reforming. The cynics assumed that it was temporary, that it was a last-ditch effort to get into a good college, but whatever the case, you could not get so much as a crushed-up Adderall off of him. And as nature abhors a vacuum, Chris Gibbons stepped up so that the students of Imperial Day would not have to do without.

Interestingly, this development only seemed to invigorate Chris and Cal's friendship so by the time Cal's tenure as Honor

Council president began, it was already a far cry from the puritanical days of Augustus and all of his nosing around off-campus parties for underage drinking. Where Augustus and Livia set out to have the school drug dealer expelled, Cal became his best friend.

The first two weeks of school passed quietly enough, though, and I lulled myself into the belief that maybe Cal had only been interested in the Honor Council because it would allow him to do whatever he wanted without consequences.

While that part was certainly true, Cal's vision was more far-reaching.

He wanted what Hector and I had built. He wanted empire.

How it started was, I went to my locker at the end of the day and opened it and a note fluttered out onto the floor. I picked it up, unfolded it, and read:

CAL IS TAKING OVER HONOR WEEK. ANNOUNCEMENT TOMORROW. THOUGHT YOU SHOULD KNOW.

Before the words of the anonymous note could fully sink in, my phone was out and I was calling Hector. Because he knew me, because he knew that my stutter made me dread being on the phone and that I would only have called under the most dire of circumstances, he answered right away.

"Hector, w-w-where a-a-are you?"

"I'm . . . in the parking lot. Just leaving actually."

There was a weird hitch in his voice. At first I thought it was because he was surprised to hear my voice over the phone, but then I realized.

"You're with someone," I said.

"I, uh—"

I could actually hear his ears turning red.

"Are you free later tonight?" I asked. "We need to talk."

In most relationships, the phrase *We need to talk* means *Something is wrong with us*. With Hector and me, it meant *Something is wrong with the Senate*.

Whatever cute-girl spell had rendered Hector moony and red-eared was broken the moment he knew this was Senate business.

"What happened?" Hector asked.

"I can't talk about it," I said. "Not if you're with the person I think you're with."

There was a pause, then Hector said, "I am."

"Call me back this evening when you're alone."

Apparently, that wasn't soon enough for Hector. By the time I got home, he was already there, sitting on my front porch, his car parked in the driveway, no sign of Esme.

"What's going on?" he asked, leaping to his feet as I came up the driveway. I hadn't thought I sounded serious enough on the phone to warrant a house call, but then again, this was the Senate we were talking about.

I showed Hector the note, and immediately he burst out a rapid-fire line of questions I didn't have the answers to: Who sent this? What do they mean, *take over Honor Week?* How? What should we do?

"I don't know. I don't know. I don't know. And finally, and in sum, I don't know," I said when he was done. "I don't know what any of it means."

"How can he take it away from us?" Hector asked.

I nodded in agreement. "It's ours. It was your idea. We started it. We did all the work. Do you think Cal wants to do all that work? He does not."

I explained my theory to Hector about how Cal would probably lose interest in trying to be in charge of anything, but by the time I got to the part about how everything would be back to normal by Christmas, I could tell Hector's brain was working in a different direction.

"Maybe we need to remind people that we started it. Maybe that's the way to stop him."

"What are you talking about, Hector?"

"I need to go home," Hector said, getting up from the porch.

"What are you going to do?"

"I don't know."

This was a lie, and I knew it. Even if the plan wasn't fully formed in his head, even if I knew he'd be staring at his ceiling at two in the morning hashing it out, I knew he had some idea.

"Hector, we don't even know who gave me the note. We don't even know if it's true."

If he'd told me then what he had planned, I would have stayed up all night helping him. Or I would have stayed up all night trying to talk him out of it.

Instead, I did my AP Psychology homework and read half of *Beowulf*, then went to bed.

The next morning, I was eating toast and looking at my phone when I saw something that made me aspirate crumbs.

Between 1:46 and 2:37 a.m., Hector had posted the following message on every social network he could think of:

Big announcement tomorrow about Imperial Day Honor Week!!! It's a surprise, but it's going to be even bigger and better than last year!!!

If there was one thing that made Hector Estrella more awkward than girls, it was social media. Give him a microphone and an audience, give him five minutes and a face-to-face conversation, and he could convince you of anything. Give him a Facebook account, and you'd swear he was an octogenarian who'd just learned the internet existed.

The number of exclamation points varied, but by and large, it was the same message posted everywhere. When I checked my Imperial Day email, it was even worse. Hector had sent a mass email about his big announcement to the entire student body at 3:19 a.m. It was punchy and unhinged and about five paragraphs too long.

Curse your insomnia, Hector Estrella, I thought. *You desperate, beautiful fool.*

And then, before I could text Hector to ask what he'd been thinking, all of a sudden, there was a message from Cal in my inbox. It read:

Thanks to the Senate for drumming up a little suspense . . . Honor Week was great last year, but we thought it would be even better if it came back where it belongs—under the leadership of the Honor Council.

More details to come, but it's going to be excellent.

Go to sleep, Estrella.

That was it. The first time Cal wanted something that was ours, he just reached out and took it. Hell, we practically handed it to him. The worst part was, I could tell it had been fun for him, thwarting us, watching us flail. I knew that he'd do it again for no other reason.

Whoever put that message in my locker may have thought they were doing me a favor. Instead, we'd ended up doing the very thing I'd tried to avoid. Hector and I hadn't kept our heads down. We'd gotten on Cal's radar in the worst way possible.

XXXIII

Ask Someone

Now it was Zelda Parsons walking through the halls of Imperial Day with fingers wrapped around Cal's arm, giggling and batting his hand away when he tried to grab a fistful of her ass like it was his due.

Zelda Parsons, of all people. It was like Livia had never existed.

If Zelda had dressed like Livia before, now she looked more like the girls Cal usually tormented with his attentions. She'd added silvery-blonde highlights to her hair, did a smoky eye, and wore tight jeans. She did hold on to the horn-rimmed glasses though.

The main thing that was different about Cal's Honor Week was that it was mostly about Cal. He and Zelda presided over every event like royalty, smiling for every camera they saw. Hector had abolished the car wash because he thought it was insulting to the teachers. Cal took things one step further. He assigned a team of Imperial Day students to each teacher, and for the duration of Honor Week, each team was required to get the teacher's lunch, clean up the classroom, run multiple-choice tests through the Scantron machines, carry bags out to their cars. Cal said he did this to engender goodwill between educators and students, and also because he thought it might encourage the teachers to participate.

The funny thing about the word *encourage* is that people often use it when the word they're really looking for is *force*. I've always found that the easiest way to find out what the person "encouraging" you really means is to refuse to do it.

Jesse Nichols, stupid as ever even in his junior year, was assigned to Ms. Yee, who very politely but firmly stated that she had no need of his services. Jesse Nichols went away and that was the end of it. Except the next day, Cal went to see her and asked why she'd insulted Jesse when he was just trying to be helpful.

"It isn't necessary," Ms. Yee said.

"Will you be helping out at the Homecoming dance on Friday?"

"I'm afraid not," Ms. Yee said.

"It would mean a lot to your students if you were there," Cal said.

"I'm not entirely sure it would be the best use of my time," Ms. Yee said, or at least that was how the conversation was reported later at her hearing.

While Cal couldn't exactly *make* you do Honor Week, he could pay attention to whether you showed up or not, then let you know he'd filed that information away for future reference.

Of course, my Honor Week activities—or lack thereof— were also the subject of his scrutiny. I was getting books for first period when suddenly, Cal was there, leaning up against my locker and blowing spearmint-gum breath in my face.

"Have I done something to offend you, Claudia?"

How to even begin to answer that question? I said nothing, but shook my head.

"When the Senate president and vice president can't even be bothered to put in an appearance at Children's Hospital, it sends a bad message," he said, peering inside my locker.

He studied the pictures I had hung up inside the door, peeling off one of Eleanor Roosevelt and putting it in his pocket. There was a tube of ChapStick on the top shelf of the locker. He twisted off the cap and applied it to his lips before putting it back. The whole time he did this, he hummed a tuneless little song to himself, like he'd momentarily forgotten I was there.

Why did he do it? Why did he do the things he did? I've had a lot of time to think about it, and I think I understand now. Augustus wanted a legacy. Ty wanted people to respect him. Livia wanted power. And Cal? I think Cal did the things he did because it amused him. It amused him to be in charge. It amused him to have people do what he said. It amused him to annoy people, to play with them, to hurt them. He enjoyed all of it equally, and by the time we realized how much he enjoyed it, we were all much too scared to stop him.

"We had a lot of Homecoming dance s-s-stuff to take care of," I said.

That was really what Cal meant when he said Honor Week would be bigger and better. He meant he was going to steal Hector's ideas, take all the credit for himself, then top the whole thing off by throwing a dance just like old times. The real insult was, Cal took over everything, but left all the grunt work to us. While Cal got his picture in the *LA Times* petting stingrays at Heal the Bay, we were trying to find a DJ and bribe freshmen into stringing up decorations.

"You and the Mexican are going to Homecoming, though, right?"

How does every offensive remark start? With the jerk who wants to make it looking over his shoulder to make sure nobody within ass-kicking distance is listening.

"He has a name, asshole."

"A-a-a-asshole. You're funny, Claudia," Cal said, chuckling as he mocked my stutter. Apparently, the looking-over-the-shoulder thing didn't apply where I was concerned. "So, are you two going?"

This would actually be my first dance at Imperial Day. Last year's had been cancelled, and it never would have occurred to me to go my freshman year. This year was different. As Senate VP, Honor Week co-founder, and the person assigned to deliver the check to the caterers at precisely 11:15 p.m., there was no getting out of it.

I didn't actually own a dress. My mother had stopped trying to make me wear them when I was about ten. If anyone asked, I told them it was because my legs were two different lengths and dresses called attention to that, but that wasn't strictly true. When I wore a dress, I felt like I was wearing a bad costume, one that wasn't fooling anyone. It didn't make me feel pretty. Nothing did, but when I put on jeans and my political campaign shirts—or even my dress shirts and neckties—I felt like myself. I hadn't quite figured out how I was going to feel like myself at a Homecoming dance.

I was thinking about that when Cal asked if Hector and I were going to the dance, so without thinking, I answered, "Not together."

"Horrors," Cal said, gripping his t-shirt in his fists. "C-C-Claudia and her Latin lover on the outs! Alert TMZ!"

Cal's insults always did operate on so many horrible levels. First, there was the way he managed to say at least one racist thing whenever he mentioned Hector, and then act like his progressive white-boy irony made the whole thing hilarious. Second, there was the fact that he never said Hector's name, like he didn't know it or couldn't be bothered to learn it. Third was how obvious it was that he didn't even care—and acted like, *Who would?*—whether Hector and I were going to the dance together or not. Fourth was his acting like the relationship he'd imagined us to be carrying on was funny, either because it was ludicrous and sad that anyone would want me, or because we were two losers who'd found one another so we could be losers together. Possibly it was both of these things at the same time. When Cal insulted you, he was always thorough about it.

At lunch I found Hector and pulled him aside. "Cal is . . . displeased with us."

"What? Is our Honor Week homage to his greatness insufficiently groveling? Does he want us to play with his balls a little bit, too?"

"Something like that," I said, laughing ruefully. "He wants to make sure we're going to the Homecoming dance."

Hector looked across the cafeteria to the table where Esme Kovacs was sitting with her friends, all of whom would have been described first and foremost as "nice."

"Yeah, we're going," Hector said, clasping at the back of his neck with his hand like he was sheepish about this, like there was something embarrassing about going to a dance with Esme Kovacs. I had no doubt she would be a vision in petal pink with freshly manicured nails and perfectly coiffed curls.

"How about you?" Hector asked, which caught me off guard.

"I don't think I have a choice," I said, but that wasn't what he was asking about, I knew. "I'm not going with anyone."

Hector looked thoughtful for a moment, then said, "You should ask someone."

"Like who?" I scoffed.

"Like whoever you want to."

"But . . ." I was about to go on about how no one would want to go to a dance with me and I didn't know who to ask anyway, but Hector held up his hand to stop me.

"What if instead of saying whatever horrible thing you're about to say about yourself, you just asked someone? You're smart, you're interesting. You're a good conversationalist. Not now, maybe, but in general."

"Why do you care?"

"Because I'm tired of watching you tear yourself down. I know you think that nobody would want to go with you, but I'm saying that you're wrong."

Oh god, I thought. *He knows. He knows I almost kissed him last year. He knows I was in love with him.*

Or worse, what if he felt guilty? In the couple of weeks since he'd gotten together with Esme, I'd been spending a lot more time by myself. No more Saturday night treks to The Last Bookstore or eating greasy slices of pizza on Hollywood Boulevard. This was probably his way of prodding me out of my solitude so he could enjoy going to the dance without worrying about whether I was going to be okay.

"I do not tear myself down. I would be a lovely Homecoming date," I told Hector, my chin raised haughtily.

"Then ask somebody to go with you."

"I will."

Hector knew me too well to let it go at that.

"I dare you," he said. As coercion techniques went, I was a sucker for this one every time.

I scanned the cafeteria until my eye fell on the first person with whom I could imagine spending an evening at a high school dance without actively wishing for death.

Soren Bieckmann looked surprised to see me when I presented myself at his lunch table and told him I thought we should go to the dance together.

"Are you serious?" he asked.

"Yes," I said. "I am straight-up legitimately asking you."

"It doesn't sound like you're asking."

"Sorry," I said. In my nervousness, I might have been a little brusque. "Let me try again. Would you be interested in going to Homecoming with me?"

"Why?"

"Because I need a date, and I think going with you might not be without its merits."

"You know I don't do that anymore, right?"

That explained why he'd sounded so suspicious of my motives. Poor guy, I thought, realizing things like this must happen to him all the time.

"I don't want drugs, Soren," I explained. "All I want is not to go by myself."

And that's how we ended up going.

XXXIV

Raw, Naked Feelings

In the days leading up to Homecoming, the anonymous notes in the blocky all-caps handwriting started to appear in my locker again.

HELEN NORWOOD: SUSPENDED—3 DAYS

EDWIN STIRATT: BANNED FROM EXTRA-CURRICULARS—2 MONTHS

LETICIA PURCELL: CAFETERIA DUTY—1 WEEK

The Honor Council punished lots of people. None of these sentences was particularly tough, but it didn't take a genius to see what Deep Throat was suggesting: that maybe the Honor Council was punishing people who hadn't done anything wrong.

Deep Throat—that was what I'd started calling this person who left notes in my locker, in my head anyway. It was the nickname those *Washington Post* journalists Bob Woodward and Carl Bernstein gave to their high-ranking, deep-cover informant when they were reporting on the Watergate scandal.

Because that was who my informant was, right? That was who it had to be, someone inside Cal's twisted regime, just trying to make sure that someone on the outside knew what was going on.

Which one of them was it, though?

Rebecca Ibañez was no insider, having clawed her way back onto the Council after losing her seat the previous year. However, I wondered if that fact would make her less, rather than more, inclined to leak classified information. Esme would have taken the information to Hector, not me, and if it was Zelda Parsons, then her cover was even deeper than the real Deep Throat's, who had worked for Nixon but stopped short of actually dating him. Kian Sarkosian actually seemed to be friends with Cal, so that left Maddie Urrea, she of the alleged quinceañera after-party that Cal had been threatening to crash, and two freshmen, about whom I knew nothing other than their names. And then there was the possibility that Cal himself was trying to mess with me.

Not only did I not know who Deep Throat was; I wasn't sure what he or she wanted me to do with any of this information.

Not knowing what course to take, I did nothing, except worry about it. On top of that, I worried about all the last-minute details Hector and I had to take care of—the DJ who'd cancelled at the last minute, the impossibility of getting anybody who owned a food truck to reply to a text and let you know if they were going to show up.

On top of all of that, I worried about my date with Soren.

The only thing I knew about him was that he'd once been a drug dealer and addict, but now supposedly wasn't. He probably found politics and history horribly boring, and I didn't know anything about surfing or video games. There was an extremely good chance we would have nothing to talk about.

When I found him waiting for me outside of third period the day before the dance, I assumed he'd also had second thoughts and was going to back out. Instead, he asked if he could pick me up at six so we could go to dinner beforehand.

This seemed like overkill for a date I'd entered into on a dare, but I said sure.

"What color is your dress?"

"I'm not wearing a dress."

"Then what color corsage should I get you?"

Was this what formal dances did to people? Was this how they acted? Was it normal? I still don't exactly know, but I had to admit, it was strange and nice. No matter how nice, though, I wasn't wearing a corsage.

"You should donate the money to science."

"How about I buy you tacos instead?" Soren suggested, and I mentally congratulated myself on having had the good sense to ask him out in the first place. Since Soren was going full-on gentleman, I decided to make an effort, too. A dress and a corsage and a manicure were still out of the question, but so, too, was my JOHN MCCAIN IS MY HOMEBOY t-shirt.

Eventually, what I decided to wear was a pair of black satin cigarette pants with a sleeveless tuxedo shirt and a bowtie. I parted my hair and slicked it to the side, and in a nod to the festive spirit of the evening, I put on some silver eye shadow and body glitter. The result was a kind of androgynous quirk that most people probably wouldn't have called "pretty," but as I turned from side to side in the mirror, there was no denying that it worked on me.

My parents told me how nice I looked, then found reasons to hover around the front door, waiting for a glimpse of my Homecoming date. It made me nervous. For the first time in a while, I saw my parents as other people might see them. I was used to my father's coffee-stained teeth and mad-scientist hair. I found my mother's nasal Midwestern intonations to be somewhat endearing, but I was not sure what Soren would make of them.

When Soren arrived, though, I didn't care what he thought about any of us. He was dressed in faded cargo shorts and a threadbare Fugazi t-shirt, carrying a giant plastic bag, and his eyes were bloodshot.

"I'm sorry, I'm sorry, I'm sorry," he said when I opened the door.

"Are you, like, on something?" I asked, inspecting his pupils.

"Fuck no," he said, shaking his head for emphasis. "It's salt water. I was surfing all afternoon and my phone died and I totally lost track of time."

He held up the plastic bag, which I realized was a dry cleaning bag with hangers sticking out of it. "Can I change clothes here?"

"Bathroom's down the hall," I said.

As Soren disappeared down the hall, I noticed my parents whispering to each other behind their hands.

"What?" I asked them.

My mother straightened up defensively. "Are you going to introduce us to your friend?"

"Once he's dressed."

A few minutes later, Soren emerged in a black pinstripe suit, purple shirt, and a purple and navy blue necktie that I seriously coveted for my own collection. He'd combed his hair and it looked like he'd applied eyedrops, too.

"Ta da," he said, soft-shoeing down the hallway.

"Soren, these are my parents, Tessa and Jason McCarthy."

As Soren shook their hands, I saw my father clear his throat and adjust his posture so that all present would notice and recognize that he was the Father of a Teenage Daughter.

"Young man, have you been drinking?" he asked, trying to sound stern and paternal.

"I'm eight months sober, so no," Soren said, unrattled by my father's somewhat rude, if reasonable, question. "There is nothing stronger than Peet's coffee in my bloodstream."

My parents did not have shit to say to that. I don't think they felt much better about sending me out into the night with an 18-year-old who attended AA meetings, but at least they seemed to appreciate his sincerity.

"You like Peet's?" I asked, cautiously optimistic we might have something to talk about after all.

We kicked off our Homecoming dinner date with two large cups of Major Dickason's Blend, followed by tacos at a restaurant that was squeezed between a laundromat and a massage parlor. When we were both on our third al pastor, we'd run out of small talk and curiosity finally got the better of me, so I just asked the thing I really wanted to know.

"What happened to you?"

I might have found a more graceful, tactful way to inquire, but Soren didn't seem to mind. He took a big swig from his horchata, wiped the milk mustache with the back of his hand, and said, "I got tired of hating myself."

I studied Soren with a seriousness that probably looked like scowling to him. It wasn't what I'd expected him to say. Soren didn't seem like a person who hated himself.

"After Honor Week last year, I got that little taste of what it felt like to do good things, and I liked it. I liked having people look at me in a different way. No, that makes it sound like—I didn't really care what other people thought. Like, I just wanted to be good some more. And instead of covering up my feelings by getting fucked up, I just felt them. And because I didn't have drugs anymore, the people who stayed around were the people who really cared about me."

His eyes shone while he talked, and I looked down at my half-eaten rice and beans, embarrassed for him. Did they make you talk like that in AA?

"Is this making you uncomfortable?" Soren asked, and I felt horrible. He'd had this conversation a few times, I guessed, and had probably gotten good at telling when people wanted to hit the eject button.

A little voice in my head cleared its throat and said, *Why did you ask if you didn't want to know? He's a person, not a sideshow attraction.*

"It's not that," I said quietly. "It's just really real is all."

"I'd rather be honest. If people can't handle it, that's cool. I just like knowing up front whether we're going to be happy chit-chat friends or what."

"I can handle it," I said.

"I'm glad," Soren said. "Because, like, for example, I didn't used to like you at all. I even thought you snitched me out to the Honor Council once."

My eyes got big. I'd almost forgotten about that day when I was hiding in the storage closet during Soren's Honor Council hearing. At the time, I'd speculated that it was Cal or Lola Stephenson who'd reported him to the Honor Council, but now I knew that Soren had developed his own theories on the subject.

"You thought *I* did that?" I asked.

"I don't think it *now*," he explained. "But you can see how it might have looked at the time, right?"

I nodded. As rats went, I certainly looked like a prime suspect. My sister had been on the Honor Council. I'd sat with half of them at lunch that year. If I'd been Soren, I certainly wouldn't have invited me to the *Little Shop of Horrors* Naked Cast Party.

"What changed your mind?" I asked.

"Because why would you snitch to those people when you don't give a fuck what they think of you?"

A stupid half-grin blossomed on my face as I basked in Soren's compliment. It was the nicest thing anyone had said to me since the note in my Valentine's Day bouquet. I'd spent a year in the shadow of the Honor Council, of Livia, even of Maisie, but now I was out from under it. That was how it felt anyway, so it was a relief to learn that an objective, outside party thought so, too.

"I have a question for you," Soren said, piling the used napkins and straw wrappers on his paper plate. "Why did you ask me to Homecoming?"

That stupid Valentine's Day bouquet. Whenever I remembered it, all I could think about was how I'd almost laid those raw, naked feelings down at Hector's feet and only just stopped in time. The memory made me cringe. I wanted to run away from it, but when I tried the thought of Hector giving Esme a pretty corsage, then taking her to dinner someplace with real silverware and plates, and as nice a time as I was having with Soren—and I was!—all I could think about was—

"Because I'm in love with Hector Estrella," I blurted out. "That's why I asked you to Homecoming."

The words hung in the air between us. It was the first time I'd spoken them aloud to anyone, even Maisie. Afterwards, I couldn't say anything else, but just sat there in a state of shock while Soren looked at me, a bemused smile on his face.

"Does he know?"

"No."

"Then you should tell him."

"He has a girlfriend."

"It's high school," Soren said, the first note of cynicism I'd heard from him all night. "Give it a month."

"I'm glad I asked you, though," I said. "I'm glad we're doing this."

"Me too."

Maybe tomorrow I would go back to acting like I didn't have feelings, but in the spirit of the evening, I decided to embrace sincerity.

Given what happened later that night, this would prove to be entirely the wrong frame of mind.

XXXV

THE KIND OF FACE YOU MIGHT MAKE AT A FIRING SQUAD

Stuffed with coffee, al pastor tacos, and horchata, Soren and I made our way toward Imperial Day Academy. With the austere budget we'd been given, it was the only place we could afford to have the dance. Still, Hector and I had done a smashing job with what we had to work with. We moved the dance from the gym to the courtyard, which I couldn't believe had never been suggested before. That alone made the whole affair exponentially less grim.

We'd enlisted a group of volunteers to fish every last turtle out of the pond and put them in a tank in the main office for the night. I'd made the decision to move them, not wanting to see any of the little creatures accidentally trampled to death on my watch. I made sure everyone washed their hands before and afterwards, that the turtles were not over-handled, that no one threatened to swing them by the tail or put them down the back of anyone else's shirt. I made sure that every last one of them was accounted for when we wheeled the tank down to the main office.

We'd strung fairy lights up everywhere, convinced Chris Gibbons to DJ for free as his Honor Week tribute, and hired some food trucks to come out with tamales, grilled cheese, kogi tacos, and ice cream sandwiches: basically, the four LA food groups washed down with aguas frescas ladled out of big plastic containers.

It looked amazing. When I saw Hector and Esme standing across the courtyard, I was so excited about what we'd done that I forgot about the confession I'd made to Soren and dragged him over to them.

"Who plans the best motherfucking Homecoming dance?" I asked as I bounced up to Hector, half-singing and half-dancing, the best I could manage of either.

"*We* plan the best motherfucking Homecoming dance," Hector replied, fist-bumping me before looking sheepishly at Esme, who glared at him. I couldn't tell if she disapproved of Hector swearing or of Hector talking to another girl, even if it happened to be me.

She was wearing a hot-pink strapless mini-dress and strappy silver heels. Looking at those shoes, all I could think was that if she stepped in a sewer grate, her ankle would snap like a twig.

"Hi, Esme. You look pretty," Soren said, and the sour look on her face turned sweet.

"Thanks, Soren," she said.

Hector put his arm around Esme's waist, then asked, "Can you do a walkthrough of the food trucks, make sure the fire marshal isn't going to shut us down?"

"Want to come with?" I asked Soren.

"I could eat," he said.

"You just ate half a dozen tacos," I said. "I watched you do it."

"I'm just saying I could eat again is all."

As we set off to inspect the food trucks, I realized there had been something off about my conversation with Hector.

Ordinarily, he would have done the walkthrough himself. He'd let you help with things if you asked, but Hector Estrella would never ask you to do something he could do much better himself.

Tonight was different. Tonight Senate President Hector Estrella was on a date.

"You *guys* have fun," Esme called after us, and maybe I imagined the extra emphasis she put on the word *guys*, but I do not think that I did. For a split second, I wondered if maybe I should have just sucked it up and worn a stupid strapless dress like everybody else.

But then Soren slipped an arm over my shoulder in a way that was friendly, yet intimate, and whispered, "That girl does *not* like you."

I smiled and put my arm around his waist as we headed toward the food trucks. No one had ever viewed me as a threat before. For some reason, this pleased me.

At the grilled cheese truck, we ran into Cal and Zelda Parsons, who was wearing a dress that made Esme Kovacs look like a nun. It was spangly and silver and backless, and I was not entirely sure what was keeping it affixed to her body. It was the first time I'd ever seen her without her horn-rimmed glasses. I waved at her. She squinted back.

"That's a nice suit you're wearing, McCarthy," Cal said, nodding to Soren. "Is this your beard?"

"I'm her date," Soren said, and this seemed to shut Cal up, about what I was wearing anyway.

Cal surveyed the hallway, the decorations, the food trucks, the courtyard. I couldn't help joining in, proud all over again of how good it looked.

"So, this dance . . . ," Cal said, his lip curled, "was clearly planned by a Mexican."

"Dude," said Soren at the same time I said, "The fuck?"

Zelda Parsons stared off into the middle distance like her body was present in our conversation but her mind was somewhere else entirely. With his proclivities toward the easily manipulated, I guess I wasn't totally surprised Cal was drawn to her.

"We rented a penthouse at the Standard afterwards, if you'd like something to eat that isn't served in a cardboard boat. It's fifty dollars a person. Zelda is collecting the money. Soren, perhaps you can bring a snack to share with the rest of the class?" Cal mimed smoking a joint, then threw an elbow into Soren's ribs, just as Mrs. Lester walked past, making her rounds on chaperone duty. Ever since her failure to contain the P-P-P-PLEDGE incident during the election assembly my freshman year, I did tend to seek her out any time I needed faculty for an undesirable task, such as, say, chaperoning a Homecoming dance. To her credit, she always agreed and never quite had the nerve to look me in the eye, so I suppose being disappointed by her was not without its upsides.

"Everything in order, Ms. McCarthy? Mr Hurt?" she asked.

"Just kidding around, miss," Cal said. "Everything's perfect."

Then, as soon as Mrs. Lester had moved on, Cal turned to Zelda, reached up her dress and pinched her thigh.

"Come on," he said. "We're done here."

Robotically, Zelda turned and followed after him.

"What's got into him?" Soren asked, as they walked away.

"That's how he always is."

A slow smile spread over Soren's face. Then he started to laugh, and once he got going, he couldn't stop. He doubled over, clutching onto the back of a folding chair to keep from slumping over on the pavement.

"What's so funny?"

"I am no longer a person Cal has to be nice to." When he caught his breath again, he added, "I mean, I always suspected he was a piece of shit, but he used to make far more of an effort to hide it around me."

I still had my eye on Zelda Parsons, tottering away on her high heels. If Livia could have seen her now, she would have found her to be beneath contempt. Was that what had caused this, I wondered? Was the disgrace of her former mentor so shattering that it had completely destroyed Zelda? Stranger things had happened, I supposed, and for less cause. What was she getting out of it, though? Being Livia's flunkie was certainly less degrading than being Cal's.

Soren got a helping of kogi tacos and an ice cream sandwich while I checked in with the vendors. Then we circled back toward the courtyard, where attendance had almost doubled in our absence. What had looked like a perfectly pleasant gathering a few minutes before was now a legitimate party in full jubilant swing.

The sophomore senators, Lucy Lin and Veronica Ollenbeck, started a conga line around the courtyard while Chris Gibbons spun records competently, even though he looked like a self-important prig while he did it. In the hallways, there were long lines for the photo booth, the caricature artist, the aguas frescas. The fact that we hadn't had enough money to hire a security guard in addition to the four teachers who were chaperoning nagged at me, but everybody seemed to be in a good mood, having a good time. There was nothing to worry about, I told myself. People danced, they ate, they talked to their friends, and then they went out to dance again.

Soren pointed toward the courtyard conga line and asked, "Want to?"

"Sure," I said, caught up in the moment enough to forget about my limp. Once around the courtyard wasn't going to kill me. I grabbed Soren's hips and fell in line. It was my victory lap.

The song ended and the line dispersed as Chris Gibbons put on a slow song. People paired off, and gradually, the dance floor filled up with swaying couples. Soren held out his hand to me and I took it. Everyone around us mashed their bodies together like horny music-box toppers, but Soren put one hand around my waist and held the other and led me in a proper waltz, slow and simple enough for me to keep up without stumbling.

I had to reach up to touch his shoulder. He was almost a foot taller than me, but I couldn't help thinking that we looked good. I liked him, and we were having such a good time that when I saw Hector and Esme dancing with their fingers entwined, their foreheads pressed together, eyes closed, mouths mumbling unheard endearments, I almost felt happy for Hector. Almost.

Then the music came to an end and while the next song faded in, one wall of the courtyard lit up. Sappy instrumental music began to play and a picture of Cal ladling soup at a homeless shelter appeared on the wall. For the next five minutes, Chris Gibbons played a slideshow of Honor Week. It had been carefully curated. Neither Hector nor I appeared in any of the pictures. No senator at all did, even though they'd done just as much as the Honor Council members and planned a whole dance on top of it. Cal was in at least half the pictures. At the end of the song, there was a smattering of polite applause from people who wanted to get back to dancing.

"Is everyone having a good time?" Chris Gibbons asked. The crowd humored him with a murmur in the affirmative.

"Okay, this next part is a little bit cheesy, but we've had a slideshow and Christmas lights and fruit punch, so I say let's go with it. Embrace the cheese. Could I get Hector Estrella and Claudia McCarthy to come up here?"

I went. What else could I do? Hector met me at the front and whispered, "What's going on?" before we joined Chris at the microphone. I shrugged, and Hector frowned at me like I should be more concerned that we didn't know what was happening at the dance we'd planned. In hindsight, he was right.

"What's this all about?" Hector asked into the microphone Chris handed him with a nervous chuckle.

"Very funny," Chris said, producing two envelopes. He handed one to Hector and one to me. "You can't have Homecoming without a king and queen, right?"

For one horrifying moment, I thought he meant to crown Hector and me king and queen right there, but then I realized whatever was about to happen would be much, much more humiliating than that.

"I don't remember voting," Hector said into the mic, still friendly, still chuckling, but with just a hint of misgiving in his voice.

"A panel of students, faculty, and staff did the voting. It was meant to be a surprise," Chris said, adding with saccharine glee, "Surprise!"

A murmur went through the crowd because at this point, they didn't care about the legitimacy of the election. They just wanted to know whose names were in the envelopes.

Chris Gibbons threw an arm around each of us and said, "Let's all give a big hand to everyone who made this great night possible. And while we're at it, everyone who made this great week possible, this great school possible. It's all of *you*. So give yourselves a big round of applause."

Hector and I exchanged a look, and I knew that I'd get an earful from Crabby Hector later that night. Like, would it have killed him to thank us by name? Or at least to thank the whole Senate for busting our asses for the past month? But then Chris Gibbons said, "Claudia, why don't you do the honors?"

Chris Gibbons was our DJ. We'd hired him, and absolutely none of this was in the plan we'd discussed. So, whose plan was it? I didn't have to look very hard to find out. No further, in fact, than the name in the envelope Chris Gibbons had handed to me.

"The Homecoming King of Imperial Day Academy is . . ."

Chris Gibbons forced the mic into my hands and played a drumroll. My classmates stared at me expectantly at first, then with impatience. Hector watched to see what I was going to do because we knew that there had never been any vote taken to determine the names in these envelopes. But if I didn't open mine, someone else would.

I opened the envelope, looked at the slip of paper inside to confirm what I already knew, and stuttered into the mic, "C-C-Cal."

Applause tore through the courtyard, loud and raucous this time, as Cal ran from the back, high-fiving everyone in his path, and joined us in front of the DJ booth. He pumped both of his fists and let out a whoop, then jumped up in the air and clicked his heels together like a leprechaun because, sure, why not.

Cal took the microphone from me and said, "Who's my queen, Estrella? Don't keep the people waiting."

Apparently he could remember Hector's name if there were other people watching.

Hector's face went stony as he opened the envelope. Cal shoved the microphone in front of his face and hopped from one foot to the other, antsy for his next photo op to get underway.

When Hector drew the embossed notecard out of the envelope, his face crumpled, though he recovered so quickly I'm not sure if anyone spotted it besides me and Cal, who was expecting it. Hector pasted on a fake smile as he looked out into the crowd and said, "I'm so happy for you, Esme. Come on up here."

Esme began to thread her way through the crowd, but in her three-inch heels, it was slow going. Cal dashed out to meet her halfway, swept her up in his arms, and carried her to the front, where at least a dozen people took their picture before he finally put her down. Chris Gibbons produced two crowns and handed them to Hector and me. I put the tiara on Esme's head while Hector gritted his teeth and crowned Cal.

Chris Gibbons crowed into the microphone, "Ladies and gentlemen of the Imperial Day Academy, I give you your king and queen."

More wild applause as Cal kissed Esme on the cheek, then picked her up in his arms again like she was something he owned, and now Hector and I were standing awkwardly in the middle of cheers that were not for us. Hector was looking at Esme and Cal like he wanted to be ill. If my girlfriend looked that happy about having Cal's hands on her thighs, I guess I'd feel ill, too.

"Come on," I said, taking his hand and leading him back into the crowd before he made a face that someone other than me could decipher.

Once we were safely in the hallway, almost deserted now that everyone had filed into the courtyard to celebrate Imperial Day's royalty, Hector's face registered the full shock of what had happened.

Yes, it was just a stupid dance, but the truth of what had just happened was too big to ignore: Cal had schemed his way onto the Honor Council, ratfucked his way to the presidency, then crowned himself king of the damn school. Because he could.

The whole thing had been orchestrated to deliver maximum insult. Having us up there to announce the so-called results like we'd had something to do with them. The fact that out of all the girls at Imperial Day he could have chosen, including his own girlfriend, he'd picked Esme, then made Hector send her running into his arms.

"Did she know this was going to happen?" Hector looked up at me, his eyes pleading.

I wanted to give him a hug, and not even one that had ulterior motives in it. I just felt bad for him.

"Of course not," I said. Esme had looked happy enough with that crown on her head, but I couldn't help wondering what was going through her mind when Cal picked her up and lifted her onto the stage. Did she want to be there? Was she just smiling because that was what you were supposed to do when people were watching you?

Before I could say more, Soren appeared with a look on his face that said he knew something was the matter even if he didn't understand its full scope.

"I can't find Zelda Parsons anywhere. I don't know, maybe you want to . . ." Soren made a gesture like he was patting someone on the back. "Or something?"

And then there was poor Zelda Parsons. When Cal scooped Esme up in his arms, I'd been so focused on Hector that I'd almost forgotten that Zelda had to watch it happen, too. What's more, she had to watch everyone in the whole school watch her watch it happen. While I did not consider Zelda Parsons a friend, neither did I think of her as my enemy, so I left Soren and Hector and went looking for her. The hall was empty, but there was a bathroom at the end of it, the eternal refuge of girls crying in public places. I opened the door, and sure enough, I could hear someone sobbing in the last stall.

"Zelda?" I called out.

The snuffling stopped, but there was no reply.

"Zelda? It's Claudia."

A long pause, then I heard her voice from the stall, teary and cold all at the same time.

"I know who it is."

I suppose there weren't a lot of people at Imperial Day with a voice that sounded like mine.

"Are you okay?"

"No, Claudia. I am not okay."

One minute her quasi-boyfriend, or whatever Cal was, had been reaching his hand up her dress; the next he was sweeping Esme Kovacs up in his arms. That there'd never even been an election meant that Cal could have picked her, but he didn't. He'd picked her friend. I imagined that must have been hard to watch.

"You're too good for him, Zelda," I said.

She let out a cracked little peal of laughter, then emerged from the stall. Her makeup was smudged under her eyes, her hair was disheveled, and whatever adhesive had been holding up her backless silver dress had come loose. She clutched the front against her chest with one hand as she punched the stall door so hard with the other that she cried out and grabbed her knuckles. The dress slipped down to her hips, and she yanked it back up, smearing the silver bodice with blood.

As soon as she'd lost control, though, she regained it, sneering as she walked over to the sink and turned on the faucet, dripping blood onto the ceramic.

"Is that what you think this is about?" she asked, still holding up her dress with one hand as she rinsed her bloody fingers.

"You think I'd cry in the bathroom at a school dance over a boy?"

When she'd finished cleaning up her knuckles, Zelda cupped her hands under the faucet and splashed the water on her face, scrubbing her skin as if she wanted to tear it off. Finally, she tugged her dress up and leaned against the bathroom stall with her head thrown back and her eyes closed. I turned off the running water.

"Zelda, what happened?" I asked. I took two steps back, made my voice soft and low, afraid that any sudden movements would make her bolt right out of the bathroom.

She lowered her chin and fixed her eyes on mine, the kind of face you might make at a firing squad.

"Let's say the Honor Council president corners you after a meeting and says you should hang out some time. You tell him you don't think that's such a good idea. Then he tells you, 'You're so good at your job. The Honor Council is really going to suck when you're not on it anymore.' And maybe he doesn't come right out and say it, but you know what he means."

"Oh, Zelda . . ." I put my hand on her shoulder, but she shook it off.

"You can't make a deal like that and expect it to save you. Not for very long. Somebody should tell Esme Kovacs that."

"Is there anything I can do?" I asked. I was thinking about immediate things, like getting her out of the bathroom unobserved or finding some gym clothes for her to borrow, or a bandage. But Zelda didn't care about anything like that.

"You have no idea how much worse it's going to get, Claudia." She shuddered, then looked at the back of her hand.

"What do you mean?"

Before she could answer, we heard a scream from the hallway. Not a playful scream. Not a surprised one. Something terrible was on the other end of that scream. Zelda and I looked at each other, and ran out of the bathroom toward it.

Trixie Pappadou and her girlfriend and fellow senior class senator, Sarah Reisman, crashed into us. They were hysterical. Nothing they said made any sense, though eventually we ascertained that they'd snuck past the barricades into the hallway by the main office. When Zelda and I started down the hall in that direction, they screamed again and begged us not to go.

We got them to sit down and breathe, and while Zelda was calming them down, I got up and went to investigate. I wasn't alone. The girls' screams had attracted a few people from the dance, and together, we rounded the corner and made our way toward the main office.

The perpetrator had not tried to conceal what they'd done. The main office door had been flung open. Monday morning, people would say that the lock should have been fixed years ago rather than standing as a testament to how trustworthy Imperial Day students were and how well the Honor Code worked.

The carpets were soaked. There was broken glass everywhere. The smell was horrible, marshy and wet. It clung to the insides of my nostrils for the rest of the night.

Someone threw up in a trash can.

Mr. Woolf came running up behind us and said, "I'm calling the police."

The teachers rounded all of us up in the courtyard, and we waited for the police to arrive. Everyone was in a state of shock. Some people looked shattered. More than a few people cried.

The office had been vandalized. The windows were broken, the aquarium smashed.

Someone had killed the turtles.

Every last one of them.

XXXVI

STALIN USED TO LOVE A GOOD SHOW TRIAL

These were the verified facts:

At 10 p.m., senior class senators Trixie Pappadou and Sarah Reisman found the main office ransacked, the windows broken, the aquarium smashed, the turtle corpses scattered around the room.

Fifteen minutes later, when the police arrived to question us, Zelda Parsons was seen wandering the hall with ruined makeup, disheveled hair, and a torn dress. The officer who took her statement noticed cuts on her hand, as well as flecks of blood on her dress and shoes. Zelda said that the blood was her own.

A few minutes after that, Dr. Graves arrived at the school in a three-piece suit even though he'd clearly just gotten out of bed. He yelled at Mr. Woolf for calling the police. Then he told the police to go, that we had our own way of dealing with things here, and that it wasn't a criminal matter until he said that it was. Much to the surprise of everyone, they listened to him.

As soon as the police cars had pulled out of the Imperial

Day parking lot, Dr. Graves and the Honor Council representatives huddled together. After a brief and whispered meeting, they herded all of us into the auditorium.

Dr. Graves stood in front of us on the stage and said, "You will all text this exact message to your parents and this message only: 'Vandalism incident at school. Everyone is safe. I will be home as soon as the hearing is over.'"

We were shocked. We were confused. It was clear that some Imperial Day students sitting in the auditorium had no idea why they were there. The information that swirled its way up and down the rows morphed slightly with each telling. I heard that the turtles had been poisoned, that their bodies had been pinned to the bulletin board, that their aquarium had been emptied into the aguas frescas.

I heard that Zelda had done it out of spite that she hadn't been crowned Homecoming queen. I heard that Zelda had done it to make the Senate look bad. I heard one person say that it was a class prank, but in almost every story, the criminal was Zelda.

Had the Honor Council decided to make its move now, to make a decision that was firm and fast and binding while everyone was still in a muddle?

I had my own theories about what had happened, but kept them to myself. After all, Cal had been front and center all evening long, all eyes on him. An airtight alibi, and yet, I couldn't think of anyone else at the Imperial Day Academy who was enough of a psychopath to murder a tank of much-beloved turtles, the closest thing to a mascot the school had.

And then, not even an hour after their bodies had been discovered, Cal was standing on the stage next to Dr. Graves, ready to conduct a hearing to find the killer.

It was my third time before the Honor Council (if you counted Soren and Julia's hearing, which I'd eavesdropped on), and the most disturbing yet. Cal began by announcing that the crime that had been committed was so horrific that the Honor Council proceedings should be conducted in the open, right here, right now, in front of everyone. No hiding behind anonymous testimony. No one would leave until the perpetrator was found.

Zelda was the first person called up onto the stage. Someone had given her a cardigan, but she was still clutching her spangly silver dress to her chest to hold it up. She said that she'd been in the bathroom when it all happened, that she'd bloodied her knuckles punching a bathroom stall. When they asked if she had any witnesses who could verify this, she said me. When they asked why she punched a bathroom stall, Zelda said she didn't recall. She didn't say anything about Cal threatening her into being his girlfriend for a month.

When it was over, she descended from the stage, ignoring the whispers that circulated through the air as she passed down the aisle. Instead of taking a seat in the auditorium, though, she continued on through the double doors.

"Young lady," Dr. Graves shouted after her, "you are not dismissed. No one is dismissed until this matter is settled."

She ignored him, letting the doors slam shut behind her. Dr. Graves stood there a moment, his eyes bulging, until Cal tugged on his sleeve and he sat down again. Cal whispered something in his ear, Dr. Graves nodded, and then they called me up to the stage.

I had never really spoken to Dr. Graves before. He had deep-set eyes, querulous eyebrows, and wiry white hair that grew over his ears and curled at the back of his neck. He was still furious that Zelda had left the auditorium without permission, and looked prepared to take it out on me.

Cal, on the other hand, appeared to be enjoying himself immensely.

"Tell us what happened, Claudia," Cal said, tenting his fingers and leaning forward in his seat. "On your honor."

I told Dr. Graves and Cal and the rest of the Honor Council and the whole school what I told you: that I'd seen Zelda in the bathroom before the turtles were discovered and that she seemed upset. I told them that her dress was dry, that I'd seen her punch the bathroom stall, and that she didn't seem like she'd just smashed an aquarium full of turtles to death with a hammer.

I could have shared the rest of what Zelda had told me, but I feared that would only make things worse for her.

They told me to take my seat.

After me, Chris Gibbons said that from his perch in the DJ booth, he had not seen Zelda on the dance floor during the slideshow or crowning of the Homecoming king and queen.

Then they called up a freshman boy whom everyone called Macro for some reason. He claimed to have heard the sound of smashing glass coming from the main office, then seen Zelda coming down the hallway shortly thereafter. No one asked him why he didn't investigate. No one asked why he didn't go for help. No one except me seemed to think he was telling anything but the truth.

Joseph Stalin used to love a good show trial. He'd have his political rivals, real and imagined, arrested for plotting to assassinate him or colluding to bring down the Soviet Union. The guilty verdicts were all but assured, and when they were delivered, the accused were executed or sent to Siberia. Some people say that Stalin even hid himself in a dark corner of the courtroom so he could watch them. He just sat there, smoking his pipe and getting off on watching people beg for their lives.

Whatever this was, it was a joke, of course. They didn't call up Trixie Pappadou or Sarah Reisman or anyone who might have seen something useful. They called up the people they wanted to, and over and over again, nobody knew anything. Nobody had seen anything, but if they'd seen even the tiniest, slightest thing, it had something to do with Zelda. If I hadn't spoken up for Zelda, nobody would have.

At the end, Cal sighed and apologized and thanked all of us for our time, and said that the investigation was ongoing, but everyone knew there was only one suspect.

Shortly after midnight, Soren drove me home.

"Weird night," he said, giving me a hug across the car seat after he'd parked in the driveway.

"Worst night," I said.

I would later realize what a stupid thing this was to say.

✳✳✳

Zelda wasn't in school on Monday or Tuesday, and then, on Wednesday, Cal got on the loudspeaker before first period, and with a triumphant note in his voice, told everyone to report to the auditorium for a special announcement.

When we got there, Zelda Parsons was standing on the stage, lit by a single spotlight. She stood perfectly motionless as we drifted in and took our seats, the whispering so loud it engulfed the entire auditorium. When she spoke, we all shut up. Nobody blinked, nobody breathed.

"I resign my seat on the Honor Council," she said, her voice shaking. "To the student body, I apologize for letting you down and failing in my charge. To my colleagues on the Honor Council, I also apologize. I ask your forgiveness and your understanding as I seek the help I need. Thank you."

Everyone was watching Zelda, the way she paused to wipe her eyes. How it looked like she hadn't showered since the Homecoming dance. I wasn't watching Zelda, though. I kept my eyes on Cal, watched as he sat back, legs crossed, arms folded, a sulky expression on his face. Whatever Zelda's humiliation here was, it hadn't been enough for him. I wondered if it was because she'd stopped short of an actual confession. I wondered what he'd wanted her to do, but regardless, because he hadn't gotten everything he wanted, he was now happy about none of it. I wondered who he'd take his disappointments out on next.

"If it wasn't Zelda, then who do you think did it, Claudia?"

"I like to think there are two kinds of people at Imperial Day, and probably in the world: those who are capable of killing a dozen turtles with a hammer and those who are not."

"Who at Imperial Day would you include in the former group?"

"Cal. Livia. Maybe Chris Gibbons, but I don't know."

"All people who couldn't have done it."

"Exactly. Or in Livia's case, people who weren't even there in the first place."

"Do you think it's possible it was someone you hadn't even considered?"

"As a frequent victim of elementary and middle-school cruelties, and as a politician, I make a habit of identifying the psychopaths in my environment as quickly as possible."

"Do you consider yourself to be a good judge of character, Claudia? Have you ever been wrong about someone?"

"What do you think? Have I?"

XXXVII

Moira Riggs's Bra Strap

Perhaps as a reward for his testimony against her, Cal appointed the freshman boy called Macro with Zelda's vacant seat on the Honor Council.

There should have been an outcry. There should have been a special election. At the very least the seat should have gone to someone in the junior class, but everyone kept their opinions to themselves, and the only remotely critical letter to the editor that appeared in the *Weekly Praetor* was published anonymously. I suspected that even this tiny protest would enrage Cal and found an excuse to swing by the newspaper office the day the letter ran. Sure enough, Cal was there, badgering editor-in-chief Ruby Greenberg for a name.

"I can't tell you," she said. Was it my imagination or did I see a look of relief flash across her face when I walked into the room? "It was submitted anonymously."

"Shouldn't the newspaper have a policy against that?" Cal asked, pacing back and forth in front of Ruby. "Aren't you encouraging people to say any irresponsible thing they want to without repercussions?"

"We don't print the irresponsible ones," Ruby stammered.

"And who decides? You?"

"We all do," Ruby answered. "The whole editorial staff."

"So the whole editorial staff agreed with the decision to print this letter?" he asked.

That was when I heard that dangerous edge creep into Cal's voice, the one that meant his ranting was about to become specific and personal. He hadn't noticed me yet, so I cleared my throat to let him know there was a witness to whatever he was going to say to Ruby next. He looked back over his shoulder at me, then said, "I don't remember the editorial staff losing their shit last year when Claudia and Hector took over the Senate."

"Nobody is losing their shit, Cal," I said.

Except you, I thought.

"What do you want, Cal?" Ruby asked, looking eager to have the conversation done with.

"A voice," Cal replied. "A column where I can explain myself, and maybe keep the *Weekly Praetor* from turning the school against me."

To anyone else, the appropriate response would be "No one is trying to turn the school against you," but the way Cal loomed over Ruby, the way he'd gradually backed her up against a row of computer tables as he paced, kept her from arguing.

"Write something up and send it to me," she said. "I'll take it to the rest of the staff and we'll see if we can run it."

Cal glared at her. It didn't matter that she'd said "maybe." All he heard was that she *hadn't* said "Yes. You're right. Of course, Cal. Whatever you want."

Within a week, Esme Kovacs revealed character—and perhaps foresight—I had not known she possessed, and resigned from the Honor Council in protest. Cal made no move to stop her, and wasted no time bringing back the spineless, witless Jesse Nichols to take her place.

I don't know how Cal sold another special appointment to Dr. Graves, but ever since his swift—and almost certainly unjust—handling of the Homecoming Turtle Massacre, he was a golden boy to Imperial Day administration. We were a bunch of turtle-murdering sickos, but there was Cal Hurt to keep us in line. He made problems like us go away, quietly and forever, and in return, they gave him whatever he wanted.

If you stood in the third-floor hallway after school on Tuesdays and Wednesdays when the Honor Council heard testimony, you would see a nonstop stream of sycophants, cowards, liars, rats, and reprobates going in and out the door. No one cared if they were seen because the Honor Council brought charges against so many people, it became almost impossible to guess who was testifying against whom. People disappeared right and left, and no one knew why.

Though not yet the darkest time, it was well on its way there. Everyone was on edge. Hector wasn't the only one with insomnia—it became endemic. Some people picked at their lunches, developed nervous tics, and cried in the bathroom between classes when it became too much. Others began cutting class and partying too much. Chris Gibbons was in higher demand than Soren had ever been. People figured it was only a matter of time before they were brought up on Honor Council charges, so they might as well have done something to deserve it.

Meanwhile, Cal and his friends—Chris Gibbons, Astrid Murray, and the underclassmen who aspired to their delinquency—roamed the school like apex predators, looking for anything smaller and weaker, anything that confirmed what they already suspected: that they could do whatever they wanted.

One day, Cal and Chris Gibbons were making their daily procession down the hall to Ms. Yee's fourth-period AP European History. This was always a raucous affair that involved checking each other against lockers, leaping in the air to whack any sign or ledge within jumping distance with the palms of their hands, and bothering freshman girls.

There was one girl in particular, Moira Riggs, who was a frequent target because her locker was right outside Ms. Yee's room. We had five minutes between classes, and Moira's fourth-period class was on the other side of the building. If she got in and out of her locker by the two-minute mark, she was fine, but if she stopped to use the bathroom or was late getting out of third period, she was still there when Cal and Chris came by. Moira wasn't an especially pretty or popular freshman, but she did have an enormous rack, and it was for this that Cal and Chris sought her out.

They would bounce down the hall toward her, chanting, "Boingy, boingy, boingy!" and then they would surround her. Don't get me wrong. They were *nice* to her—sort of, if you thought that an aggressive combination of teasing and flirting was nice. In fact, many upperclassman girls at Imperial Day loathed Moira because of the attention that Cal and Chris paid to her.

But then Moira would start trying to extricate herself from that attention so she wouldn't be late to class, and they would barricade her at her locker. The whole time they'd say things like, "You don't have to go yet," and "You can be late," and "If you get in trouble, we'll get you out of it." They could do that because their fourth-period class was right there, and the second the bell rang they could slip in the door and be in their seats before Ms. Yee even started taking roll.

It was all friendly, it was all in fun, but you could see

Moira's face turn panicked as the seconds raced by, and then the bell would ring and her panic would turn to resignation as Cal and Chris ran into Ms. Yee's room without even saying goodbye to her.

This went on until one day, Ms. Yee was standing out in the hallway between classes and watched the whole thing happen.

"Mr. Gibbons! Mr. Hurt!" she barked, hands planted on her hips like Napoleon. "Leave Miss Riggs alone and get in your seats this minute."

"The bell hasn't rung yet," Chris Gibbons said.

"Even so," said Ms. Yee, her voice drawing a line on the linoleum that even Chris Gibbons should have known better than to cross.

Moira Riggs had taken advantage of the distraction to gather her books and slam her locker door shut. She'd only taken a step or two down the hall when Cal caught her by the bra strap and tugged her back.

"You aren't even going to say goodbye?" he asked, as if Ms. Yee wasn't standing right there.

"You'll get in trou—" Moira started to say.

I was not there that day, but I heard from an eyewitness that Ms. Yee marched over to them, pried Cal's fingers from Moira Riggs's bra strap and barked, "Get to class."

"Get your hands off of me," Cal said, pulling away from Ms. Yee like she'd struck him. "I didn't do anything."

It was then that five years of teaching at Imperial Day, being pestered for extra credit and grade changes, badgered to participate in Honor Week and chaperone dances, tasked with maintaining order over students who felt free to ignore or question even the most reasonable of requests—it was then that it all finally caught up with Ms. Yee.

"Oh for fuck's sake," she said, rolling her eyes. "Get out of here. Get out of my sight."

Moira Riggs stood rooted to the spot until Ms. Yee turned to her and added, "You. Get to class."

According to my eyewitness, Cal pointed at Ms. Yee and said, "You don't talk to me like that."

She didn't reply, but turned and went back into the classroom, slamming the door shut behind her. Cal's reptile smile spread across his face as he ran down the hall after Moira, probably already thinking about how he was going to get even.

The handful of people still in the hallway when it happened stared after them, still half-stunned by what they'd seen. Later, Cal would call them all as witnesses, and they would confirm certain portions of his story: that Ms. Yee had grabbed his hand, sworn at him, turned her back to him, and slammed a door in his and Chris Gibbons's faces.

In mournful tones, Cal would explain to Dr. Graves and the Board that Ms. Yee had been rude to him in the past, that she'd snapped at him when he asked her to participate in Honor Week, ignored him when he asked her about grades he'd received.

Nobody said a word about Moira Riggs's bra strap, not even Moira Riggs.

Rumor has it that Ms. Yee refused to speak on her own behalf, refused to defend herself against any of the charges.

Maybe she thought that a teacher with an advanced degree from an esteemed university, five years of experience, a track record of impeccable student AP scores, and no prior complaints need not dignify such accusations with a response. Maybe she didn't think anything would come of it. I mean, it wasn't like what she'd done was that terrible. It wasn't like Cal didn't have it coming.

But that's where I was wrong.

After the Board recommended that she be suspended without pay for two weeks for improper conduct toward a student, Ms. Yee tendered her resignation.

"That you would blindly accept the word of a tyrant and a bully who has cowed your student body into the service of his whims and vendettas through fear and intimidation, that you would place so much power in the hands of such a person, leaves me with little choice but to conclude that Imperial Day is not the place I thought it was when I accepted this position five years ago."

She wrote a letter to Dr. Graves, to the Board, and to Ruby Greenberg, who was fool enough to print it in the *Weekly Praetor*.

Around the time of Ms. Yee's disciplinary hearing, Rebecca Ibañez finally had enough and quit the seat she'd fought to win back, and Cal had the gall to bring Chris Gibbons in to replace her. That did it. The Honor Council was officially a mockery, and the most frustrating thing was, Hector and I couldn't do anything about it. It wasn't like the previous year when we'd swept in with an ambitious agenda and made things happen, while the Honor Council stumbled under Ty's leadership. Now we had twice as many senators and got half as much done. Cal had us so on edge, we couldn't act; we could only react.

Macro Stinson, Jesse Nichols, and Chris Gibbons began showing up to every Senate meeting, not just the Tuesday ones that were open to everyone, but the closed, senators-only Thursday meetings, too. The three of them never talked. They never explained what they were doing there. They didn't have to. They recorded a lot of things on their phones and wrote a lot of things down, and there was nothing we could do about it. Every idea we mentioned, whether it was something innovative like planting a community garden, or something mundane like buying a senior class gift to the school, Cal would make a big show of announcing the idea as his own in his new weekly newspaper column.

I could tell that having to weigh every word was starting to exhaust Hector. The thing was, no matter how careful we were, it was only a matter of time before they would find some way to take something out of context and use it to smear us.

So when we talked about how the mock trial team would carry on until a new advisor could be found, or who would chaperone the Model UN trip to the University of Southern California, we never mentioned Ms. Yee's name. We spoke like she'd vanished and our memories had been wiped and no such person had ever existed.

Cal's message was clear: there was no one he couldn't touch, and if you stood up to him, he'd come after you.

That was why I decided to run away.

XXXVIII

RESPECT

History is filled with stories of people who fled oppressive regimes. The Marquis de Lafayette saw Robespierre's mob gathering up their kindling and pitchforks and got out of town before they could kill him. After English prisons and homophobia broke Oscar Wilde, he fled to France, not that it fixed anything or unbroke him. And Trotsky fled Russia more times than anyone can keep track of, though they did eventually find him in Mexico City and put an ice axe through his head anyway.

So I knew that running away wouldn't necessarily make things better, but it would have the advantage of getting me out of the way during an extremely crucial time.

I remembered the Honor Council hearing during my freshman year, when they'd blindsided Soren with the ridiculous indecent-conduct charges. They'd done it quietly, right before Thanksgiving break. It was a classic Livia move, and I knew there was a very good chance that Cal would use it. I knew there was a very good chance he'd use it on Hector and me.

"When are you doing your college visits?" I asked Hector one day at lunch.

He looked at me like I was insane. "Spring break? Summer? I don't know. Why?"

"Because I was thinking about going to visit Maisie before Thanksgiving, and I thought maybe you'd want to go with me."

It wasn't a normal suggestion, but it also wasn't the most unreasonable thing in the world to ask. We were college-bound juniors. No teacher ever did anything important the two days before Thanksgiving break. We could fly out Saturday, come back Wednesday, and be munching turkey with our families on Thanksgiving Day. Hector looked at me like I'd suggested we run off to Paris together instead of to Sarah Lawrence.

"I don't think so," he said. "But thanks."

I wouldn't let it drop, though. This was our one hope, our escape. If there was one place Cal and the Honor Council couldn't follow us, it was on a plane to New York.

"We don't just have to go to Sarah Lawrence," I said. "We could tour NYU, Columbia . . ."

Hector cut me off. "I am well acquainted with the schools in the greater New York metro area, Claudia."

"Then why don't you want to go?" I asked. "I can help with your plane ticket. My parents have a lot of miles they can cash in."

"It's not the money, Claudia." His eyes narrowed, and I could tell that I'd pushed past Crabby Hector into a Hector I'd never seen before. "Maybe your parents are cool with you taking a week off of school to jet off to New York with a boy, but mine will not be. Mine would flip their shit, as would my girlfriend once she got wind of it—which she would. So, no, it's not happening. I am not going to New York with you."

"Fine," I said, and that was all I said to him for the rest of the day.

Was it because of the money? Was he on edge? Were things strained between him and Esme? I didn't know why the invitation had upset him so much.

That night, I couldn't sleep. I couldn't stop worrying about Macro and Jesse and Chris and whatever they might be pouring into Cal's ear from our Senate meetings. He'd twist their words to justify whatever it was that he wanted to do to Hector and me.

I sat up in bed and reached for my phone.

I'm worried, okay? Getting out of town seems like a good idea. For both of us.

Nothing came back even though I knew there was at least a 45 percent chance Hector was also awake, still staring at his ceiling and doing his usual insomniac rituals. Esme was probably his late-night correspondent now, not me.

I had to give the girl credit. I thought she'd fall into the same trap Zelda had once Cal set his eye on her, but Esme saw through it. She stood by Hector, rejected Cal, and resigned her seat on the Honor Council rather than let Cal take it from her. She'd lost, but at least it was on her terms. I had to respect that.

I was about to give up and go to bed when my phone buzzed. Hector had written back:

I know what you're trying to do and I'm not going to run from him. If he wants me he can come get me. I hope you have fun in NYC.

I had to respect that, too.

XXXIX

STRONGER AT THE BROKEN PLACES

When Maisie picked me up at JFK Airport, she had a very conspiratorial look about her.

"On a scale of 1 to 10, how much does your enjoyment of this week hinge upon spending a lot of time on a college campus?" she asked.

"Zero," I said, because my enjoyment of the week hinged entirely on being with my sister and not at the Imperial Day Academy.

"Brilliant," she said, grabbing my luggage off the carousel. She didn't even have to ask if it was mine, it being the only suitcase plastered with 1992 Jerry Brown presidential campaign stickers.

Even though Maisie carried my suitcase, I could tell that New York City was not going to be easy for me. Everyone walked so fast here. As Maisie and I made our way through the airport terminal toward the shuttle that would take us into Manhattan, Maisie explained that one of her friends from school lived in the city and that she and her family were out of town for the holiday. They'd offered Maisie the run of their Gramercy Park apartment in exchange for the care and feeding of two geriatric cats and some light plant watering.

"If you absolutely need to tour some colleges, we can do that, but otherwise, the city is ours. We can totally rage."

For a minute, I had fearful visions of Maisie dragging me, stuffed into a midriff top, to a club where we'd brandish fake IDs and do shots.

"Want to go look at some Caravaggios?" she asked, and I was relieved to discover that college life had not changed my sister, at least not in any dull or predictable ways.

After dropping my suitcase off at the apartment, our first order of business was to go uptown to the Metropolitan Museum of Art, then afterwards, to a wood-paneled Viennese café, where we drank something called a Kaiser Mélange that was basically coffee with whipped cream and ate chocolate-hazelnut torte. There was even a chamber music quartet.

The next day we went to the Tenement Museum, Grand Central Station, and a diner that used to be a hotel ballroom. We refused to eat in any restaurant that was not at least fifty years old. My sister had always been good to indulge me in the occasional history bender, but this time, she'd outdone herself.

It wasn't until the third night that Maisie asked about Imperial Day, and by then, I'd almost forgotten about it. We were dressing up to go see *Chicago*, Maisie in a swingy green dress, me in the tuxedo shirt and cigarette pants I'd worn to Homecoming.

"How is school, anyway? Is Cal still terrible?"

She asked like he was a distant memory. A distant, distinctly bad, but ultimately harmless memory, and not the boogeyman of the waking nightmare that was my current life at Imperial Day.

"Even worse than you remember him," I said. "Let's talk about absolutely anything else."

The weekend melted away, and then the week filled with sleeping in, lavish meals, museums, and history, and I hardly thought about Imperial Day at all. Hector texted me once to ask about the holiday food drive, but Maisie and I were at the theater and I didn't even see it until three hours later.

Maisie had lobbied hard for our parents to meet us in New York for Thanksgiving, and eventually they gave in. We ordered a complete Thanksgiving dinner from Whole Foods, and Maisie and I made pumpkin pies and brewed one pot of coffee after another. While the pies baked, we went up to the rooftop with our hands clamped around mugs to keep them warm. Downstairs, our parents did something I'd never seen before: they put on sweatpants and watched television while doing nothing else.

"Can I ask you something?" Maisie's voice was serious, and even as I nodded, I felt my chest tighten up because I had a feeling that whatever was coming next, I didn't want to talk about it. This whole week was about not talking about it. That was the whole point.

"What are you staying there for?" she asked.

I didn't reply. I hadn't realized it up until then, but the answer to that question had gotten so tangled and messy. If you could get it, a diploma from Imperial Day would allow you to spend the next four years pretty much wherever you wanted to go. But that wasn't why I stayed. It was more than that. I'd built something during my time there, or at least I'd started to. Under Hector and me, Imperial Day could be a place where people tried to make the world better, where they helped each other instead of ratfucking each other's campaigns and lives.

I didn't want to walk away from that without a fight.

"Is it Hector?"

I didn't answer that either, but Maisie wouldn't let me off the hook.

"I listen to you when you talk, Claudia, and for a person who never likes anyone, you really seem to like him."

"He's my best friend," I said, holding the coffee cup close to my chest to ward off the cold. If there was one thing I wanted to talk about less than the situation at Imperial Day, it was the situation with Hector.

"And?"

"And he has a girlfriend. I invited him to come on this trip with me, but he said no."

"Because of her?"

"Partly. Mostly it was because he didn't want to abandon his post. Like I'm doing."

Maisie's brow furrowed as a gust of wind blew her bangs back.

"You can quit, you know. It won't ruin your life," Maisie said, her eyes serious in a big-sister-wisdom-imparting kind of way.

Whatever damage Imperial Day had done to Maisie, she had healed now. Hemingway said that the world broke you and that afterwards, some people were stronger at the broken places. Maisie looked like that now, wise and beautifully scarred, and for a split second, I wanted it for myself—until I thought about what Maisie had done to get that way, what she was suggesting I do now.

Maisie was telling me to abandon Hector the way she'd abandoned me. She was telling me to save myself. I never would have called Maisie a selfish person, but in that moment, I realized how much different my life would have been, what a different place Imperial Day would have been, if Maisie had stayed. If she'd beaten Ty in the Honor Council presidential race like I knew she could have if she'd really wanted to. If she'd actually tried.

The hatchet job on Oberlin St. James would never have happened. Cal would never have lasted out the year on the Honor Council, much less been elected president. Hector and I would be regular, ordinary senators, not officers with targets on our backs. Zelda Parsons would have been spared humiliation. Esme Kovacs would have been spared harassment. All the people who'd been wrongfully accused would have clean records. Ms. Yee would still have her job. The turtles would still be alive.

That was what running away got you. A list of wrongs you could have righted. I was tired of waiting for the worst to happen, then reacting when it did. I didn't want to run away. I wanted to take a stand against Cal, against the whole poisonous, paranoid police state that my high school had become.

I could do it, but only if I didn't care what happened to me, and in a reckless moment, standing on top of an apartment building staring out across Manhattan, I didn't.

There was nothing I wanted, nothing I was afraid to lose anymore.

"Claudia?"

I shook myself back to the present moment. Maisie watched me, a nervous expression on her face.

"We should go inside," she said, tugging my arm with false cheer. "The pies will be done soon."

Our parents were still watching football when we went back downstairs. It was strange to see them this way, but we all passed a pleasant two days together in this other family's apartment. We went to Times Square and the top of the Empire

State Building and did all of our Christmas shopping at the same stores we had in LA, and when my leg started to hurt, we went back to the apartment for a Tim Burton movie marathon.

During that time, I became more resolved than ever. I would return to Imperial Day with a mission: to eliminate the threat of Cal and save the school, even if something terrible happened to me in the process.

It was only after my parents and I got through airport security at JFK that I began to have doubts and to worry about what had happened at Imperial Day in my absence.

As we waited at the gate, I checked my email and made the internet rounds, and as far as I could tell, things had been quiet. Too quiet, really. I'd only had the one text from Hector, and that was days ago. What if something had happened to him while I'd been gone? What if something had happened to me? What if I returned to Imperial Day to find that I'd been charged, convicted, and sentenced without my knowledge? Before we boarded the plane, I texted Hector: *On my way home—what's going on?*

Then the flight attendant made me turn off my phone before Hector texted back. The whole flight back to LA, I ran through every possible scenario I could think of. In some of them, Hector had to step down as president or got expelled. In others, I did. And in between terrible, worried thoughts, I imagined how I was going to stop Cal. Sort of. I could visualize myself setting out to do it, then my brain would flash forward to the students of Imperial Day lifting me up onto their shoulders to celebrate their liberation. It was the part in between that I couldn't picture.

When the plane touched down, though, my silly little plans and fantasies hardened into something real and necessary.

I had five texts from Hector when I turned my phone on. There was also one from Esme, one from Lucy Lin, and two from numbers I didn't recognize.

Something terrible *had* happened.

I'd been right to be afraid, right to run away, but I'd been afraid of the wrong things. I'd been afraid for the wrong person. If I'd known what was going to happen, I would have done it all differently.

I would have invited Soren Bieckmann to come to New York with me, and if I had, he'd still be alive today.

XL

NOT AN ACCIDENT, NOT ON PURPOSE

I wasn't there when it happened, but here's what I know.

On Thanksgiving Day, Soren left his home at around 10 a.m. and went to the LA Food Bank, where he passed out turkeys and canned cranberry sauce until 3 p.m. He returned to his house at 6 p.m., where he ate his last meal—a frozen bean and cheese burrito and a spinach salad—and played video games. At 8 p.m., he left his home again and went to a party at the home of an actor who'd once been on a Nick Jr. show, but had since gone into DJ'ing.

Nobody saw him drinking anything except coffee at the party, but there were a handful of accounts saying that he'd appeared to be slightly intoxicated. Whatever happened, he knew better than to drive himself home. His car was found parked in the Hollywood Hills near the actor/DJ's house two days later.

Soren punched in his front door security code at 1 a.m. Someone wearing a gray hoodie can be seen in the security footage walking him to the door, but you can't see his face, and in the footage, he doesn't follow Soren inside. Whoever that person was, he was the last person to see Soren alive.

Soren's parents were in Park City when it happened. They found him on Saturday morning when they got home. There was no drug paraphernalia around, but the toxicology report showed that Soren had ingested hydrocodone and diazepam. He had a prescription for the latter, for anxiety, but not the former. He died sometime around three or four Friday morning.

People speculated that he'd relapsed, that he'd used that three-hour window between volunteering at the food bank and returning to his house to obtain the painkillers illegally. Some people said it was an accidental overdose, while others said it was on purpose. Soren's grades weren't good. He'd lost a lot of his old friends since he'd gotten clean. He spent a lot of time alone. He hated being sober. His parents had left him alone at Thanksgiving.

People theorized that the person in the gray hoodie, his or her face hidden from the camera, was an unlicensed cab driver or some minor celebrity who'd decided to be a Good Samaritan and make sure Soren got home, but was afraid to stick around. Police questioned everyone at the party, but nobody admitted to going home with Soren and nobody remembered seeing anyone in a gray hoodie.

I didn't buy any of it. Not Soren. Not accidentally. Not on purpose. It wasn't possible.

I know that sounds naïve. My mother was raised by a family of drunks, and has spent my entire life drilling into my head the two things that addicts do: they relapse and they lie. But none of that sounds like Soren to me.

Why would he spend five hours helping other people on Thanksgiving, then leave depressed? And if he was lonely and it took him three hours to get home from the food bank, wasn't it equally possible that he went surfing or to a coffee shop or to an AA meeting? He wasn't upset that his old friends had fallen away. He was happy about it. He hated those people, and he'd told me as much at Homecoming when he realized that Cal didn't have to be nice to him anymore. He was relieved.

Not an accident. Not on purpose. Not Soren.

We drove home from the airport, my parents peppering me with questions I didn't have the answers to yet while I sat in the backseat, too shocked and numb and angry to cry. They'd met Soren, but they didn't know him. Their concern was based on curiosity, that a thing like this had happened to a student at their daughter's school. I didn't have it in me to answer questions like that, so eventually, I handed the phone to my mother and told her to call Hector herself.

She and my father had him on speaker when we pulled into the driveway. I jumped out of the car and ran toward the house without waiting for them, without helping with the bags. The last thing I heard before I slammed the car door shut was Hector asking, "Is Claudia there? Is she okay?"

I was not okay. I didn't want to talk to anyone, not even Hector. I wanted to run up to my room, pull the covers over my head, and stay there until someone came to tell me that none of it was true.

I unlocked the front door and dashed into the foyer, where our house sitter had stacked the mail. Behind me, I could hear my mother asking questions that no teenage boy except Hector Estrella would have known the answers to: *Where were the services going to be held? Was his family asking that money be donated to a charity in lieu of flowers?*

That was as far as I made it. That was when it hit me.

That Soren Bieckmann was dead.

My floppy-haired, reformed drug dealer Homecoming date. My friend. I thought about the way he'd put his arm around my shoulder at the dance, the way his eyes had gone intense when he said, "I'd rather be honest."

Someone else is responsible for this, I thought. The person who gave him the hydrocodone. The person who drove him home without bothering to make sure he was okay. His parents, for not being home when it happened. Everyone at Imperial Day who'd turned their backs on him the second he got sober. Me, for not taking him to New York with me.

I'd rather be honest.

When the universe looked down and said, *Which one of these lives should I blot out today?* that's who it picked. The guy who said things like that.

The rest of us got to live.

XLI

A GOOD PERSON

The funeral wasn't until the next weekend. There were about two seconds of a police investigation, and then the coroner had to do some toxicology reports before they'd release the body to Soren's family.

The body.

It was so strange, that was all he was now. All anyone at school could talk about was how sad and stupid and tragic and awful it was. I couldn't bring myself to talk about any of it, but I heard things. It had been one of those big, sprawling parties that started early, ended late, and ranged indoors, outdoors, upstairs, downstairs. Certain names began to bubble up to the surface consistently enough that I believed the accounts to be accurate, but it was impossible to know when they'd left, what they'd seen or hadn't seen.

Chris Gibbons had been there. And Kian Sarkosian. So had Cal. So had Esme Kovacs. And so had Hector.

Those were the names I heard whispered again and again.

I just never heard it from Hector.

He was out sick with a cold half the week, and when he returned, he wouldn't talk about it.

"Did you see him?" I asked after an especially muted and brief Senate meeting. "Did you talk to him?"

"Claudia, I'm not ready to talk about it," he said.

"Was Cal fucking with him? Did you see them together?"

"Claudia, stop it," he said in a way that made me feel like a vulture for asking in the first place.

I wasn't a vulture, though. I wasn't one of the people who spoke of nothing else that week, who cataloged every known fact or rumor of the night Soren died like they were his fucking biographers. *Those* people were the vultures, and of course, I talked to them so I could learn what they knew. I hated it, I hated them, I hated myself, and yet, I needed to know.

Because I was never going to be able to know what Soren was thinking the night he died. I would never know if he felt lonely when he got home from volunteering at the food bank or if he was happy to be going to a party or if he went out that night intending to get fucked up or if the thought never entered his mind.

I was never going to get to know any of that, so this was all I had.

The funeral was at Forest Lawn in Glendale, where all the old movie stars are buried. It was a chilly gray day, little flecks of rain spitting down on everyone's faces. The service was outside, which was fine because it felt right. Nobody wanted sunshine.

Hector and I went together. He offered to drive as an olive branch, and since Esme had stayed home, I accepted (she said she had to meet her SAT tutor, but I suspected that she just didn't want to be there). I didn't want Hector to be angry with me for asking too many questions, and I didn't want to be angry with him because he wasn't ready to talk. If he wanted to pretend there was no unspoken business between us, I would let him.

Attendance was spottier than I would have guessed it would be. I'd expected hordes of people who'd never even talked to Soren huddled together and making a spectacle of their grief, making his death all about themselves. That was how it had been at school all week.

Maybe it was the weather or how long it took to drive from the Westside to Glendale. Maybe it was the seediness of Soren's previous affiliations or the fact that so many Imperial Day students had purchased from Soren on at least one occasion the very narcotic on which he'd OD'ed. Chris Gibbons did not have the nerve to show his face, but Cal did.

I wouldn't say I was surprised.

That was the other reason I asked so many questions. When I found out Cal had been there the night Soren died, I wanted to know how he'd been involved with it. Not if. *How.*

I realize that's a very serious accusation to make, but just listen.

I'm not saying that Cal ground up a fistful of pills and snuck them into Soren's cup of coffee. I am not even saying that he gave Soren the painkillers.

What I'm saying is that I know Cal, and as I've told you, I know that he did the things that he did because it amused him, and the idea of taunting a recovering addict who was alone on Thanksgiving, drinking coffee at a party where everyone else was doing shots, walking around by himself because he remembered too late that none of these people were really his friends anymore?

I think that is an idea that would have amused Cal very much.

I'm not calling Cal a murderer. What I am saying is that if he hadn't been at the party that night, Soren would still be alive.

So maybe I *am* calling him a murderer.

Cal stood in the second row of mourners, right behind Soren's parents, wearing a suit and looking somber and reflective. Soren's mother turned and whispered something to him, and he turned around, scanned the crowd. When his eyes fell on us, he said something to Soren's mother, then waved us up to the front.

What do you do in a situation like that? You go. You do not make a scene at your friend's funeral and upset his parents. You go up to the front and you sit next to the person you hate most in the world, the person you suspect is responsible for your friend's death, even if you're not sure how.

Soren's parents turned and clasped our hands and thanked us for coming with a practiced formality, like they'd stayed up all night saying the words over and over so they wouldn't fall apart when they had to say them for real.

Soren's mother was bird-thin, but wore layers and layers of flowing, gauzy clothes that enveloped her. His father had a shock of white hair and a tan that suggested he surfed almost as often as his son did. As his son used to.

On our way up to the front, one person stood out in the scattering of mourners, one person I hadn't expected to see. Not there. Not ever again.

Livia was wrapped in a gray woolen coat and a dusty rose scarf with a matching beret. She sat alone in one of the back rows, speaking to no one, looking at no one. I'd never seen her look so invisible before. I didn't know she was capable of it. The only flash of the old Livia came when Hector and I walked past and she met my eyes for a second before looking down at her lap. In that glance, I knew that nothing had been forgotten and nothing had been forgiven. I knew that if Livia had it to do over again, she would have spent a few more minutes scrambling my insides with the heel of her boot last spring.

But why was she back? And what was she doing here?

Before I could stop to wonder, a non-denominational preacher got up and said some oatmeal words about tragedy and those left behind to carry on in the wake of it and how we should always keep our good memories of Soren close to our hearts. Then Soren's father got up and talked about how all he'd ever wanted was for his son to have all the things he never did, but maybe he'd been wrong. He wished he'd done things differently; said that if he had, maybe Soren would still be here. Then his face crumpled and he broke down in tears, and everyone just sat there watching him until Cal went up and took him by the shoulder and led him back to his seat. After that, no one felt much like talking.

Soren's parents each threw a handful of dirt into the grave, and then we all lined up behind them and followed suit, and after that, people started to drift away. If there was a wake, nobody wanted to go to it. I suspected that a lot of people would be seeking obliteration that night, but they were going to do it in private. Soren's mother looked around as it was ending, disappointed and panicked all at once. If we left, it was really over and he was really gone.

"I'm afraid I don't know you," she said, extending a hand to Hector to keep him from leaving. He introduced himself and said he was sorry for her loss, and then she turned to me.

"I'm Claudia McCarthy," I said. "Soren and I went to H-Homecoming together."

"Did you," she said, her voice suddenly crisp and suspicious like she thought I might have been one of Soren's friends from the bad days, part of the reason he was here in a hole in the ground.

I pulled my jacket tight to my chest to keep out the chill and looked out over the cemetery, the line of cars parked by the side of the road. Livia was gone.

"We thought very highly of your son," Hector said, bowing his head solemnly.

Mrs. Bieckmann's lip curled and I watched as she bit back a bitter remark, smiled graciously, and said, "That's so good of you to say."

That was the moment something in me broke. Soren had looked inside himself, and when he hadn't liked what he saw there, he'd been brave enough to change it. He'd worked hard. He'd sacrificed things to stay sober, and to watch his mother stand there in the cemetery burying her son and thinking he was a fuck-up was more than I could bear.

"Soren was a good p-p-person," I burst out. It was louder than I'd meant it to be, and Mrs. Bieckmann studied me with a mixture of horror and pity.

"Thank you, dear," she said, and then she started to excuse herself to go somewhere, anywhere else, but I wouldn't let her.

"He was a good person," I said again. "And honest. He was the most honest person I ever met, and this is not what it looks like. Soren was sober. He didn't want to relapse. Whatever happened to him, it wasn't that. Maybe he took something by mistake. Maybe he didn't know what he was taking."

My voice pitched up, fast and manic and punctuated by staccato stutter-steps. Mrs. Bieckmann's eyes grew wider and I felt Hector's hand on my arm—a warning that I was going too far, but in my mind, this wasn't far enough. I wanted to tell her my suspicions that Cal must have been involved, that he must have said something that had driven Soren to it. I wanted to throw anything I could at Mrs. Bieckmann to at least make her consider the possibility that this wasn't a stupid junkie overdose.

"That's enough," Mrs. Bieckmann said, clutching the sides of her face with her hands. "Please."

"We're sorry," Hector said, even though he hadn't had anything to do with it. "We're so sorry for your loss, Mrs. Bieckmann."

He led me away, past the rows of white folding chairs, past the stragglers who'd stayed to look for Humphrey Bogart's grave or vape in their cars before heading back to west LA. Hector unlocked the car and said, "Get in," a little more forcefully than I would have expected from him.

He got in on his side, slammed the door shut, and grasped the steering wheel, his arms ramrod straight, his teeth gritted. He wouldn't even look at me.

"What is wrong with you, Claudia? You can't talk to people like that."

"Like what?"

"This was her son's funeral." He slammed his palm down on the steering wheel, and something inside of me reared up.

"I know what the fuck it was, Hector. I was there."

I saw a middle-aged couple walk past the car and stare at us, as if trying to decide whether this was a situation where they should intervene. I glared at them, and they kept walking.

"What was I supposed to do? Let her think Soren was a selfish, stupid addict?"

"Look, I know he was your friend . . ."

"Then why won't you tell me what happened?" I interrupted. "Yours is the only story I'd believe anyway."

My voice caught in my throat as I realized how angry I'd been with Hector all week, almost without realizing it. He *knew* me. He knew how my brain worked, that having facts and dates and names and quotations to piece together was the only thing that would comfort me. It was only words—it seemed like such a small thing, and he wouldn't even give me that.

Disgust clouded Hector's face as he turned even further away from me, looking out the window across the dismal cemetery.

"I don't want to talk about it so you can feel better, Claudia." His voice started out a quiet, quaky calm, but it didn't take long before he was yelling again. "I already talked to the police. I talked to my parents. Separately, so I got to do that twice, and it was equally fucking fun both times. I saw him that night, Claudia, and I didn't know, and so he died. That is why I don't want to talk to you about it. That is why I never want to talk about it again. Do you fucking understand?"

I wanted to explain myself. I wanted to tell Hector that I understood how he felt, that I blamed myself, too, but instead I lowered my head.

"Stop yelling at me," I whispered.

As soon as the words were out, the part of me that had started to break at Soren's grave broke all the way. I wrapped my hands around my knees, put my head down, and sobbed until nothing else would come out.

The same thing must have broken in Hector because I heard him crying in the seat next to me a moment later. We didn't look at each other. We didn't offer each other our shoulders for comfort. We sat there with our separate grief and guilt, and when it hurt too much to sit there bearing them any longer, Hector started the car and drove me home.

"I stand by what I told Mrs. Bieckmann. The notes you're taking, whatever you end up doing with them, keep that part in, please. Keep in the part where I said that Soren Bieckmann was a good person because it's the truest thing I've told you so far."

XLII

A STORY LIKE THAT COMING FROM YOU

By Christmas, Bradley McCord and Trina Gaines, the two freshmen, had resigned from the Honor Council. Both made official statements about needing more time to commit to their studies, but I knew it was either that they no longer had any stomach for Cal's brand of justice or that he'd driven them out. Within days, he'd appointed Astrid Murray and some sycophant freshman to fill their seats, and the only person left who'd actually been elected was Kian Sarkosian, whom I was beginning to suspect had Stockholm syndrome.

People dealt with Soren's death in different ways. Hector threw himself into Esme and, to an even greater degree, the Senate. Sometimes I wondered if he was doing good works just to keep himself from going insane. He got the senior class to agree on a gift—a row of cypress trees to be planted on the school grounds in Soren's name. He organized a memorial scholarship in Soren's name. Even the goddamn Valentine's Day flower sale was to be held in Soren's name.

The Senate had been my refuge and my inspiration the previous year, but now, all my work as Senate vice president just felt like going through the motions. Ms. Yee was gone, the Honor Council was a sham, Soren was dead, and Cal larked around the school doing whatever he felt like. Even Hector's most ambitious ideas seemed hollow when it was so obvious that the best thing we could do for our school, the thing that we most needed to do, was find a way to get rid of Cal.

Deep Throat must have felt the same way because the day we came back from winter break, there was a note in my locker that read:

CHECK THE ATTENDANCE RECORDS

You'd think they might have fixed the lock on the front office door after the Homecoming Turtle Massacre, but to do that would be to acknowledge that there was a problem. It was easier for the school to do nothing, to tell themselves the turtles were an isolated incident and everything was fine.

Anyway, it was easy enough to lag behind after a Senate meeting one Thursday afternoon, to pace the hallways until they were empty. The hard part was convincing myself that I was any better than the Watergate burglars Nixon had hired.

I wondered if my Deep Throat was one of the front office's student volunteers, or one of the staff, or possibly even Dr. Graves himself. What if our school principal was so terrified of Cal that he was actually turning to me for help? Far-fetched though it was, the last thought chilled my blood enough to send me through the office door.

I was breaking and entering to save my school.

It didn't take long to find the attendance records for the fall semester. Eventually, it all got entered into a computer, but whatever scholarship kid whose job it was to shred all the paper records had apparently been hoarding them instead.

I wracked my brain trying to remember who the student workers were, but they were all quiet, helpful, agreeable types. You signed in late, you signed out early for the dentist, and by the time you were in the parking lot, you'd already forgotten their faces.

Or maybe not *you*. Maybe that was a me thing.

Cursing myself for being the kind of person who overlooked the kind of people I apparently thought were less important than me, I found the file folder in the first drawer I opened. Not only was it neatly labeled, but somebody had already done the math for me. So helpful! So agreeable!

20 SUSPENSIONS

5 EXPULSIONS

The school year was only halfway over. If these records were to be believed, that meant the Honor Council was suspending or expelling more than a student a week. There were only four hundred people at Imperial Day—did any other elite private school in Los Angeles have disciplinary numbers like that? I wondered what the Board would think about that if they got wind of it.

That was what Deep Throat wanted me to know. What was implied was that Deep Throat expected me to do something about it.

When I pitched the idea to Mr. Prettinger, though, he looked skeptical.

"You haven't been on the newspaper staff in two years," he said, looking for a way to hedge out of the conversation. I reminded him of all the times my byline had appeared on stories as a personal favor to him.

"Is that what this is?" he asked. "Another favor? How's that going to look, Claudia—a story like that coming from you?"

"Get someone else to write it then, I don't care. I'll give you the numbers."

"Numbers you're not supposed to have."

"Check the office records," I explained. "They'll hold up."

"And so what if they do?"

"What do you mean, what if they do? What about exposing the truth? What about Nixon and Watergate and Woodward and Bernstein?"

Mr. Prettinger sighed the sigh of a man who had watched his profession, tenuous though his connection to it may have been, turn to dust.

"Claudia, no one except you and I even know who Woodward and Bernstein are," he said. "And let's say we do run it. What if the only thing that happens as a result is that they shut down the newspaper?"

A little voice in my head whispered, *If Ms. Yee was still here, she'd know who Woodward and Bernstein are.* Then again, look what had happened to her. I suppose I shouldn't have expected Mr. Prettinger to willingly throw himself in front of the 18-wheeler that was Cal and the Honor Council.

"Then what should I do?"

"The Board knows your face well enough by now. Go tell them yourself."

I thought about going to the Board, but Prettinger was right about one thing: this was information I wasn't supposed to have. When they asked where I'd gotten it, what was I going to tell them? The truth? That an unknown person sometimes wrote things down on pieces of paper and stuffed them into my locker? When they heard that, they'd ask, "How do you know what they're telling you is true? And how'd you get those attendance records anyway?"

And I wouldn't have an answer for that.

Mr. Prettinger saw the look on my face and sighed.

"I'm sorry, Claudia," he said. "I just can't get involved in this."

There was no one who could help me, and I didn't know where to turn. I felt like an animal in a zoo, a shitty one, the kind with a shitty habitat that drove the creatures into a pacing, ferocious madness.

XLIII

IT'S NEVER ENOUGH

I didn't expect Livia to be the one to help spring me from my cage.

The day Livia came back to Imperial Day, I found her standing in front of my locker at the end of eighth period, arms folded at her chest, jaw set. She looked like she'd been waiting there since lunchtime.

"So you're back," I said, because otherwise I think she would have stood in front of my locker glaring at me for another ten minutes without saying a word.

"Are you happy with the way things turned out?" she spat, like it was my fault.

I held up my hands in surrender. Whatever Livia thought had happened between us, I had too many other things on my mind, and the last thing I wanted was another enemy.

"Livia, whatever you think I did to you, you're wrong."

"Sure," she said, bumping my shoulder with unnecessary roughness as she shoved past me and stalked off down the hall.

In the three weeks following her return, Livia moved through the halls with an unblinking calm, daring anyone to ask where she'd been or to bring up the circumstances surrounding her exile. People whispered about it, but no one was bold enough to ask her to her face.

Livia sat alone at lunch. I never saw her speak to anyone except teachers. The only person she seemed to make any kind of exception for was me. Since her return, she'd slammed the bathroom door in my face, spilled a cafeteria tray full of chicken teriyaki and rice down my front, and stepped on the back of my heel in a way I couldn't prove was on purpose, but knew wasn't an accident.

When I ran into her in an empty stairwell one day after school, I clutched the railing and braced myself for the inevitable shove, but instead, Livia took me by the elbow, gave it a tug, and said, "Come with me."

"Why?" I asked, digging in my heels.

"Because we're going to do something."

"What?"

"You know what's the best thing in the world about having the worst thing happen to you?" she asked with a smirk. "After that, it doesn't matter what you do. So come on."

I felt a shock go through me as she said this. It was the same feeling I'd had when I broke into the front office, the same feeling I'd had that night on the New York City rooftop with Maisie. I didn't care what happened to me if it meant I could put a stop to this. Even if it meant working with Livia. She led me up the stairs to the third floor, into the Honor Council meeting room. We were not expected. We were not invited. We walked past the witness-holding cell, rounded the corner, and took seats on two of the wooden chairs while Astrid Murray gaped like a fish.

"You're not allowed to be here," said Macro, Cal's pet freshman. Livia shrugged, daring him to do something about it.

Jesse Nichols and Chris Gibbons came in next, the latter scowling at the sight of us.

"Leave," Jesse Nichols said. God, what an insipid person. Has anyone ever listened to anything Jesse Nichols has ever said?

Again, Livia and I said nothing, not even when Chris Gibbons made an obscene gesture at Livia or when Astrid Murray started doing her best impersonation of my stutter and limp, which I had to admit were fairly spot-on. I guess since her parents were actors, maybe she'd accidentally learned something.

"What are you even trying to prove?" Astrid asked as I turned away, repulsed by her bug eyes and mottled jowls.

Livia and I remained silent because we knew that ultimately, there was one person whose thoughts on this subject actually mattered, and until he arrived, it was pointless to engage his minions.

A few minutes later, Cal arrived with Kian Sarkosian. When they entered the room, everyone let out a raucous cry.

"CAL!!! CAL AND KITCHEN BOY!!!"

It was a far cry from the days of Augustus. I remembered how Soren had arrived at his ambush hearing, half-expecting to find the Honor Council representatives in robes and wigs.

I wondered why they'd started calling Kian "Kitchen Boy." I also wondered what about him was so broken inside that he felt compelled to stay even after everyone else had resigned in disgust.

"To what do we owe the honor, Claudia?" Cal asked. He acted like Livia wasn't even in the room, like she'd ceased to be an entity of any concern the moment she left Imperial Day and the Honor Council behind.

"We're staying," I said somewhat stupidly. Talking to Cal never got any less intimidating for me.

"Sure, that's great. You'd be taking up space somewhere, it might as well be here."

"What about the confidentiality of the court?" Astrid Murray piped up, suddenly a privacy advocate even though just a week before, I'd heard her gossiping about a juicy case they'd tried.

"Claudia and Livia are not here to spy on us." Cal said it like he was addressing the Honor Council, but it was clear he was talking to Livia and me. "They are here because their minds are small and twisted, and we should show them today that whatever they think is going on in this court is simply not true. Jesse, your client is waiting outside. Let's get started."

Jesse Nichols went around the corner and I heard the door to the witness room swing open. A moment later, he came back, a terrified-looking Ruby Greenberg trailing behind him. If Jesse Nichols was my appointed representative, I'd be terrified, too. I wondered what she'd done, then I remembered that she was the editor of the *Weekly Praetor*, that she'd hesitated before offering Cal his weekly column, that she'd run that letter from Ms. Yee before she resigned. None of that was a crime, but I didn't doubt it was the real reason Ruby Greenberg was here.

"Why are *they* here?" Ruby asked, her eyes darting over toward us, then back to Jesse, who, being 75 percent barnacle, looked to Cal for an answer.

"These girls are here today as impartial observers of the court," Cal said. "That's all right with you, isn't it?"

Ruby nodded, and Cal began the hearing by reading the charges that had been brought against her.

The case against Ruby Greenberg was serious, and also, it wasn't. In addition to her newspaper-editing gig, Ruby hung 't with Imperial Day's art scenesters and literary types and was always doing countercultural, subversive things, but only if she thought they would get her into RISD. No punk had ever taken so many Princeton Review SAT courses or earned so many attendance awards.

She was accused of painting a mural on the side of Imperial Day. It was a beautiful mural, everyone agreed on that, and no one wanted to take it down, but because it defaced the cornerstone that had been laid by homophobic tit Paul Chudnuff himself, and because no one seemed to remember authorizing the mural, it was technically a crime.

Jesse Nichols offered an indifferent defense against the facts of the case: Ruby thought she had permission. It was clear she hadn't acted alone, but had been singled out to make an example of and she wasn't naming any names. Chris Gibbons grumbled that she was uncooperative. That was what some of them really wanted, I could tell, an excuse to bring in more students and make them beg for mercy. There was nothing Cal liked quite so much as a girl who was afraid of him. Especially if she wore thigh-high boots and fishnet tights.

"Any closing statements?" Cal asked.

"Please," Ruby said. "Please, I didn't mean to do anything wrong. I'll sandblast it off. I'll do anything. Just please don't suspend me."

"Let's not get ahead of ourselves," Cal said with a wry smile that reminded Ruby and everyone else in the room that according to the Imperial Day Student Code of Conduct, the sentencing for vandalism started with suspension and went all the way up through expulsion.

Jesse Nichols led a near-tears Ruby back to the holding cell while the Honor Council prepared to deliberate. Astrid Murray and Chris Gibbons glared at me, like that might make me follow them, but Cal anticipated their irritation and said, "We have nothing to hide."

As soon as they were out of the room, the Honor Council members circled up their chairs and fell silent until Kian said, "One-week suspension," like it was the opening bid at an auction, or taking the temperature of the room to see what kind of justice people were hungry for that day.

There was a moment of silence, and then Chris Gibbons said, "One day. It would accomplish the same thing—you heard her."

Oh Ruby, I thought, *you should have held your cards closer to your chest. Never let them know what you're afraid of.*

"What if we told her to pay to have the mural removed?" Macro posited.

"What if she had to do it herself?" Chris suggested. "Obviously she didn't act alone. If her friends' consciences get the better of them, they'll come out to help her."

"Are we happy with this?" Cal asked. The others nodded their approval at Chris's suggestion, then Cal raised his hand and said, "Clean-up duty it is."

I thought, Is *this* it? I'd been looking for scandal and injustice, and what I'd seen was even-handed discussion. Thoughtful deliberation. Mercy. Not what I expected.

"Should I go get her?" Jesse asked.

"I'll break the news to her," Cal said. "No need to drag her back out here in front of all of you and do the whole suspense thing. We're done here—you can all go."

Cal disappeared around the corner and I heard the door to the holding cell click shut behind him.

"Was it all you hoped it would be, Claudia? Was it more?" Chris asked, his voice taunting. "Lots of good gossip to take ˑk to your boyfriend?"

Astrid Murray chortled, and the two of them slung their bags over their shoulders and left together, still mocking us. I didn't care. They could say whatever they wanted because in that moment, I actually felt like I'd done some good. Because Livia and I had been there, the Honor Council had decided to go easy on Ruby, to show us how merciful they were capable of being.

Before I could pat myself on the back too much, though, Livia got up from her chair and inclined her head toward the door. "Come on," she said.

"Seen enough?" Kian asked. Oddly, it seemed like he was really asking. He was the only Honor Council representative besides Cal who hadn't been irritated by our presence.

Livia made no distinction, though, turning on him like an owl that's just spotted a rabbit.

"I saw that *you* wanted to suspend that girl for a week for painting a mural *that everyone likes*."

Kian smirked at her. "Wasn't that how you used to do it, Livia? Start high on the sentencing, then see if there's anyone willing to argue down? That's how I remember it being."

Livia's eyes flashed, and for a moment, I thought she was going to tear into him, a sophomore talking to her that way. Macro and Jesse Nichols watched, bloodlust in their eyes, but Livia disappointed them by marching out the door. I got up and hurried after her, not wanting to be left alone with those three.

The holding cell was empty, and when I looked out into the hallway, there was no sign of Ruby or Cal.

"Where are they?" I mouthed to Livia. She didn't answer, but picked up speed as she headed out into the hallway, slamming the door shut behind us.

The last time Livia and I had been in this hallway together,

I was lying on the floor gasping for breath, my ribs and sides aching where she'd kicked me. Now, when she looked at me, there was no rage, no hatred.

Instead, she said, "If you were Cal, where would you take Ruby Greenberg right now? If you wanted to 'tell her something'?"

My eyes widened. Livia didn't explain further, but she didn't have to.

There were bathrooms on this floor, but they were the ones the Honor Council would have used. Tryouts for the spring play were going on in the theater, so the auditorium was out. The orchestra room was locked up.

It would be somewhere isolated, somewhere deserted, somewhere no one would have any reason to go. Somewhere far enough removed that they would not be seen or heard.

"The West Gym," I said.

Livia nodded. "Locker room," she added.

Together, we went down to the first floor, Livia racing down the halls toward the practice gym and me doing my best to keep up with her. This wasn't the main gym with its glossy waxed floors and padded bleachers, filled every Friday night during basketball season. The West Gym had been untouched since the days of homophobic tit Paul Chudnuff when they tossed around medicine balls and climbed ropes. Now it was where we did yoga or self-defense or any physical activity deemed insufficiently masculine for the main gym.

Livia opened the door and closed it softly behind us. We slipped off our shoes and padded across the floor toward the locker room without speaking. We looked at each other once 'efore reaching out together and pushing the door to the boys' 'er room open.

It was a cavernous room with high windows and poor ventilation. A hundred and ten years of stale sweat hung in the air. From behind a row of lockers, we heard a moan echo off the mosaic tile walls.

We closed the door behind us without a sound and crept around the corner, where we saw Cal sitting on a bench with his back to us. His pants were around his ankles. All I could see of Ruby were her fishnet tights and boots. The rest of her was hidden behind Cal's torso.

"Isn't this better than getting suspended?" Cal asked, then moaned again.

I turned my back on the scene and almost collided with Livia as I made for the door. She glared at me and raised a finger to her lips.

We could not be caught, she was saying. We had to leave the way we'd come in, undetected.

But Ruby, I thought. We couldn't just leave her there.

"No," I whispered, and then I ran for the door, making as much noise as I could, slamming doors behind me as loudly as they would slam. I picked up a half-inflated basketball and flung it at the locker room door, then Livia and I ran out of the gym.

I didn't breathe until I was out of the locker room, out of the West Gym, down the hall, and out in the parking lot, struggling to keep up with Livia. And when I did breathe, I realized that we hadn't made anything better. We hadn't saved Ruby from anything. Instead, Cal did what he wanted, took what he wanted, just like he always did. I thought about Ruby. She thought her sentence was going to be a suspension. She'd never know that the rest of the Honor Council ruled for community service hours. I felt myself shudder involuntarily.

As I caught up to Livia in the parking lot, I braced myself for another earful accusing me of sabotaging her campaign, blaming me for everything that had happened, screaming that all of this was my fault, up to and including what Cal had done to Ruby Greenberg.

It didn't happen. Instead, Livia froze in place. Her shoulders hunched forward and her mouth fell slack. Her arms hung limp at her sides until she drew one of her hands up, bringing it to rest on her cheek.

"We just left her there," Livia said.

"No," I said, "that's not what happened. That's not how it was. We tried."

"It's not enough. It's never enough," she said, and then her chin sank down into her chest and she began to cry.

It is a strange and terrible thing to watch your enemy cry when you know exactly how she feels. I was repulsed, disgusted, angry, frustrated, and I didn't know what to do about any of it. I didn't know how to make it stop. I understood completely why Livia was crying.

Her pain was my own, and if she had been anyone else, I would have tried to comfort her.

XLIV

THERE BUT NOT THERE

There was nothing I could do to stop this or change it. I walked around school for the next few weeks, there but not there, my head spooling out ideas, each one more impossible and ineffective than the last. I was too ashamed to tell Hector what Livia and I had seen. I didn't want him to know that we'd run out of the room without screaming our heads off or pulling a fire alarm.

I managed my Senate duties in a haze. During the Soren Bieckmann Memorial Valentine's Day bouquet sale, I botched one tag after another, and probably contributed to at least one breakup through my negligence.

When I went to eighth period, there was a bouquet on my desk, once again with a card that read, YOU ARE A FORCE FOR GOOD IN THE UNIVERSE, and all I could think as I stuffed it back into the envelope was, *I can't even stop a high school despot from forcing a girl to suck his dick in the locker room.*

I'm not a force for anything.

XLV

A FORCE FOR GOOD IN THE UNIVERSE

The day before spring break was one of those shitty, stir-crazy, overcast days that everybody entered into with nobler intentions than they were able to realize. I had two midterms, a brutally dull discussion on *Hard Times*, which no one had read, and a physics lab before lunch, and not one teacher had had the decency to show a movie.

On my way to lunch, I stopped by my locker to drop off books before going to the cafeteria, and a note from Deep Throat fluttered out:

COME TO THE COURTYARD AFTER SCHOOL. THERE'S SOMETHING I NEED TO TELL YOU.

Deep Throat's messages always had a sense of urgency about them, but this was unusually intense and cryptic. What was going to be waiting for me out in the courtyard? Another message? An ambush? Or was Deep Throat actually suggesting that we meet face to face?

It was burrito day in the cafeteria. No, I don't remem-
ʳ what my grandmother looked like, but I remember that
ʟay before spring break was burrito day. Probably the

detail sticks because before receiving the message from Deep Throat I had expected the burritos would be the highlight of my afternoon.

There was a commotion as I approached the cafeteria, a scrum of bodies packed tightly around the door, the weird silence paired with scuffling feet and grunting and gasps that could only mean there was a fight happening.

Fights were rare at Imperial Day. They were considered gauche and simply not done, so things went on for a few moments before someone had the presence of mind to get an adult. By the time Mr. Woolf came barreling down the hall shouting, "Break it up! Break it up!" the novelty had worn off, and the crowd peeled back to reveal none other than Astrid Murray and Macro circling each other like wolves.

I pushed my way to the front and nudged a shell-shocked freshman named Jacob Lockhart.

"What happened?" I asked.

"She just went after him," he whispered, keeping one eye on Astrid and Macro to make sure they didn't hear him. "She grabbed him by the backpack and pulled him *down*."

On the other side of the hallway, I saw Livia taking in the scene, her face twisted with equal parts contempt and frustration, and I had no trouble guessing what she was thinking in that moment: *If I'd been elected president instead of Cal, none of this would be happening.*

It was strange and sobering to find myself agreeing with the person who'd knocked me to the ground and kicked me hard enough to bruise my ribs. Livia was a corrupt, power-hungry, manipulative liar with a violent streak, and yet, under her watch, Honor Council representatives would not be attacking each other in the hallway like feral dogs; no one would have smashed up a tankful of turtles; no one would be demanding sexual favors for the promise of a lighter punishment.

Mr. Woolf took Macro, and a moment later, Mrs. DiVincenzo emerged from the cafeteria to escort Astrid to the main office. Even though the teachers kept them more than arm's length apart, they snarled and swore at each other as they went down the hall.

In case you were wondering, both of them got off with a warning. I'm sure it was all extremely fair and impartial.

For the rest of the day, all anyone could talk about was the fight and what it meant. People theorized that factions were emerging; that having run out of civilians to prosecute, the Honor Council was finally turning on itself.

During my afternoon classes, I thought about Deep Throat's note and wondered if it had anything to do with this. Where did Cal stand in all of it? Had he instigated the fight? Was there some sort of power struggle brewing?

I was so lost in thought that when the final bell rang, it took me a moment to realize that it was time, that soon I'd have some of the answers I'd been looking for—key among them, who had been passing information my way for the past two years.

The halls emptied out quickly as people burst from Imperial Day, eager to escape and taste freedom for ten days. I walked more slowly. I didn't want to be the first to arrive in the courtyard. I wanted to have a chance to peer in through the window and see what I was walking into first.

It didn't happen that way, though. We turned the corner at the same time, me from one hallway, him from the other. We walked toward each other, met at the courtyard door, and he said, "You came."

"In my head, I've been calling you Deep Throat," I said, remembering that I *had* seen him working the attendance desk in the front office. Really, it was the perfect job for a trusty, incorruptible Honor Council representative.

Kian Sarkosian stared blankly at me. Perhaps he had not thought about how this conversation was going to go because he looked down at his feet and stammered, then looked up and mumbled something in my general direction, and then finally shoved his hands into his pockets.

"You know—Nixon, Watergate," I said, not expecting him to get those references either, but needing something to fill the silence. "You're the one who called this meeting, you know."

He recovered, and in that moment, I saw the difference between the bystander who'd watched Cal taunt Hector and me at The Last Bookstore and done nothing to stop it, and the steely-eyed Honor Council rep who'd held his own when I mouthed off to him.

"Woodward. Bernstein. I know," he said, then added, "So you've been getting my notes?"

"That's why I'm here."

I hated the harshness in my tone, which was only there because I felt guilty. If I'd managed to do more—or anything— to stop Cal, Kian wouldn't have to ask if I'd been getting his notes. He'd know.

He held the door open for me and we walked out to the courtyard in silence, taking a seat on the bench by the pond. Some of the underclassmen senators had raised the idea of getting new turtles, but Hector and I had vetoed it. It felt wrong somehow, too soon, so there was nothing in the pond now except for some hideous goldfish with bulging eyes that reminded me just a little of Astrid Murray.

"Why me?" I asked, softening my voice.

For a minute I thought he was disappointed in me, like he'd trusted me with all of these secrets, and I'd failed to make anything different. Like I'd let him down. But then he looked down at his feet and a streak of pink crept up past the collar of his white button-down shirt, and he said, "Because you are a force for good in the universe."

And that was when I realized that when Kian asked if I'd been getting his notes, he wasn't just talking about the ones from Deep Throat. He was talking about how he'd felt about me for the past two Valentine's Days and who knows how much longer before that.

Time slowed down as I combed my brain for a response.

I'd spent the past year trying to bury my feelings for Hector Estrella. Now, when I tried to dig them up, they were gone. I didn't notice when it happened exactly. Once, I'd been the kind of person who could lose a weekend devastated because the boy I liked didn't buy me flowers for Valentine's Day. Once, I'd been the kind of person who fell in love, who wanted romance, even though I was afraid of it. All I wanted then was to be left alone, to have my books, and maybe a little space in my life for someone who cared about me, if that person existed. Now, those Valentine's Day bouquets and those simple little wants seemed like things that had happened to another person.

Of course I didn't say any of it out loud. As far as Kian knew, I was sitting there trying to figure out how to let him down easy.

"I'm sorry," he said. "Forget I said anything about it."

"You don't even know me."

I'd always thought my best shot at love was to get to know someone and slowly win them over until they liked my quirks right along with the rest of me. That someone would fall for me from a distance was incomprehensible. It did not fit into my worldview. It was like handing an iPhone to the Salem witches and telling them to use it to save themselves.

Maybe Kian realized that, or maybe because he'd already revealed so much, he figured he didn't have anything left to lose by saying the rest.

"Do you want to hang out over spring break?"

The weird thing was, I was intrigued. It was intriguing to be wanted like that.

If Hector had wanted me, he would have done what Kian was doing. If he'd cared, he would have tried.

"What about after that?" I asked.

I already knew the answer, and that was the other thing that made it so appealing. It could only be spring break. It wasn't like I could start dating my informant, but during those ten days, we could be away from Imperial Day, the Honor Council, the Senate. We could be other people together. We could get to know each other like none of the problems that currently engulfed us even existed.

"We could see," Kian said.

"The last person I went out with died," I said.

"I know," Kian said, and immediately, I wished I could take it back and say what I actually felt instead of these tossed-off, callous things.

"You were there that night, weren't you?"

Along with Cal and Chris Gibbons and Hector and Esme, his was the name that I'd heard enough times to believe it might have been the truth.

"Not as a guest. My cousin owns a catering company, and she was short-staffed, so I said I'd help her out. I didn't know there were going to be Imperial Day people there or I wouldn't have done it."

So that was why they called him Kitchen Boy, I thought. Lovely that Cal and Chris Gibbons's main takeaway from the night Soren died was a cruel new nickname for their colleague.

"Cal came into the kitchen and started hounding my cousin for booze. Then he tried to get her to go into the pantry with him."

I curled my lip in disgust. Knowing Cal, he probably thought that the help were his to harass and fondle at will.

"When he saw me come around the corner with an ice bucket, he was, like, 'Nice apron, Kitchen Boy,' and I said, 'Thank you,' and that was the last I saw of him that night."

"Did you see Soren, though?"

"He came into the kitchen at about ten looking for a cup of coffee. There wasn't any made, but I told him I'd brew a pot, and he wouldn't let me. He went into the pantry and found the filters and made it himself. He wasn't fucked up, Claudia. We sat there and he asked me about the chess team. I didn't even know he knew I was on the chess team."

I could almost see the story unfold before my eyes as he told it, Soren's hands wrapped around the coffee mug, the intense way he had of looking at you when you were talking to him, like he was listening as hard as he could. At 10 p.m. on the night he died, Soren was still Soren, and even though it didn't change anything, knowing this flooded me with peace.

That was when I knew for sure that I wanted to know Kian Sarkosian, the person who had been my ally all along. Since my sophomore year, he'd warned me of danger, tipped me off, given me insider information that no one else was supposed to know, steered me through the minefield that was my Honor

Council hearing. And on top of all of that, he'd even bought me flowers.

"Why do you always wear the same thing?" I asked. I knew the question was a little blunt, but Kian Sarkosian and I seemed to be in blunt territory now.

He considered his answer for a minute, then grimaced. "It's weird."

"You're talking to a girl who wears neckties and Nixon t-shirts," I reminded him.

"I don't like using my clothes as a shortcut way of telling people what kind of person I am. I like things simple. No affectations."

"Isn't the absence of affectation an affectation?" I asked, smirking to let him know I was just messing with him a little bit.

He smiled, and I felt myself melt.

"For what it's worth," he added, "I like your neckties."

I thought about what freshman-year Claudia might have said. That was who I wanted to be when I was with Kian, the person who'd never run for Senate or fallen for Hector Estrella or gone out for tacos with Soren Bieckmann.

"What do you want to do over spring break?" Kian asked me.

"Old things," I said at last. "I want to go look at some old things."

XLVI

YOU DESERVE BETTER

The first time Kian texted, he asked me to go to the silent movie theater on Fairfax. We watched a Rudy Valentino movie from the 1920s, then afterwards he took me to the Jewish deli down the street for pastrami sandwiches and pickles. We paid at an antique cash register that was operated with a hand crank, and even though we were the youngest people in the restaurant by at least three decades, I looked at Kian and said, "Older."

The day after that, we went to the Central Library and looked at microfilm and found out all the horrible crimes that took place on our birthdays during various years of the 1800s.

"Older," I told him.

The third day, we met at the Los Angeles County Museum of Art. Kian led me through the German expressionists, the French impressionists, the Flemish portrait painters, the Italian Renaissance, medieval England, past all of it until we came to a room with two giant Assyrian reliefs covering the wall. The sculptures were part bird, part horse, part human, part god. They'd been taken from a palace in Nineveh, the city Jonah, in the Bible, was supposed to save from its wickedness before he chickened out. Kian stood before the reliefs, his eyes soaking up every detail, every feather on the eagle's neck, like he was storing up the view until next time.

"This is my favorite place," he said. "I come here when I need to think."

"Why here?"

"Because these are 17,000 years old, and they were basically some king's wallpaper. It puts things in perspective. Nobody knows what's important or what will last."

I nodded. "Everything we do matters. Nothing we do matters."

"Exactly," Kian said, and that was when he kissed me.

Assyrian reliefs are not very popular in museums. You can kiss in front of them for at least a minute before someone comes barging into the room. You can slip a hand up under a sweater, clutch a hip. You can feel a person's breath on your neck, the nip of his teeth on your earlobe.

It was spring break. Everything mattered. Nothing mattered.

I don't remember our walk to the car, only that by the time we got there, I was breathless. I climbed into the backseat and he climbed in after me and slammed the door shut, and beyond that, I do not think what happened is relevant to my testimony.

On Saturday night, I invited him over to my house to watch documentaries, much to the astonishment of my parents, who were going to some kind of company party in Santa Monica, one of the ones where they got all dressed up and came home after two. I could tell this scenario hadn't crossed their minds and they had a moment's hesitation about leaving me alone in the house with a boy. But they were computer nerds. I saw them calculate the risk in their heads based on what they knew of me, what they could deduce about Kian from a first impression, and I guess they liked the odds because they gave Kian some stern looks, made some vague comments about trusting me, and then left.

Five minutes later, my phone buzzed three times in quick succession, then Kian's did the same. I assumed it was my parents doing a paranoia check, but it was Hector. Some people were going over to Esme's to watch movies, and I was invited if I wanted to go. And where had I been all week?

I smiled as I looked up at Kian.

"Who was that?"

"Esme," he said. "Inviting me over. You?"

"Hector. Same thing." My smile widened. "Nobody knows where I am."

Kian smiled back. "Nobody knows we're doing this."

The thought was delicious, not only for this reason, but because no one anywhere would have suspected that I was alone in my house with Kian. He was my secret.

"If Cal knew I was with you . . ." Kian trailed off, the smile fading from his face in a way that made me realize he'd been about to add *he'd kill me.*

That was when I realized the other reason I couldn't resist doing this. I liked Kian. In fact, the better I got to know him, the more I liked him. What was not to like? A guy who thought up elaborate places to take me, the way he hung on everything I said like he really did believe I was a force for good in the universe. And then there was the way he kissed. Not that I had much—or any—prior experience in that field, but when his lips touched mine, I felt a shock from the back of my neck to the base of my spine. My toes curled up in my shoes. I felt reckless, electrified, not just the first time he kissed me, but every time.

If it would be dangerous to be caught together, I didn't care. I took his hand and led him upstairs to my room.

An hour or so later, we went back down to the kitchen and made an oven pizza, a bag of popcorn, and root beer floats, and ate everything. It was there at the kitchen table, sluggish and content with the dual pleasures of eating junk food and fooling around, that Kian decided we needed to talk and basically inject a dose of horrible reality into what had been an otherwise unimpeachable week.

"What are we going to do?" he asked.

"Watch some television?" I suggested. "Or a movie? I don't care."

"I mean next week. At school."

It was the conversation we'd been putting off, the thing I'd managed to avoid thinking about altogether. I thought about trying to carry what we had over into the real world. Was that possible? And more than that, was it even what I wanted? Kian had already surprised me plenty of times in the past week, but I was in no way prepared for what he said next.

"Because I think we should keep doing this. In public."

"We'd be arrested," I said, because making a stupid joke prevented me from having to answer the question. Kian knew what I was doing, though. Kian knew exactly what I was doing and rolled his eyes.

"Never mind. Forget I said anything."

If I'd left things alone there, it might have turned out differently. I would have hurt Kian, he would have hated me for a while, but in the end, it might have been preferable. Instead, though, another impulse took hold of me. I was exhausted. I was sick to death of pushing everything away. I was tired of acting like there was no one I needed and nothing I wanted.

Kian deserved better than that. And I imagined that maybe Soren was watching, that wherever he was, he'd be proud of me for trying to tell the truth.

"I'm sorry," I said. "It's just . . . this week. This week was such a good thing in such a year of shit."

Every one of those words stuck in my throat, unwilling to be pried out. My tongue was unused to sincerity, and it did not come easily, but I kept going.

"I like talking to you. I like kissing you. I like your stupid face. I want us to be together, too."

Kian's face lit up as I spoke, his smile spreading almost to his ears. I hated that I had to keep talking.

"But it can't happen. As long as Cal is running things at Imperial Day, I don't see how this can work."

"I don't care what he does to me," Kian said.

"You should," I said. It was bold and reckless and romantic for Kian to say something like that to me, but it was a terrible idea. A year's tuition at Imperial Day was more than most people in the world earned in a year, and if Kian's parents could afford to send him there without a scholarship, it was only just barely. They were banking on him. He was an investment. They were sending him to Imperial Day so he wouldn't have to spend holiday weekends rolling canapés at a Nick Jr. star's house party.

So that was part of it. I wasn't going to let Kian throw away his life for a chance to hold my hand in the hallway at school.

But it was also more than that.

"You want to take Cal down, right?"

"Of course I do," Kian said.

"The only way we can do that is if we go on like we've always been. If you and I are a couple, Cal will be suspicious. We want him thinking that everything is normal and fine."

"Do you have a plan?" Kian asked.

"I'm close to one," I lied, and for a second, things felt back to the way they'd been. He was Deep Throat; I was Woodward and Bernstein. Nothing more.

Kian looked impressed, and I reminded myself that I was doing him a favor. I was protecting him from whatever he thought he was willing to sacrifice to be with me.

"And if it works? What about then?" he asked, leaning toward me, and I let my kiss be my answer.

I'm sorry, Soren, I thought. *I'm not as good at the truth as you were.*

In one of the moments in between kissing and talking, Kian picked up a Whole Foods receipt from the kitchen table and started nervously fiddling with it. He wrapped it around his index finger as many times as it would go, then he folded it up into a triangle, then he unfolded it and smoothed it flat.

"Is that a nervous habit?" I asked.

"Sort of," he said. Then he picked up a pencil from the table and wrote in the blocky letters I'd come to know so well:

SOMETIMES YOU MAKE ME NERVOUS

I laughed. Kian served on the Honor Council week after week with Cal Hurt, an unpredictable psychopath with a hair-trigger response, and *I* made him nervous?

DON'T BE NERVOUS, I wrote back. I HAVE NO IDEA WHAT I'M DOING.

"It doesn't seem that way," Kian said, in a slightly eyebrow-waggling tone of voice that I supposed was a compliment.

I LIKE YOUR EYES, he wrote next.

YOU'RE A GOOD KISSER, I wrote back.

"This paper is magic," Kian said. "You can say anything on it, as long as it's the truth."

Then he wrote, I WANT YOU TO BE MY GIRLFRIEND.

I'VE NEVER BEEN ANYONE'S GIRLFRIEND BEFORE.

IT DOESN'T MATTER.

But it did matter. I acted like the reason I'd never been anyone's girlfriend before was because I wasn't pretty enough. Or because of my stutter or my limp. But for a long time, I'd been beginning to suspect it was something else.

WHAT HAPPENS WHEN YOU FIGURE OUT I'M A TERRIBLE PERSON?

YOU ARE A FORCE FOR GOOD IN THE UNIVERSE.

Would he ever get tired of saying that? I wondered.

Yes.

He would.

Once he got to know me, it wouldn't take long before he never wanted to say it again.

YOU DESERVE BETTER, I wrote.

Kian took my hands across the kitchen table and said, "I can't do this, Claudia. Write one nice thing about yourself. One nice thing, that's it."

I stared at the Whole Foods receipt, imagining the frivolous things on the other side of it: sea salt, rice crisps, and infused olive oils that no one in my house would ever use. I made no move to pick up the pen.

"The magic paper is a safe space, Claudia."

For a moment, I thought about picking up the pencil and doing what he'd asked, but instead, I shook my head and pushed the receipt back across the kitchen table at him.

"You should go," I said, and when he started to protest, I pressed my fingertips to his lips. "My parents will be home soon. I'll see you on Monday."

Kian's goofy smile disintegrated, was replaced by his indifferent Honor Council poker face, which, since we're being honest here, I actually preferred.

"If that's what you want," he said. The chair scraped along the tile floor as he got up from the table and walked out of the kitchen. He let himself out. I waited until I heard his car starting in the driveway to get up from the table and lock the front door.

I was glad Kian was smart, that he'd gotten it on the first try and hadn't made me say out loud that when I saw him on Monday, it would be like none of this had ever happened.

I didn't know then what was coming or what was going to happen, but there was one true thing I knew and it was this:

Whatever Kian thought this was, however he thought he felt about me, I needed him to know that when the time came, and all of this came crashing down, he should save himself. He shouldn't bother wasting the truth on me.

"What if you and Kian had walked in to school that Monday holding hands? What do you think would have happened?"

"Cal would have made his life miserable."

"But Kian didn't seem to care."

"He would have been off the Honor Council within the month—either kicked off or forced to resign."

"He didn't seem to care about that either."

"Well, then I would have lost my informant, wouldn't I?"

"Was that all he was to you?"

"I wasn't going to let him throw that away for me."

"Wasn't that Kian's decision?"

"It would have been the wrong decision."

"Which part?"

"All of it."

"Which part, Claudia?"

"The part where he decided that he wanted to be with me."

XLVII

The Part of the Story Where You Will Like Me Less

We are all the heroes of our own stories, aren't we? There is always a reason we act as we do, and when we act in a way that is less than admirable, the contrast to the rest of our lives provides the context.

All of this is to say that we are approaching the part of the story where you will like me less, which is not to assume that you like me now.

I am telling you what happened. The fact that these things happened near me makes me look bad enough even if they were not caused by me. At this point, all I can ask is that you try to separate the things I did from the things that happened, to remember that these are, in many cases, two completely different sets of things.

What I told you I said to Kian was really all that I said. It's not like I told him we could be together once Cal was out of the way. Besides, the way we left things that night probably killed any lingering desire he had to be my boyfriend.

I never told him to do anything except leave.

XLVIII

BETTER OFF BEFORE I CAME ALONG

It was around the time we came back from spring break that Cal's grip on reality became increasingly tenuous. He was suspicious of everyone, even his closest friends. One day he'd be walking down the hall with his arm thrown around Chris Gibbons's shoulder, the next, he'd stand up in the cafeteria, knocking Chris's chair over backwards and accusing him of undermining his authority in some way.

He announced that he was overriding Hector's decision and instead of a row of cypress trees honoring Soren's memory, the senior class gift would be a row of lemon trees honoring Soren's memory. Not that it mattered, not that Cal even cared about anything except getting his own way.

People were like mice around him, tiptoeing past, trying to avoid his attention because if Cal was aware of you, Cal would find a way to punish you. If you were weak or shy or vulnerable, he loved that, but if you were confident or powerful or popular, he loved that even more. By April, everyone on the Senate except for Hector had been called up on some minor charge, most of them bogus—using cell phones during class; plagiarizing math homework; unexcused absence from school

(I had the flu the day we came back from spring break, and while the timing was undeniably convenient in allowing me to avoid Kian, a firmly worded note from Dr. Christina Xiu, head of pediatrics at Cedars Sinai Hospital and my longtime physician, absolved me of Cal's charges).

I often thought about what Livia had said to me her first day back at Imperial Day: *Are you happy with the way things turned out?*

Livia and I blamed each other for Cal's power grab. We blamed each other for not being able to stop him, but I wondered, did Livia blame herself the way I did? When she passed me in the hallway, did she think about that afternoon in the West Gym and how we'd run away instead of doing something?

The Tuesday Senate meeting after spring break was the first time I'd seen Hector in two weeks. After we'd dispatched our business and everyone had cleared out of the room—even Macro and Jesse Nichols, who always stayed until the bitter end—it was just Hector and me. It was weird to think how sophomore year we'd been inseparable, and now, I couldn't remember the last time we'd been alone together.

Did I still have feelings for him, or were they just gone? Would they come back if he and Esme broke up? I'd fallen for Kian, I cared about him—whatever you think about what I did, you should know that I *did* care about him—but it wasn't the same as the secret, all-encompassing, desperate thing I'd felt for Hector last year. I'd chosen Hector. I'd seen him patiently dealing with his misspelled, ratfucked campaign posters freshman year, and the first time I talked to him, something inside me sat up and took notice.

"Where were you over spring break?" Hector asked, taking advantage of our rare unstructured solitude to actually talk. "Did you get grounded? Were you trapped under something heavy?"

"I—" I felt the blush creeping up my cheeks until they tingled, and the truth just came out. "I met someone. It was weird. In a good way."

Even if I couldn't tell him the whole truth, I didn't want to lie to him any more than I had to. Besides, a secret like that? You just want to tell someone. It's too good to keep to yourself.

As for what Hector thought about it, I couldn't tell exactly. He half-chuckled, then ran his fingers over the close-shaved hairline at the nape of his neck and looked down at the desk.

Finally, he looked up and smiled at me. "That's great, Claudia. Who is it?"

And you see, that's the problem with telling people things. It makes them want to know more things.

"He doesn't go here. He might live in Canada. He might be a figment of my imagination."

That would be the easiest thing to believe, right? That no one would want to be with me? But Hector just shook his head, like he was disappointed in me.

"Fine, don't tell me. I wish you'd have come over to Esme's last weekend is all. It was boring without you."

"It was boring being with your girlfriend?"

"It was boring being with my girlfriend and all of her friends, none of whom likes me very much."

"Why not? You're Hector Estrella," I said. "You're delightful."

"They seem to think she was much better off before I came along."

"Well, that is demonstrably true," I said.

The past few months had not gone well for Esme, as if Cal was punishing her for choosing Hector instead of him.

She'd been suspended once for tardiness and sent home twice on dress code violations. Between the harassment, the turtle murders, and Soren's death, her parents were one step away from pulling her out of Imperial Day midyear.

"The only way she's allowed to hang out with me anymore is if a whole shield-like legion of her friends is there. It's awful."

"Is it worth it?" I asked, and I wasn't just asking for Hector's sake. Why did Esme stay with him? It would be so much easier on her if she let him go.

"Actually, we broke up."

"When?"

"Saturday. She sent everybody else home, and for a minute, I thought I was actually going to get to be alone with her. I was, but only because she was about to dump me. I tried getting ahold of you, but . . ."

But I was up in my room with Kian.

"I'm so sorry," I said. "I had no idea."

"It's okay. Maybe we're both better off this way."

It was the way he said it that pissed me off, like he was just going to give up because this was the way things were now. I wasn't going to let Hector Estrella go around thinking that this was just one of those normal things that happened. This was something that had been done to him. It had been done to all of us.

"You know it's all his fault," I said.

"Whose fault?"

"Cal's," I said. "Who else? He's the one who basically tried to coerce Esme into—who knows what—at Homecoming and he's made her life a living hell ever since. Your relationship, Esme's life, Soren, the whole school walking around like they're expecting to get a hatchet between the eyes, and it's all that fucker's fault, every last bit of it, and if we can find some way to take him down, impeach him, recall him, have a vote of no confidence, I don't know, we should make it our life's fucking mission to do that."

A strange look passed over Hector's face. Did he agree with me? Did he already know all of this? Did he know in his bones that if we didn't take action, no one would? The ordinary channels had failed, there was nothing else but to turn vigilante.

All Hector said to me, though, was "I think you're taking all of this too seriously, Claudia. You should rest, pull back from the Senate stuff if you have to. I can take care of things."

"What do you mean?"

"Just things. I'll take care of them."

That's what he said. That's all that he said. That's all I knew about it.

Just like Kian, just like Livia, I never told him to do anything. Whatever people are saying, I certainly never told Hector to hurt anybody.

XLIX

BECAUSE YOU'RE A RAPIST SCUMBAG

It was a Friday when it all came to an end, the Friday after I'd told Hector that Cal needed to be taken down, and it began, like so many Fridays, with a school assembly in the auditorium.

At high schools all over the country, people just like us were filing into dimly lit auditoriums, pulling up the hoods on their sweatshirts and settling in for a nap as the principal took the stage to welcome the college admissions counselor or dating violence expert or traveling circus performers who would be enriching them that morning.

At Imperial Day Academy, however, this assembly had been planned by Cal, and its featured speaker was Cal. The bastard even introduced himself. We were ostensibly gathered there that morning to honor all the seniors who'd won scholarships, but it was clear Cal had been looking for an excuse to stand in front of the student body and list off all the prestigious schools he'd been admitted to and all the scholarships he'd won so far.

"I didn't get into Harvard, by the way," he said with a wolfish grin. "And the reason I'm telling you that is to inspire you. If someone like me can apply to Harvard and not get in, the lesson you should draw from that is that if the admissions office at one school is too dumb to appreciate you, remember, *it's their loss.*"

I decided I'd had enough. I got up and walked out of the auditorium, looking back over my shoulder just long enough to see Cal glare at me, and I knew that he would file away the fact that I'd left in the middle of his speech, and that sooner or later, he'd make me pay for it.

At that moment, though, it was worth it. The hall was empty and quiet, and standing alone in it with my eyes closed, my head tilted back against the wall, I felt better than I'd felt since spring break.

I didn't hear the auditorium door open, so when I opened my eyes and saw Mrs. DiVincenzo standing in front of me, I almost jumped out of my skin.

"Are you okay, Claudia?" she asked.

"I wasn't feeling well," I said. "I needed some air."

"Do you need to go to the nurse's office?"

That sounded nice, I thought, a cool, dark room to hide out in for an hour or so. I wondered how often the nurse's office was used by legitimately ill people and how often it was just people like me who needed a rest from the bleakness and misery of the world.

"I'll be okay," I said. "I just need a minute."

Mrs. DiVincenzo nodded and had just turned to go back into the auditorium when my phone rang. I groaned. I'd forgotten to turn off the ringer, which never happened. Because at Imperial Day, we turned a blind eye to coercion, election fraud, and abuse of power, but woe upon your head if you left your cell phone turned on during school hours.

It was Kian, too, which made the whole thing worse. What made him think that I'd answer a phone call when I hadn't replied to any of the texts he'd sent since he left my house the Saturday night before? What did he want that was so important? And where was he calling me from when he was supposed to be in the assembly like everyone else?

Of course, there's no way of knowing for sure, but given what happened later that day, I have a few ideas what Kian might have been calling about.

A pained look crossed Mrs. DiVincenzo's face, like it hurt her more to do this than it would hurt me.

"Can't you let it go just this once?" I asked, even as I handed the phone over to her.

"You can come pick it up in my room after eighth period," she said, then motioned back toward the auditorium. "Just be glad it didn't happen in there, right?"

And then I realized why Mrs. DiVincenzo had followed me out in the first place. She was trying to help me. She was trying to get me back inside that auditorium before I was gone long enough for Cal to punish me for it, and I realized that if the teachers knew about it, knew what he was and what he was capable of, and this was all they could do—light damage control at best—then we were all good and fucked.

After the assembly, I saw Chris Gibbons, Astrid Murray, Macro, and Jesse Nichols huddled together in the hallway whispering. They kept their distance from Cal. None of them went up to tell him what a great job he'd done. Cal passed through the crowd with a dangerous, stormy look on his face, daring someone to get in his way. I could have sworn I saw Livia pass by, lock eyes with Chris Gibbons for a moment, then nod at him, like they were sharing some kind of secret signal.

The Honor Council goons were nowhere to be seen during lunch. People filled up every table so there were no extra seats, spread their meals out so there was no extra room. For the first time in his life, Cal ate lunch by himself.

We all knew to stay out of his way when he was like this, and today was worse than usual. Only an idiot would have engaged him when he was in this state, much less picked a fight with him—which was exactly what Kian did.

Kian walked up to Cal while he sat alone at that lunch table, leaned down, and said loudly enough for the surrounding tables to hear him, "Maybe the reason you didn't get into Harvard is because you're a rapist scumbag."

If the reason he'd called was to tell me what he was planning to do in the cafeteria that day, I would have tried to talk him out of it. It was possible he hoped I'd try to talk him out of it.

However, there is also the possibility that there was more to it than that. After all, Kian wasn't an idiot. He'd basically been an undercover informant on the Honor Council for two years, and the only person who knew a thing about it was me. Kian was the best liar I'd ever met, so why would he choose that moment to blow his cover unless there was some greater purpose to it?

Cal grabbed his lunch tray in both hands, swung it around, and hit Kian in the face, knocking him to the ground. His head smacked against the tile.

"Say that again, you little bitch," Cal said, then threw the tray down on Kian's prone body and walked out of the cafeteria like he'd just remembered he had something else to do. There was no look of horror on his face at having lost control, no fear of what would happen to him next, no regret at what he'd done or shame at what we'd think of him.

He was Cal. He did whatever he wanted, whatever he did was right, and no one ever stopped him.

A hush fell over the cafeteria as he walked out, and I saw something come over the faces of every person in the room. I don't know what to call that look exactly, so I'll call it this: *motive*.

The thing that happened to Cal later on that day—I know that some people think Kian did it, or that Hector did it, or that I told them to, but I was in the cafeteria that day, and what I know is this:

The moment Cal smashed Kian's face with the cafeteria tray in front of a room full of witnesses, none of whom had the power to stop him, everyone in that cafeteria, every single one of us, became capable of doing the thing that happened next.

L

I'm Not a Monster

This is the story of what happened to Cal, but it is also the story of how I came to be the president of the Imperial Day Academy Honor Council, and after I finish telling it to you, it will become the story of why they are putting me on trial.

They say they're putting me on trial for fraud and election tampering and for what happened to Cal, but really, it's because they realize they made a mistake in naming me president and they'd like to take it back.

A person like me was never supposed to be the face of the Imperial Day Academy. A person like me was never meant to wield that kind of power. It was bad enough that the son of a disgraced State senator was running the Senate, but to have a limping, stuttering, ugly, unpopular, foul-mouthed malcontent in charge of the Honor Council was unthinkable.

So why did they choose me?

Why was I there, in exactly that moment and exactly that place?

I swear to you, no one told me what was about to happen to Cal. I hadn't even been in the hallway by the West Gym since the day Livia and I had gone there together.

The whole week, Kian had been waiting for me in the hall-way after eighth period. Every day, I'd managed to spot him and take a different route in time to avoid whatever he planned to ask me.

The day of the assembly, the day Cal had bashed his face with a cafeteria tray, I almost had a change of heart when I saw Kian standing by my locker, his lip swollen and split, a bruise blooming on his cheek. I thought about listening to whatever he had to say to me, whether it was to ask me again to be his girl-friend or to tell me I was a rotten person for kissing him in pri-vate, then treating him like a stranger in public. I thought about it, but I didn't go to him because I realized it would require less of me to leave things broken between us than it would to fix them.

So I did what was easier, and I walked down the hall in the opposite direction.

Even so, I wouldn't have ended up near the West Gym if I hadn't remembered at that moment that I'd forgotten to pick up my phone from Mrs. DiVincenzo. I trotted toward the nearest stairwell and hobbled up to the third floor. Of course I'd been busted by the teacher with the most inconveniently located room, and of course it was a Friday, after an extraordinarily trying day and Mrs. DiVincenzo had already gone home for the weekend by the time I got there.

There was a note on her door telling me that she'd given my phone to Hector Estrella, and that he said he'd find me after school to return it.

Sighing heavily, I made my way back to the first floor and around to the other side of the school. I stuck my head out the door and scanned the lot for Hector's car. Not seeing it, I returned the way I had come, resigning myself to at least the next two hours without a phone.

That's why I went down the hallway past the West Gym in the first place.

Why I went in is another story.

I hadn't seen much of Livia since the day we crashed Ruby Greenberg's Honor Council hearing and its aftermath together. We'd avoided each other. Maybe it was out of the shared horror at what we'd seen that day and what we'd failed to stop. Or maybe it was because after that, it was so much harder to see one another as the enemy.

That was what I was thinking about when I opened the door to the West Gym and stepped inside. This time, I wasn't careful not to make any sound. I wasn't hiding.

Those were the things that led me to that hallway, those were the thoughts that led me to the gym, but what led me to the boys' locker room was the sound of running water.

Nobody used the West Gym showers. I hadn't even known that they worked. My first thought was to turn around and walk away. Whatever was going on in the locker room had nothing to do with me. It was none of my business. But then I remembered what Livia and I had seen, how we'd done nothing, and I thought, *This time I'll stop it.*

The air in the locker room was thick and swampy and I could still hear shower heads spraying full blast onto the algae-slick tile. There was a tangy, metallic scent in the air that I'd encountered exactly once before—also at Imperial Day, but I would have recognized it anywhere.

And so, even if I didn't know exactly what I was going to find when I turned the corner, it didn't come as a total surprise.

Cal's body was crumpled on the floor of the showers, being pelted on all sides. There was blood in his hair, rivulets of it coursing toward the drains in the center of the room. A single tooth lay in the middle of the puddle. One of the shower heads lay next to him on the floor. I guessed that was the weapon.

At first, I thought he was dead. I stood there, my feet rooted, but it wasn't shock I felt or fear. It was a strange detachment, and though it had never occurred to me to beat the shit out of Cal, I found I was not entirely sorry someone else had. It wasn't until he turned his head to the side and I saw his puffy, blood-smeared face, one eye swollen to a slit, and he croaked, "Help," that I screamed.

He was alive, and that was so much worse.

No one came, but I kept screaming until Cal spit a mouthful of blood in my direction and said over the streaming showers, "Get help, you stupid cunt. I can't get up."

My mouth clapped shut. I threw open the locker room door and ran out of the gymnasium and into the hall. Even if no one was there, I could at least call for help.

I burst through the main office door and found Dr. Graves standing at the photocopier. He jumped when he saw me, even before I said, "There's b-b-been an accident. Call the ambulance."

He picked up the phone and dialed. While he gave instructions to the dispatch, I wrote down the particulars, and after he hung up the phone, Dr. Graves said, "Show me."

So I'm the one who found Cal. I'm the one who got help. Even though it was Cal, I got help. Would I have run faster if it were Hector on that locker room floor? Probably. But I still went. Cal can call me a stupid cunt all he wants to, but I'm not a monster.

LI

THE KIND OF POWER THAT EVERYONE WANTS

Because of my quick thinking, Cal's life was saved. Therefore, people decided that I was a hero.

Nobody asks whether I would have been doing the world a favor if I'd turned around and walked out of the locker room like I hadn't seen a thing.

Because that is not the kind of people we are. Most of us want to be good people. Most of us are trying, and when you say something like *Things would be better if so-and-so was dead*, it fucks everything up. It makes it hard to go on feeling like you're a good person. So instead of making me regret that I'd saved Cal's life, my classmates rewarded me for it.

A special election was held. There were three names on the ballot—mine, Chris Gibbons's, and Livia's—but at the end of the day, I found a note in my locker:

IT WASN'T EVEN CLOSE

When I saw Kian's handwriting, I knew he'd accepted that what had happened between us over spring break had only been a brief respite from the way our lives were going to look. We were never going to walk around the halls of Imperial Day holding hands. He was never going to be my boyfriend. Love, friendship, a harmless hobby like the study of history—those things weren't for me. Every time I'd tried to seek them out in an effort to be happy or normal or well-adjusted, or to help save someone from themselves, something had steered me back toward politics and power, like it was my fate.

Which I suppose it was.

You're going to destroy them all. You're going to leave them reeling, their ambitions unrealized, their dearest hopes and wishes thwarted. And when all of them have fallen away, you alone will be left standing with the kind of power that people would lie and cheat and steal for, the kind of power that everyone wants. Everyone except you.

This wasn't the life I would have chosen for myself. It chose me, which I suppose is what the fortune-teller was trying to warn me about that day at Venice Beach.

By an overwhelming majority, the students of Imperial Day elected me president of the Honor Council, and because I'd fucked up so badly, because I'd failed to prevent Cal from coming to power, because I'd failed to stop him once he did, because I hadn't left him to die when I had the chance, and most of all, because there was no one else capable of fixing all the things that had gone wrong, I accepted.

"Do you have anything else to add, Claudia?"

"You're still listening?"

"It's my job to listen, Claudia. Besides, it was an interesting story. In places."

"Then you believe me?"

"It's not my job to believe or disbelieve, Claudia. I am here to listen."

"What happens next?"

"I prepare a transcript and summary of our conversation and turn it over to the Board. It is the hope of your counsel that this will offer the Board some better sense of the context in which you made the decisions you did."

"Do you think it will help?"

"I don't know, Claudia. I can only say that I wish you the very best of luck."

"With the trial?"

"No, Claudia. With your life."

PART IV
THE TRIAL OF CLAUDIA

If you are reading this, you are a student of history.

The Honor Council does not keep records. It never has in the 110-year history of Imperial Day, and a person can't help wondering, have there been other Cals before? Was there an Augustus in the 1940s, a Livia in the 1980s?

I hate it when the historical record is lost. That's when you get the Etruscans or Stonehenge, a lot of maddeningly unanswerable questions that could have been sorted out if someone had just bothered to leave a note.

I know what it's like to feel like you're owed an explanation and to know you're never going to get it, and I never wanted anyone to feel that way about me.

I didn't care that my trial would be public or that there would be a transcript. I wanted it that way. I wanted a record in the archives of Imperial Day so that you could find it. I want to share with you that most comforting lesson that history has to teach us: If you are around to tell your story, that means you survived it, you outran it, you came out the other side. Maybe not whole. Maybe not better than you were, but you lived to tell the tale.

You may notice places within this transcript where I've taken it upon myself to correct and amend the record. Because sometimes the wrong people ask the wrong questions, and the right people arrive at the wrong conclusions. Because people are mistaken. And because people lie.

If you are a history purist, you may view my commentary as a contamination of the historical record, or you may view it as delightful ephemera. Either way, let's keep it between us.

If a tank full of dead turtles wasn't enough to make them fix the lock on the main office door, I doubt my additions to this particular file will either, but let's not tempt fate.

You don't know what I mean about the turtles yet. It's about two hours into the recording, between the part where I go to Homecoming with Soren Bieckmann and the part where he dies. Do you still have flash drives? Can you even open the audio file?

In any case, know that the things I did, I did out of hope, out of frustration, out of despair. I could say that I did them for you, whoever you are, but if you've read this much, I guess I know better than to bullshit you with a line like that.

XX,

Claudia

DR. ROBERT GRAVES, PRINCIPAL OF THE IMPERIAL DAY ACADEMY: The Board of the Imperial Day Academy is assembled here today to hear the case against Honor Council President Claudia McCarthy. Board President Carson Quentin Mathers, Esquire, presiding.

Claudia McCarthy is accused of election tampering and defamation of character. Ms. McCarthy is also a person of interest in the assault on Calvin Hurt, an incident that occurred on school grounds. Ms. McCarthy stands accused of conduct unbecoming any Imperial Day student, much less its leader, and of damaging the school's legacy through her words and deeds.

We are gathered here today to determine not only whether Ms. McCarthy is fit to remain Honor Council President, but whether she is fit to keep her position as a student at this institution.

MR. CARSON QUENTIN MATHERS, PRESIDENT OF THE BOARD OF COMMISSIONERS OF THE IMPERIAL DAY ACADEMY: Ms. McCarthy, do you understand the charges against you?

CLAUDIA McCARTHY, HONOR COUNCIL PRESIDENT: I understand them. I just don't understand how they apply to me.

MR. MATHERS: And how do you plead?

CLAUDIA McCARTHY: Innocent. On all counts. I did not tamper with any election. I defamed no one's character. I told the truth, as I knew it, as I understood it at the time. I had nothing to do with what happened to Cal.

I deserve to keep my place at this school and my position as president of the Imperial Day Honor Council, and I question the motives of anyone who says otherwise.

MR. MATHERS: Please take your seat, Ms. McCarthy. And for heaven's sake, stop glaring.

Dr. Graves, would you please call the first witness?

DR. GRAVES: The first witness is Senior Class Honor Council representative Christopher Gibbons.

Except for the last part, I maintain that all of this is true. Sometimes people have motives you couldn't possibly understand at the time, as you eventually see.

MR. MATHERS: You served on the Honor Council under Ms. McCarthy. Can you relate the circumstances under which Ms. McCarthy came to be president of the Honor Council?

CHRISTOPHER GIBBONS, SENIOR CLASS HONOR COUNCIL REPRESENTATIVE: Well, someone tried to kill her predecessor in the boys' locker room.

Or to be more specific, Claudia McCarthy wanted to be Honor Council president, so she put out a hit on Cal Hurt. She convinced her flunkie, Hector Estrella, that Cal deserved to die and this was the only way to stop him.

She saw her chance, she used her friend, and she *took* it.

That is how Claudia McCarthy came to be president of the Honor Council.

MR. MATHERS: Mr. Hurt has maintained that he has no idea who his assailant might have been. You and the victim were friends, weren't you? Did he ever confide in you about the details of his attack?

CHRISTOPHER GIBBONS: No, he never told me who tried to kill him.

MR. MATHERS: He never told the school or the police either. Do you think that's strange?

CHRISTOPHER GIBBONS: He was a strange person. *Is* a strange person. When he was the Honor Council president, he'd walk out in the middle of hearings. One time, he stuck his face in front of a defendant and barked like a dog at them. I don't pretend to understand why he does anything he does.

MR. MATHERS: Erratic as his behavior was, weren't you almost relieved when Ms. McCarthy took his place?

CHRISTOPHER GIBBONS: I was surprised, not relieved.

I mean, *I* was the Honor Council VP, but whatever. I'm used to it. Claudia beat me out for a Senate seat freshman year. This wasn't any different.

MR. MATHERS: You've also maintained Claudia used the assault on Cal Hurt as an excuse to bypass the electoral process and stack the Honor Council with her friends.

CHRISTOPHER GIBBONS: When she took over, Claudia cleaned house. She kicked Jesse Nichols and Macro Stinson and Astrid Murray off because they were Cal's people. She kicked me off. She brought Zelda and Esme back.

There were no elections, even though all of this happened right around election time, but because of everything that had happened—the tragedy, the investigation—nobody said anything about it. Every single person who got on the Honor Council had been hand-picked and vetted by Claudia.

And then, once she was in charge, she stopped having hearings.

MR. MATHERS: How would you know that, Mr. Gibbons?

CHRISTOPHER GIBBONS: I was . . . around. I'd stand in the hallway outside the Honor Council room before school. After school. All the times they usually met. It was three weeks before I even caught them having a meeting.

MR. MATHERS: Isn't that the best possible outcome, Mr. Gibbons?

Isn't it possible that the Honor Council had been overzealous under its previous leadership, and these changes under Ms. McCarthy's leadership merely signified a regression to the norm?

CHRISTOPHER GIBBONS: I don't think it's possible. I've gone to school here for four years. There's no way people aren't lying and cheating as much as they ever did. People don't change that much.

MR. MATHERS: Then what are you suggesting, Mr. Gibbons?

CHRISTOPHER GIBBONS: I'm suggesting that Claudia got everything she wanted, just like she always does. She can act like it's an accident or like she's some dork with a limp and a stutter, her whole little "poor me" routine, but I promise you, everything that girl does is on purpose. None of it is an accident.

MR. MATHERS: Mr. Gibbons, are you a drug dealer?

CHRISTOPHER GIBBONS: Sir, I . . . what? Excuse me?

MR. MATHERS: So, Mr. Gibbons, let me ask more precisely: Did you provide Soren Bieckmann with hydrocodone?

CHRISTOPHER GIBBONS: We shouldn't be having a disciplinary hearing for Claudia McCarthy right now. We should be talking to the police.

MR. MATHERS: That is not what I asked you, Mr. Gibbons.

CHRISTOPHER GIBBONS: I'm done talking, sir. I'm not the one on trial.

But if you want proof that I'm telling the truth, ask anyone. They'll tell you the same thing. Claudia McCarthy doesn't care about anything except power. And herself.

He never answers the question about the hydrocodone and that tells you everything you need to know

Chris Gibbons gave my friend the overdose that killed him and basically accused me of attempted murder.

But Cal? By the end of Chris's testimony, I knew he hadn't had anything to do with what happened to Cal.

Chris Gibbons is a piece of shit, but thank god, he's also a lousy liar. Look at the way he flailed when Mathers asked him about Soren and the hydrocodone. If Chris Gibbons had dished out the beating that made it necessary for Cal to complete his senior year from a hospital bed, he would have fallen to pieces during the questioning.

That's the first reason I'm crossing Chris Gibbons off the suspect list.

The second, sadder reason is I think Cal actually was the closest thing to a friend Chris Gibbons ever had at Imperial Day.

CAL'S BEATING: SUSPECTS

~~Chris Gibbons~~

Kian Sarkosian

Hector Estrella

Livia Drusus

Zelda Parsons

DR. GRAVES: The next witness is Zelda Parsons.

MR. MATHERS: Help me to understand all of this, Ms. Parsons. How did we arrive at this point?

ZELDA PARSONS: In the 110 year history of the Imperial Day Academy, there have been ninety Honor Council presidents, and do you know how many of them have been female?

MR. MATHERS: I can't say that I do.

ZELDA PARSONS: Seven. And that's if you count Claudia McCarthy.

MR. MATHERS: I'm sure those numbers will begin to balance themselves out now that we're well into the 21st century, don't you think? But what does that have to do with anything?

ZELDA PARSONS: You asked me to help you understand all of this, and that's something I want you to understand.

When I was running for Honor Council my freshman year, Livia took me aside, and she told me something that changed my life. She told me that no one was ever going to give me permission to have power. She said that I was going to have to demand it, and that if that didn't work, I was going to have to reach out and take it.

Even before I was elected, I saw what she meant. Ty Berman was president of the Honor Council, and he didn't have a clue what he was doing. Livia had to pretend she was following his lead, when really it was the other way around.

Livia always told me that if we stuck together, it wouldn't always be that way. She said that we just had to get through that year, and after that, she'd be the president and I'd be her vice president, and we could do things the way we wanted to.

MR. MATHERS: And did Livia ever ask anything of you in exchange for this alliance?

ZELDA PARSONS: She didn't have to. Livia and I wanted the same things. That's why she was grooming me to be the president, not Claudia or Esme or any of the other underclassmen.

MR. MATHERS: Did she tell you that?

ZELDA PARSONS: She told me that she admired my work. During election season.

MR. MATHERS: What about your work did Ms. Drusus admire?

ZELDA PARSONS: Elections are not just about convincing voters that you're the best candidate. They are about convincing them that their worst fears about your opponents are all true.

And that can be accomplished by . . .

MR. MATHERS: Ratfucking.

Apologies for the language. It's a term that came up in Ms. McCarthy's transcript.

ZELDA PARSONS: That's a strange word for it. I always thought of what I did more as . . . massaging an election.

Rat massage.

How many ratfucks exactly had Zelda Parsons been responsible for?

MR. MATHERS: I'm not sure that's an improvement, Ms. Parsons.

So you formed an alliance with Ms. Drusus that eventually resulted in the two of you running on a ticket together. And as we know, that didn't work out the way the two of you had hoped.

ZELDA PARSONS: No, it didn't.

MR. MATHERS: And then there was the incident with the turtles . . .

ZELDA PARSONS: Can you not call it that? Can you just say I killed them?

MR. MATHERS: My god, it *was* you?

ZELDA PARSONS: Yes.

MR. MATHERS: You killed the turtles during the Homecoming dance.

ZELDA PARSONS: Yes.

There were Hector's INTEGRETY posters, the mysterious hits taken out on Rebecca Ibañez and Cecily Stanwick, the Photoshop job against me . . . Which ratfuck had gotten Livia's attention in th first place?

My therapist asked me if I considered myself to be a good judge of character, I'd ever been wrong about someone. I suppose now I have the answer to that question.

MR. MATHERS: Why in god's name would you do something like that?

ZELDA PARSONS: I had three reasons, and once you hear them, I think you'll understand. Maybe you won't agree, but you'll understand.

First, I wanted to discredit Claudia McCarthy, who, I might add, was such an incompetent Senate vice president that she forgot to hire any security guards for the dance. I wanted to get back at her for sabotaging Livia's campaign with that disgusting story from the Griffith School.

Second, I wanted to ruin Cal's god-awful celebration of himself, which I'd known he was planning—the slideshow, crowning himself king, the whole thing.

But the third reason I did it, the main reason I did it, is that I thought it might get some adults to step in and make it stop.

You've heard what kind of Honor Council president Cal was. You know the things he did. And you know that no one ever stopped him.

He threatened other students, he threatened teachers, and every day I thought, *Someone will notice. Someone will step in and do something. Someone will stop him.*

*parently, no
atter what I
, some people
e going to keep
sisting that I
d something
do with that
near campaign
ainst Livia.*

372

Then he threatened me into being his girlfriend for a month. The whole time I thought, *People know you. They know you would never do this. Someone will pull you aside and ask you what's wrong.*

When they didn't, I thought, *Well, if they don't care what happens to us, maybe they'll care about the turtles.* Turtles can't even feel pain, by the way. I looked it up. They never knew what hit them, and it was over in a second.

I didn't want to do it, but I thought, *If I do something bad enough, the people in charge of this place won't be able to ignore it anymore. They'll have to do something, and that will be worth a few dead turtles.*

MR. MATHERS: But the only person who was stopped was you.

ZELDA PARSONS: That was when I realized that no one was willing to stop Cal. No one knew how to stop him. Except the person who took the shower fixture to his head.

MR. MATHERS: I understand you have an alibi for that afternoon?

ZELDA PARSONS: I was in San Pedro visiting my grandmother. She was sick.

MR. MATHERS: I'm sorry to hear that. I hope she's doing better.

ZELDA PARSONS: She died. I was in the room when it happened.

Her nurses knew it was close, so they called all her family and told us to come down so we could watch it happen. It was awful. When I die, I want to die alone.

MR. MATHERS: Ms. Parsons, please. That's enough.

We all make mistakes. My first was trusting Zelda Parsons, ratfucker and turtle murderer. My second was giving her back her seat on the Honor Council. I can assure you that as of this writing, both of those mistakes have been remedied.

CAL'S BEATING: SUSPECTS

~~Chris Gibbons~~

Kian Sarkosian

Hector Estrella

Livia Drusus

~~Zelda Parsons~~

MR. MATHERS: Ms. Kovacs, I'm surprised to see you mixed up in this.

ESME KOVACS, HONOR COUNCIL REPRESENTATIVE, FORMER SENATOR: I'm not happy about it, Mr. Mathers.

MR. MATHERS: Well, why don't you help us to understand exactly what happened here. Why don't you start at the beginning. You started out on the Senate, and you've been on the Honor Council since your sophomore year—is that right?

ESME KOVACS: Yes, sir. I was really proud to have been elected and to serve my school, and of course, I knew how important the Honor Council was to the legacy of Imperial Day. It was like being a part of history. It was important to me to live up to that.

MR. MATHERS: And back when you started, did the Honor Council live up to that standard?

ESME KOVACS: Mostly, I think we did.

MR. MATHERS: Can you tell me about your working relationship with Claudia McCarthy on the Honor Council?

ESME KOVACS: A person like that should not be representing the Imperial Day Academy.

MR. MATHERS: That's a stronger response than I expected. Could you explain?

ESME KOVACS: The president of the Honor Council is the face of the school. It's the highest, most visible, most important job, and to have someone like . . . like *that*—it reflects poorly on the whole school.

MR. MATHERS: Did Ms. McCarthy do something in particular to offend you? Not to put you on the spot, but is it possible you were a little jealous of her friendship with Hector Estrella?

ESME KOVACS: No! Also, I don't even know why I'm here. I didn't do anything wrong. I'm being dragged down by these other people. I look guilty by association. I wish I'd never even seen Hector Estrella. I feel dirtied by the whole thing.

MR. MATHERS: No one thinks you've done anything wrong, Esme. You're helping us to understand what happened, that's all.

ESME KOVACS: But *I* don't even know what happened!

I walked past the Senate meeting room one day. Hector and I had broken up a few days before, but I wanted to talk to him. To see if maybe I'd made a mistake. And I heard Claudia in the room. They were alone together and having this big heart-to-heart.

And then they started talking about Cal, and how he'd ruined the

there was ny truth to ne accusation nat I'd stacked ne Honor ouncil with y own people, ouldn't I have t least picked ome who ·IKED me?

376

school. I heard Claudia blame Cal for everything from Hector and me breaking up to Soren's death.

MR. MATHERS: You saw Soren Bieckmann the night he died, didn't you?

ESME KOVACS: A couple of times.

Around eleven, I saw him talking to Chris Gibbons in the corner, and then, not too much later, he ran into me in the hall, giggling and practically falling down, and I said, "Wow, it's like the last year never happened." He staggered off, and that was the last time I saw him.

MR. MATHERS: What else did Ms. McCarthy say to Mr. Estrella in the Senate meeting room?

ESME KOVACS: She said that they needed to make it their top priority to stop Cal. To "take him down"—those were the exact words she used.

MR. MATHERS: What did Mr. Estrella say to that?

ESME KOVACS: He told her to calm down. He said she should step back and let him "take care of things."

MR. MATHERS: What did he mean by that?

ESME KOVACS: I don't know! All I know is that the next day, Hector wasn't in Mrs. DiVincenzo's eighth-period class, and that same afternoon, Cal gets

There is no group of people so thoughtless, so careless, so immune to self-examination as the people who have always been told they are "nice."

I would never say that the person who kicks the addict while they're down is a murderer, but let's dispense with the illusion that Esme Kovacs is a "nice" person.

beaten up in the locker room and he would have died if Claudia hadn't just happened to find him. And why would she do that? Why would she go into the West Gym locker room unless she knew exactly what Hector was going to do?

And I just don't . . . I just don't . . .

MR. MATHERS: It's all right, Ms. Kovacs.

ESME KOVACS: I just don't know! Did my ex-boyfriend try to kill someone? Did she put him up to it?

I won't dignify Esme's ravings with a response, but there is one more thing I'll say about her.

If I hadn't meddled her and Hector into a relationship, they wouldn't have been at that party together. They wouldn't have run into Soren at the moment they did. Maybe Esme never would have gotten the chance to say whatever shitty thing she said to Soren Bieckmann the last night he was alive.

Whether she said the words that broke Soren, the words that made him decide to overdose, or whether she didn't, it almost doesn't matter.

I put her in the room with him that night. So that's on me.

DR. GRAVES: The next witness is Livia Drusus.

MR. MATHERS: Ms. Drusus, your tenure at this school has been a rocky one, and your name has come up more than a few times today. Not in connection with the charges themselves, of course, but in league with the general culture of deceit that I have come to understand exists at the Imperial Day Academy. What do you have to say to that?

LIVIA DRUSUS, IMPERIAL DAY SENIOR, FORMER HONOR COUNCIL VICE PRESIDENT: Mr. Mathers, there are so many things that I want to say right now, but the first is that I'm sorry.

I'm not going to sit here and tell you that everything people have been saying about me is a lie. A lot of it is true. We did abuse the power of the Honor Council. We acted like the rules didn't apply to us. Worst of all, we opened the door for people like Cal and Claudia to step into those roles, and for that, I'm sorriest of all.

MR. MATHERS: You left school for a time. A leave of absence, isn't that right? Could you explain what led you to take that rather drastic measure?

LIVIA DRUSUS: Elections at Imperial Day are rough. They always have been. I've seen what people do to each other in the name of winning, but I have a thick skin. Might makes right, and if you can't handle the elections, you probably can't handle the job.

I thought I could handle it.

MR. MATHERS: Why did you want to be Honor Council president?

LIVIA DRUSUS: It wasn't even that I wanted it. I *needed* to run and I *needed* to win because the alternative was Cal.

He'd been groping and harassing and intimidating and—let's call it what it is—sexually assaulting his way through Imperial Day since his freshman year. Every girl in this school has some story about him, and nobody ever did anything about it.

It was up to me to stop him.

MR. MATHERS: And did you resort to any unconventional—any unsanctioned—tactics in your campaign against him?

LIVIA DRUSUS: What Zelda and I did to Cal wasn't a ratfuck—pardon my language, sir.

I thought Cal had gotten away with so much because people were afraid to speak up for themselves. I thought that if I could find everyone Cal had ever hurt and get their stories together, maybe someone would listen. Maybe something would change. Maybe people would at least think twice before voting for him.

MR. MATHERS: You planned to collect these stories about Mr. Hurt's indiscretions and do what, exactly, with them?

LIVIA DRUSUS: I planned to give them to you, sir. To Dr. Graves. To anyone who would look at them, really.

That was what I planned to do, but before I had a chance . . .

MR. MATHERS: What happened before you had a chance, Ms. Drusus?

LIVIA DRUSUS: Mr. Mathers, one of the great things about the Imperial Day Academy is that people come here from all over the city. It can be a place to reinvent yourself. If you're someone like me, it can be a place to start over.

When I was in eighth grade at the Griffith School, something awful happened.

There was a teacher I didn't get along with. To blow off steam, my friend and I joked about how he was creepy and gross and how in his spare time he probably wrote bad poetry to all the pretty girls in our grade. Then, because we were fourteen and bored, we wrote some.

It was just a joke. We never meant for anyone to see them, but someone fished them out of the trash and gave them to the guidance counselor, and the next thing I knew, there was an investigation. I didn't speak up because it looked like everything was going to blow over. But then, my friend, Octavia, confessed everything and the charges were dropped, and everyone hated me, but I didn't care because at least it was over.

And then it turned out that Mr. Arnold really *was* a pervert. Everything Octavia and I had been joking about was true. The only thing we were wrong about was the girl.

No one talked about that part, though. They talked about me like I was the one who'd committed a crime. I hadn't set out to ruin anyone. It was all a big, awful coincidence, and no one at the Griffith School ever let me live it down.

I think that's why I cared so much about what happened with the election and Cal. If I hadn't stumbled onto what was happening with my English teacher and that girl, it would have continued. Who knows how much longer and how many more girls? If somebody doesn't put a stop to it, it just goes on and on.

I knew what would happen if Cal was president of the Honor Council.

MR. MATHERS: And you believe Ms. McCarthy was the one who leaked this story to the student body just prior to the Honor Council elections?

Of course, leave it to Olivia to turn HERSELF into the victim of that whole story.

and the HERO of this one.

LIVIA DRUSUS: There is no doubt in my mind that she did. Only a handful of people came here from the Griffith School, and of all of them, Claudia is the only one who would do something like that to hurt me.

MR. MATHERS: What about your friend? Octavia, you said her name was? I seem to remember her name popping up once or twice in Ms. McCarthy's testimony.

LIVIA DRUSUS: She's my *friend*. She's *still* my friend. She was the only one who stood by me through everything that happened at the Griffith School. She's been loyal to me ever since. I think she even flirted with Cal for a week around election time just to keep him distracted. She did that for *me*.

Besides, when everything happened at the Griffith School, people were almost as angry with Octavia as they were with me. That was one of the worst times in our lives. In *either* of our lives. It's not a story we go around sharing.

MR. MATHERS: According to Ms. McCarthy, you and she were involved in a physical altercation after this story got out.

LIVIA DRUSUS: That is a lie. I never even spoke to her. She came into the Honor Council room after the lies

I still think Octavia did it. I think she told Cal the story about Mr. Arno during that Valentine's Day weekend when he bought her five bouquets of flowers and stuck his tongu down her thro in the hall. I'll never convince Livia of that, though. I can only hope that I've convinced yo about me went up all over the school. I don't know why Claudia came to me.

Maybe she wanted to gloat. I was upset. I threw a coffee mug on the floor and some of the shards might have bounced over near where she was standing, but I didn't lay a hand on her.

MR. MATHERS: How did you find the school when you returned from your leave of absence, Ms. Drusus?

LIVIA DRUSUS: As bad as I'd feared, sir. Worse.

I went to Dr. Graves and one or two of the teachers, but no one seemed to take it very seriously, maybe because it was coming from me. So I started going to Honor Council meetings like a UN elections observer or the Red Cross in a war zone. Knowledge is power. I felt that if I understood what Cal was doing, I might understand how to stop him.

Unfortunately, he was brutally attacked before I could arrive at a peaceful solution.

MR. MATHERS: What did you think about that?

LIVIA DRUSUS: I was sorry it happened, of course, but not surprised.

MR. MATHERS: And do you have any ideas about who might have been responsible?

LIVIA DRUSUS: I've thought about this a lot, and what I keep coming back to is Claudia McCarthy. Maybe she didn't do it herself, but I don't doubt she was involved.

She cleared a path for herself into the Senate vice presidency, and I can't help thinking, *What if what happened to Cal was Claudia McCarthy clearing herself another path?*

I think it because that used to be me. I used to want power like that. I used to chase it, spend time planning how I was going to get it. So I understand how that works. It consumes you. It makes you forget that people are people. Instead, they're obstacles.

In closing, I'd like to say that I used to feel that way, so I know where Claudia is coming from.

I don't feel that way anymore.

CAL'S BEATING: SUSPECTS

~~Chris Gibbons~~

Kian Sarkosian

Hector Estrella

Livia Drusus

~~Zelda Parsons~~

DR. GRAVES: The next witness is Honor Council representative Kian Sarkosian.

MR. MATHERS: Mr. Sarkosian, as the person who brought these charges against Claudia McCarthy, I'm sure you understand how serious they are.

KIAN SARKOSIAN, HONOR COUNCIL REPRESENTATIVE: I do.

MR. MATHERS: And so, before we go on, it's important that we rule out certain questions. You and Ms. McCarthy were close, weren't you?

KIAN SARKOSIAN: We were . . . something like that.

MR. MATHERS: What would you say if I suggested that you brought these charges against Ms. McCarthy because of hurt or unreciprocated feelings between the two of you?

KIAN SARKOSIAN: Mr. Mathers, I brought the charges against Claudia because I believe she did it.

MR. MATHERS: You think she's capable of something like that?

KIAN SARKOSIAN: She told me she was working on a plan to take him down.

MR. MATHERS: I mean physically capable.

KIAN SARKOSIAN: Maybe she didn't do it alone.

Remember what I said about people having motives you couldn't possibly understand at the time? I give you Exhibit A: Kian Fucking Sarkosian, Informant, Semi-Ex-Boyfriend, and Turncoat.

MR. MATHERS: What if I suggested that you were the one who helped her? Mr. Hurt hit you in the face with a cafeteria tray just a few hours before he was attacked in the shower? Surely you were still angry about that.

KIAN SARKOSIAN: Mr. Mathers, when I'm upset I go to the LA County Museum of Art and look at ancient Assyrian art. I don't settle scores. And I don't do things because Claudia McCarthy asks me to.

MR. MATHERS: You accuse Ms. McCarthy of unjustly firing all the Honor Council representatives, then appointing her own picks without fair elections. Yet you got to keep your seat.

KIAN SARKOSIAN: I was good at my job. I hadn't done anything wrong.

MR. MATHERS: Yet you violated the confidentiality of the Honor Council to serve as Ms. McCarthy's informant. Do you think that was ethical?

KIAN SARKOSIAN: In the darkest times, resistance is always ethical.

MR. MATHERS: Mr. Sarkosian, what is in your hand?

KIAN SARKOSIAN: Just a slip of paper, sir. Nervous habit. Something to do with my hands.

MR. MATHERS: Well, you're clearly reading it. Give it to me, please.

Thank you, Mr. Sarkosian.

WHAT HAPPENS WHEN YOU FIND OUT I'M A TERRIBLE PERSON?

YOU ARE A FORCE FOR GOOD IN THE UNIVERSE.

YOU DESERVE BETTER.

Would you care to explain what this means?

KIAN SARKOSIAN: It doesn't mean anything.

Here are the facts:

1. I don't blame Kian for what he did. I'm not even angry. Kian Sarkosian will always be my good thing in a year of shit.

2. In bringing me up on all these charges, he did me a favor.

3. Before the trial, people doubted my innocence and suspected the worst of me, but then Kian Sarkosian brought it all out into the open.

4. And after that, no one would ever again be able to question my absolute right to be exactly where I was. Sometimes I wonder if Kian thought of that, too—if he wasn't trying to take me down, but clear the way for me. I wouldn't put it past him.

5. As I said before, he's the best liar I ever met.

CAL'S BEATING: SUSPECTS

~~Chris Gibbons~~

Kian Sarkosian

Hector Estrella

Livia Drusus

~~Zelda Parsons~~

388

MR. MATHERS: Where were you between 1:30 and 3:00 on April 6?

JESSE NICHOLS, FORMER HONOR COUNCIL REPRESENTATIVE: What day was that?

MR. MATHERS: The day of Mr. Hurt's attack, son.

JESSE NICHOLS: Oh, right.

I had eighth-period English with Mr. Woolf, so that went until 2:30. Then Kian Sarkosian and I walked to my locker. I think I wasn't sure whether I needed my trigonometry book over the weekend, and Kian kept telling me to hurry up.

Oh my god, Jesse Nichols

Shut up.

Shut up.

MR. MATHERS: Why was Kian Sarkosian in such a rush?

Shut up.

Shut up.

JESSE NICHOLS: I don't know. I went as fast as I could, but he was still annoyed. Then we went downstairs.

Shut up.

MR. MATHERS: Near the West Gym?

JESSE NICHOLS: No, the back hallway by the science classrooms. We stood in front of some random person's locker for ten minutes, I don't know why, and then finally Kian said, "Never mind, let's go."

MR. MATHERS: Why were you and Mr. Sarkosian leaving school together that day?

JESSE NICHOLS: We always do. My house is on the way, so he usually gives me a ride. I haven't gotten around to getting my permit yet. I want to, but it just seems like so much work and I haven't had time and—

MR. MATHERS: What you are saying is that you and Mr. Sarkosian were together every step of the way between 1:30 and 3:00, with witnesses?

JESSE NICHOLS: Yeah.

MR. MATHERS: Well, then why in god's name didn't somebody mention that? Why didn't Kian Sarkosian mention it?

JESSE NICHOLS: Maybe he was thinking about other stuff. He's under a lot of stress. Some people really think he did it.

Except that part, Jesse Nichols. That was all you needed to say.

CAL'S BEATING: SUSPECTS

~~Chris Gibbons~~

~~Kian Sarkosian~~

Hector Estrella

Livia Drusus

~~Zelda Parsons~~

MR. MATHERS: Claudia McCarthy has been a patient in your care for how long?

DR. CHRISTINA XIU, PEDIATRICS, CEDARS SINAI MEDICAL GROUP: Since she was five, shortly after her second heart surgery.

MR. MATHERS: In your professional opinion, is Claudia McCarthy capable of carrying out a physical assault against a five-foot-ten-inch male who weighed 170 pounds?

DR. CHRISTINA XIU: Excuse me?

MR. MATHERS: Do you believe she could have done it?

DR. CHRISTINA XIU: You mean I was called away from my practice to answer a question that—it seems to me—the school nurse, or any of Ms. McCarthy's peers, or anyone who has met Ms. McCarthy could have answered?

MR. MATHERS: Which is to say . . .

DR. CHRISTINA XIU: Which is to say I would find a scenario where the young man happened to be standing in the shower, the fixture fell on his head, and he fell to the floor and knocked his skull on the tile to be far more plausible than one where my pediatric, asthmatic heart patient with leg-length discrepancy carried out an attack.

Is that all?

CAL'S BEATING: SUSPECTS

~~Chris Gibbons~~
~~Kiau Sarkosian~~
Hector Estrella
Livia Drusus
~~Zelda Parsons~~
~~Claudia McCarthy~~

Just so you don't think I'm
trying to put one over on
you by leaving myself off the
suspects list altogether.

MR. MATHERS: Dr. Graves, based on what I've heard so far, of what exactly am I supposed to convict Claudia McCarthy? Being disliked? Being in the wrong place at the wrong time? Ambition?

DR. GRAVES: I apologize, Mr. Mathers. You've been more than patient.

MR. MATHERS: What I'd like to know, Dr. Graves, is, Is there anyone here who can tell me anything useful? Anything that doesn't contradict every other piece of testimony? Anything that isn't wrongheaded, misinformed, misinterpreted, or an outright lie?

DR. GRAVES: There's only one person left to go.

Mr. Estrella? You can come up. We're ready for you now.

MR. MATHERS: Mr. Estrella, it's been a long afternoon and I think it's fair to say that we'd all like to go home, so I'll keep this brief. Your name has already come up a few times today, so I feel like I have some sense of who you are and of your relationship with Ms. McCarthy. Would you say that depiction was more or less accurate?

HECTOR ESTRELLA, SENATE PRESIDENT: I'm afraid I don't understand, sir.

MR. MATHERS: Would it be accurate to say that without Ms. McCarthy's . . . interventions, you would not be Senate president right now?

HECTOR ESTRELLA: I don't think that's necessarily accurate, sir.

MR. MATHERS: So you might have aspired to that position even without her encouragement?

HECTOR ESTRELLA: It's hard to say what I might have aspired to when I was a freshman. I wanted to make the school a better place, and being on the Senate seemed like a way to do that. My peers elected me to represent them three times, and Claudia didn't have anything to do with that.

MR. MATHERS: Why do you think they elected you? What special skills do you bring to the leadership of the Imperial Day Senate?

HECTOR ESTRELLA: Sir, I believe I was elected because people thought I'd do a good job.

MR. MATHERS: And have you?

HECTOR ESTRELLA: Sir, I'm afraid I don't understand. Have I done something to offend you?

MR. MATHERS: In my role as president of the Imperial Day Academy Board of Commissioners and as an alumnus of the school, I take a personal interest in the health and growth and development of the students here, so when someone comes in from outside and through his influence harms our children—

HECTOR ESTRELLA: What do you mean "comes in from outside"? I transferred here my freshman year.

MR. MATHERS: I am aware of the circumstances surrounding your transfer.

HECTOR ESTRELLA: I was accepted to Imperial Day just like everyone else, sir. I pay my tuition just like everyone else.

MR. MATHERS: You mean your parents pay your tuition.

HECTOR ESTRELLA: Just like everyone else's.

MR. MATHERS: Mr. Estrella, you are here today because your friend, Ms. McCarthy, is facing some very serious charges. Assault, attempted murder, corruption, election tampering. In fact, the most serious charges I've seen during the time I've been affiliated with this school, which is three times longer than you've been alive.

I find it difficult to believe that you, as Ms. McCarthy's closest friend and ally, weren't at least somewhat complicit in all of this. So if it seems like I'm being hard on you, it's because I am.

HECTOR ESTRELLA: I see, sir.

MR. MATHERS: And how would *you* describe your relationship with Ms. McCarthy?

HECTOR ESTRELLA: Claudia was my best friend.

MR. MATHERS: Was?

HECTOR ESTRELLA: Is. I don't know.

MR. MATHERS: According to both Ms. McCarthy's and Ms. Kovacs's testimony, shortly before Mr. Hurt was beaten in the boys' locker room, you told Ms. McCarthy to take a step back. You told her that you'd "take care of things." What did you mean by that?

HECTOR ESTRELLA: I meant that I'd take care of the Senate. Claudia doesn't always take care of herself, and I was worried about her.

I was trying to protect her. The situation with Cal couldn't have gone on much longer. He was graduating in a month and a half. It was all about to be over if she could just outlast him.

MR. MATHERS: In the version of the story Ms. McCarthy tells, it almost sounds like you offered to take care of Cal for her. And that is a version of the story that's supported by the testimony of your girlfriend. What do you have to say about that, Mr. Estrella?

HECTOR ESTRELLA: I had nothing to do with what happened to Cal.

MR. MATHERS: You weren't in your eighth-period class that afternoon. Not according to Ms. Kovacs.

HECTOR ESTRELLA: Mrs. DiVincenzo wrote me a pass to the guidance office. I was doing college research.

MR. MATHERS: Would you be able to prove that? Would anyone in the guidance office be able to confirm your whereabouts during that window of time?

HECTOR ESTRELLA: I don't know.

MR. MATHERS: You don't know.

HECTOR ESTRELLA: But the Admissions counselor at Northwestern can.

MR. MATHERS: Excuse me?

HECTOR ESTRELLA: We spoke on the phone from 1:30 until 2:15. After that, I went back to class. Mrs. DiVincenzo gave me Claudia's phone that she'd confiscated during the assembly. I waited around at Claudia's locker for a few minutes, but Kian Sarkosian and Jesse Nichols were standing around glaring at me, so I went out to my car and went home. I ran into Mr. Prettinger in the parking lot. We talked about the Dodgers for a few minutes, then I went home.

So, that's where I was.

MR. MATHERS: All of these things just happened around you and you went blithely on, unaware of it all? Is that right, Mr. Estrella? None of this touches you. None of this is your fault. Is that how you see things?

HECTOR ESTRELLA: No, sir.

MR. MATHERS: Would you care to elaborate in more than a monosyllable?

I've thought about this part a lot, and at first, I wondered why Mr. Mathers was being such a dick to Hector. Was he frustrated that his last credible suspect had just produced an airtight alibi? Was he a racist?

Possibly. But then I remembered that Mr. Mathers is also a lawyer, and since he went to Imperial Day, I'm going to guess he's a pretty good one. And Hector had told the truth. He'd told almost all of the truth. But he was holding one more thing back, and even though I didn't know it at the time, Mr. Mathers did.

That's why he pushed him, I think.

HECTOR ESTRELLA: There's something I need to say.

It doesn't have anything to do with Claudia or Cal, but I need to say it here and now while everyone is listening.

The night Soren Bieckmann died, I was the one who drove him home from the party. The guy in the gray hoodie who walked him to his door, then left—that was me. I had no idea he was going to overdose. I don't even know what that looks like.

Esme and I ran into him at the party, and he looked like he'd had a couple of drinks. That's what I thought, anyway, but Esme turned to me and said, "I'm surprised it took this long," and I know Soren wasn't completely wasted then, because he heard her. He looked right at us, and he had this expression on his face like he was going to cry.

We kept walking, but I couldn't get it out of my head, so about half an hour later, I told Esme I was going to find him and take him home. She was worried about what would happen if we got pulled over with him in the car. I get pulled over, uh, slightly more than the average Imperial Day student, so I told her she didn't have to come, that I'd go back to the party for her after I dropped Soren off, and have her home before curfew.

That's even more brutal than what Esme says she said. Between you and me, I'm going to believe Hector's account on this one.

When I found Soren, he said he was fine.
He said he could get himself home, and I
told him, "No. I'm not going to let you do
that." When I said that, his face crumpled
and he started to cry, and he said, yeah,
that I should probably give him a ride.

He was fine in the car, though. Slurry,
but mostly making sense. We talked about
some idea he'd had for a documentary
about the hip-hop artists who sell their
CDs on the Venice boardwalk. He told me
he was thinking about adopting a dog
from the shelter. He acted like he hadn't
just been crying in front of me.

We got to his house, and I asked if he
was all right, and he said yes. I walked
him to the door. I didn't even think to
ask him if there was anyone else home.
I didn't invite him to spend the night
at my house because we weren't really
friends like that.

I wish I had. I wish I'd taken him home
with me or offered to stay there with
him. I wish I'd left him at that party
and hadn't offered him a ride home.
The worst part is, if I'd just left him
there, there would have been a ton of
people around. He wouldn't have been
alone. Maybe he wouldn't have died.

I know Claudia wants to believe that Cal
was responsible for Soren's death. If
he was the one who gave Soren all that
hydrocodone, maybe I *would* have beaten
the shit out of him in the boys' locker

room. But I never saw Cal go anywhere near him that night.

What I know is that the person most responsible for Soren Bieckmann's death is me.

MR. MATHERS: I see. Well, thank you for that, Mr. Estrella.

Before I let you go, there's something I'd like you to think about. You are the last person to testify in this trial today. You are the last person who can help me make sense of this. You seem like a thoughtful young man, so I'd like you to think about this: Do you think the testimony we've heard has painted an accurate picture of Ms. McCarthy and her culpability in any and all of the matters we've discussed today?

HECTOR ESTRELLA: I see what you're doing, Mr. Mathers.

You're running out of time to find someone who's responsible for all of this. You hoped it could be me, but since it can't be, you'd like me to help you decide that it's Claudia.

The problem with your story is, I don't think it's the right one.

If you ask me, the reason Claudia is here today is because, despite everything that happened, she refused to be a victim. She didn't always do the right thing, but she did the best she could.

MR. MATHERS: Did you know how she felt about you?

HECTOR ESTRELLA: Excuse me?

MR. MATHERS: She never told you?

HECTOR ESTRELLA: Told me what?

MR. MATHERS: Nothing. It's just that Ms. McCarthy lied to you as well.

HECTOR ESTRELLA: The person Claudia lies to more than anyone else is herself. She doesn't deserve to be found guilty. She doesn't deserve to be punished.

MR. MATHERS: What does she deserve?

HECTOR ESTRELLA: Claudia deserves to be happy.

CAL'S BEATING: SUSPECTS

~~Chris Gibbons~~

~~Kiavi Sarkosian~~

~~Hector Estrella~~

Livia Drusus

~~Zelda Parsons~~

~~Claudia McCarthy~~

VERDICT

MR. MATHERS: At the beginning of this trial, it was the severity of the charges brought against Ms. McCarthy that made me fear for the future of this school.

However, the testimony I have heard today makes me question whether a governing body like the Honor Council should exist, whether you have, through your own treachery and bad faith, forfeited your right to self-governance.

I believe that you have.

As Imperial Day Board President, I have no choice but to find Ms. McCarthy NOT GUILTY of all charges.

As Imperial Day Board President, I have no choice but to take to the rest of the Board members my recommendation that the Honor Council be abolished for a minimum of four years until the lot of you cycle through this institution and go off to poison other wells, hopefully a long way away from here.

I have nothing else to say.

Get out of my sight.

So, unknown future reader, student of history, that was my trial, which raised as many questions as it answered and left Mr. Mathers wishing he'd never asked in the first place.

While I was on the Senate, I did as much as I could. During my time as Honor Council president, I accomplished only one thing, but it was the thing that needed to be done: I brought down the empire.

That spring, I ran for Senate president after Hector announced he would not seek reelection. Between his dad and his time at Imperial Day, politics no longer held any good associations for him. This is a great loss, for which I partly blame myself, because Hector was one of the good ones. Twenty years from now, he'll probably be curing cancer while Cal Hurt and Chris Gibbons are dumping toxic waste into the ocean and laughing about it.

I remember a poster that Ms. Yee had on the wall of her classroom. Sitting at my desk listening to her spin stories about Assyrian kings and Roman emperors, I hadn't understood it, but now I do.

The poster said, "A true historian will always rise superior to the political disturbances of her day."

When it was all over, when the smoke had cleared and I found myself left standing, I resolved that even if I was no longer a historian in practice, I would try to remain a historian in my soul. I would move in the circles where I needed to move, I would run the Imperial Day Academy to the best of my ability, I would pay attention to the things that went on here, and I would tell you about them.

So that maybe there is a chance, there is a hope, that when nothing makes sense, my story will speak clearly and boldly to you and show you a way out of whatever mess you're in.

Maybe it will show you how to be a better person than I know how to be.

XX,

Claudia

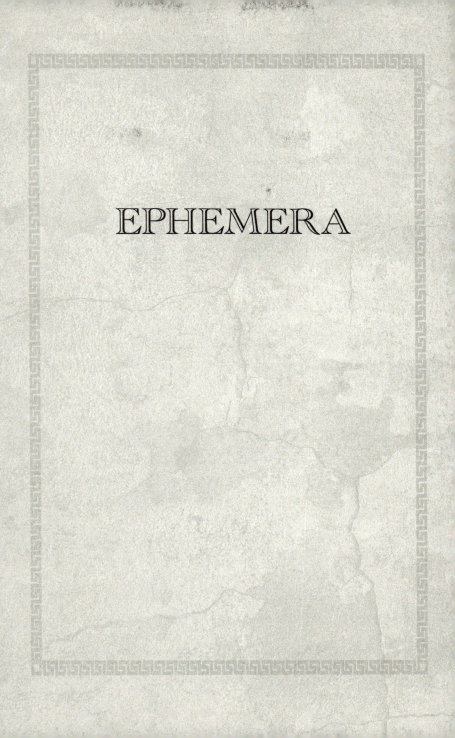

EPHEMERA

Dear Hector,

The person I lie to the most isn't myself. It's you. It was always you.

I'm not expecting you to say I loved you, too, or I'm sorry, I had no idea, which is exactly how you'd tell me you didn't love me because it's the kindest way you could think of to say it.

Either way, it wouldn't be fair to you, so while I'm glad you know the truth now, I think it would be best if we pretended it never happened.

I wish I could say I had something to do with the way my trial turned out, but the truth is, I didn't know what people were going to say up there. I had no idea Zelda Parsons killed the turtles. I really believed that Cal had something—a little something, but something nonetheless—to do with Soren's death. I didn't know about what Esme said or what you did or felt like you didn't do.

So what do I know now that I didn't know then?

I know that in a parallel universe with fewer complications and disasters, where I have room in my life for a great love or at least a friend with benefits, Kian Sarkosian and I are a terrifying, fierce power couple.

I know that there is no one less deserving of the second chances he has received than that hydrocodone-dealing douchebag Chris Gibbons.

I know that if Zelda Parsons had a little more spine and a little less psychosis, she'd destroy us all.

I know that Esme Kovacs was more of a monster than I gave her credit for.

I know that Livia had better intentions than I gave her credit for, even if she was still a monster.

I know that we are, all of us, monsters in our own way.

Except you, Hector.

Did I know that you were the one who dropped Soren off at home the night he died? No. What I do know is that if you hadn't gotten the weight of that decision off your chest, it would have ruined your life.

I don't blame you for what happened, Hector.

You might believe that if you'd left him at the party or invited him to spend the night with you, he'd still be alive. But what if he hadn't gone to the party? What if his parents hadn't gone out of town? What if I'd invited him to go to New York with me? What if he'd never gotten sober in the first place?

I know that if you spend too much time asking yourself questions you have no way of finding out the answer to, you'll go crazy.

I know that a person can be beautiful and Zen and sober and true, and still make a stupid, horrible decision that fucks up all those true and beautiful things irrevocably. I know that now.

I also know that a person can be vile and false, a liar and a manipulator to the depths of their heart, and get away with it.

But I've always known that.

Mr. Mathers never took the girls very seriously as suspects in what happened to Cal, and he should have.

I'm dangerous even though I've never been violent. Zelda is violent without being dangerous (to humans). Esme is living proof you can hurt people without being violent or dangerous. And Livia? I've always said Livia is capable of anything.

I went over to Livia's house after the trial. I suppose you could call what I went over there to do "blackmail," but I thought of it as more of a truce.

When I knocked on the door, it was almost like she'd been expecting me.

"Tell me how you did it," I said. No sense in pretending this was a social call.

For a moment, I thought she was going to close the door without saying a word, but then a little smile played across her lips.

"I'll show you," she said.

She led me through her house, out the back door, and into the yard. There was a shed tucked away behind a cluster of lantana and lavender bushes, and Livia produced a key and opened the door.

"After you," she said, and I stepped inside to see a riding lawnmower, jugs of organic fertilizer, terra-cotta pots. It was only after Livia had stepped in behind me, turned on the single, bare overhead light bulb, and shut the door behind us that I noticed the bags of peat and potting soil stacked in the corner.

Every one of them was burst open, the plastic flayed into strips.

Livia picked up a crowbar from the corner of the shed and grinned at me before lifting it over her head. I only had time to gasp and throw my hands up in front of my face (like that would have done anything to help), before she brought the crowbar down on the stack of bags with a meaty thwack and sent a shower of dirt in my direction. I felt little chunks of it pelt my hands and chest.

"I was too angry that time with you," Livia said, as I brushed the dirt off my front and tried to keep my hands from shaking.

She was talking about that day in the Honor Council room when she'd thrown the mug at my head and kicked me in the gut. Her emotions had gotten in the way that day. It was only after the initial burst of rage had faded that her blows started to land. Once there was cruelty and calm intent behind those kicks and punches, Livia could hurt me.

"So you practiced," I said.

"Then I put a note in his locker telling him to meet me there. Signed it with Ruby Greenberg's name."

"I'll bet that made it easier when he showed up," I said.

"You have no idea," she said.

Cal never said who'd cracked him on the head with the shower fixture, and without his word, there wasn't enough evidence to prosecute or punish anyone for his attack, and so the person who actually did it—the only person who'd never been a suspect in the first place—got away with it.

Livia always did have a way of coming out clean.

When I think about what I know now, and how I'm never going to tell anyone about it, I wonder, does that make me as bad a person as Cal?

At my trial you said that I deserved to be happy. You said that the problem with the story Mr. Mathers was telling was that it was the wrong one.

The thing is, Hector, I think you're telling the wrong story about me, too.

Maybe you think I was pulled unwillingly into politics and had no choice but to stick around until I'd saved the school from itself.

Or maybe you think I got caught up in the power, and that now I need someone—that I need you—to save me from myself.

But if that's the kind of story you think this is, then fuck you either way, Hector Estrella.

This is the story of how I survived.

This is the story of how I evolved, how one day I crawled out of the ocean up onto dry land and became the political animal I was born to be.

I'm not like you, Hector. I'm never going to be the kind of leader that everyone loves. When you're someone like me, there's always someone gunning for you, always someone who thinks that you're easy pickings or that you don't deserve what you have. I don't look like much, but nei- ther did Abraham Lincoln, or Joan of Arc, or Charles I. A postmaster; a farmgirl; a stammering, limping invalid. That's what they used to be until the day they decided to step up and embrace their fates.

I used to be a historian, but now I'm something bigger than that, more important, and I'll keep going as long as I can, doing this, surviving, and you don't get to save me, Hector Estrella.

And just like Lincoln, Joan of Arc, Charles I, King Wenceslas, Julius Caesar, Ashurnasirpal II, Richard Nixon, and all the rest of them, when the inevitable knife between the shoulder blades comes for me, I'll be ready for it every single time.

Right up until the time I'm not.

I know what happened to all those people, Hector. I'm not an idiot, but this is what I want, and you don't get to save me.

You don't get to save me.

I might not be brave enough to give you this letter. I might just leave it in a file tucked away with the rest of the Imperial Day records that no one's ever going to look at. If someone does, though, I hope it's someone like the person I used to be back when I first met you, back when all of this could have turned out differently. I hope I can explain it to that person even if I can't bring myself to explain it to you.

I loved you. I'm sorry I loved you. I'm not sorry for any of it.

Which part is the truth? All of it, every word, and Hector, that's the truest thing I've told you so far.

xx,

Claudia

Acknowledgments

Alix Reid, thank you for your wonderful guidance on this project, for helping me to untangle Claudia's brain snakes and understand her crooked little heart. You lit the path, then let me wander where I needed to wander to get where I needed to go.

Patricia Nelson, you saw me through this book's unanswered questions, off-the-rails moments, and acts of turtle murder. Thank you for letting me go over the top, and then reeling me back in.

Leah DiVincenzo and John Woolf, thank you for being the kind of friends who would lend your brains, your turns of phrase, and even your names to this novel, and thank you for being the kind of teachers I would follow into battle.

Angela Serranzana and Mark Walker, I am indebted to you for your sharp insights and notes, and for giving me perhaps the greatest piece of advice on character development that I've ever received. Kian Sarkosian and Soren Bieckmann are five times cooler because of you.

Thank you to Marc Weitz, whose thoughts on the Nicolas Cage and John Travolta vehicle *Face/Off* brought much-needed focus to my world-building, and to Vi Ha, who came through with wisdom, kindness, and origami tutorials.

Thank you, John Darnielle, for your words and music. For every character in this book, there is a Mountain Goats song that helped me understand them better.

Shelby, I started writing this book when you were 4 weeks old, in the strange, manic little snatches of time between your naps. The years I spent writing this book were the first years I spent with you, and they've been the happiest ones of my life. You inspire me.

Brady Potts, thank you for every bit of back porch conversation, couch deliberation, and train car correspondence that brought this book to life. Even if you were the only person who ever read *I, Claudia*, that would have been reason enough for me to write it.

Topics for Discussion

1. Why is it important to the story that Claudia considers herself a historian? How does it affect how she narrates the story?

2. How is the book formatted, and why? How does it affect the reader's experience?

3. How does Maisie and Claudia's relationship change throughout the book? What causes it to change?

4. Do you think Claudia uses humor and sarcasm as a defense mechanism, to disguise her discomfort, or for another reason? What are some examples?

5. Consider the fortune-teller scene early in the book. What parts of the prediction come true, and how?

6. Do you think Claudia's actions are influenced by a desire for power or something else entirely? Why?

7. How would you describe the differences between the Honor Council and the Senate?

8. Is Claudia a reliable narrator? Why or why not?

9. How is Soren's death a turning point for Claudia or any of the other characters?